Data and Statistics Cookbook
with Excel 2007

First Edition

Larry A. Pace
Argosy University

Prentice Hall

Boston   Columbus   Indianapolis   New York   San Francisco   Upper Saddle River
Amsterdam   Cape Town   Dubai   London   Madrid   Milan   Munich   Paris   Montreal   Toronto
Delhi   Mexico City   Sao Paulo   Sydney   Hong Kong   Seoul   Singapore   Taipei   Tokyo

Executive Editor: Jeff Marshall
Editorial Assistant: Courtney Elezovic
Marketing Manager: Nicole Kunzmann
Production Assistant: Caitlin Smith
Manufacturing Buyer: Debbie Rossi
Cover Administrator/Designer: Kristina Mose-Libon

CIP information not available at time of publication.

10 9 8 7 6 5 4 3 2 1   BRR   14 13 12 11 10

Prentice Hall
is an imprint of

www.pearsonhighered.com

ISBN-13: 978-0-205-84067-0
ISBN-10: 0-205-84067-1

Preface and Acknowledgements

Over the past several years, I have noted an increased interest in the use of spreadsheets for teaching and learning basic statistics. This movement began in business schools, where spreadsheets are used extensively, but has recently expanded to the sciences and more recently, the social sciences. This book about using a widely available spreadsheet program for basic statistics can be used as a course supplement or as a standalone text. Topics covered include those commonly taught in a first course (or two-course sequence) in basic descriptive and inferential statistics. Although the text makes repeated use of certain datasets, each chapter serves as a standalone module, so instructors can skip the topics they do not wish to cover.

The nature of a spreadsheet, with rows for participants or cases and columns for fields or variables, makes it easy to visualize and implement simple data structures and basic data analysis. The unified problem space of the spreadsheet allows the creation of templates that can be transparent teaching tools. These models allow the student to see the data, the formulas, and the results in the same place at the same time. The student can learn the definitional formulas for statistics and implement these in the worksheet without fear of rounding errors and computational mistakes. In the process, the student can avoid complicated and confusing computing forms entirely. For these reasons, spreadsheets are superior to handheld calculators and dedicated statistics packages for teaching and learning basic statistics.

While there are pedagogical reasons for using spreadsheets for statistics, some of the growing interest is more pragmatic in nature. Dedicated statistics packages such as SPSS are often quite expensive, and the licensing requirements sometimes restrictive, making it often difficult for teachers and students to have access to the latest version of the commercial software. Availability for students is frequently limited to partial versions or restricted to computer laboratories. Spreadsheets, on the other hand, are inexpensive or even free. Most working professionals do not have easy access to a dedicated statistics package, but virtually everyone has a computer with a spreadsheet program installed. As a bonus, the student who has learned basic statistics using the spreadsheet approach with built-in functions and formulas as described in this book will typically find the transition to a high-level statistical language such as R to be smoother than will the student who learned statistics using either a calculator or a dedicated statistics package.

This book had modest beginnings. A few years ago, I was asked to teach statistics online. The students did not have access to SPSS, and I was unable to troubleshoot hand calculations at a distance. After polling the class as to the availability of computational resources, I determined every student had access to a computer with Microsoft Excel. I began to write tutorials showing the students how to complete their homework assignments using Excel. At the end of the class, the students asked me to produce a small book from all the tutorials. The first iterations of this book were short, self-published, and very much of the "cookbook" variety.

Over the past several years, I have come to understand Excel is not only a decent (though quite far from perfect) computing tool for basic statistics, but also an excellent statistics teaching tool if used properly. As a result, this book is far more complete than its predecessors were, and is now more of a handbook than a simple cookbook. Coverage now includes discrete probability distributions, nonparametric tests, and confidence intervals. In the discussion of confidence intervals for proportions, instead of the traditional approach, I demonstrate the use of the more accurate "plus four" method. There is improved coverage of z scores and the standard normal distribution. I have also included an appendix with instructions for reporting the results of statistical tests in American Psychological Association (APA) style based on the latest sixth edition of the *Publication Manual of the American Psychological Association* (APA, 2010). Finally, there are more and more varied examples and exercises. An appendix contains the answers to all odd-numbered exercises. Most of the larger tables and datasets for most of the exercises in this book are available from the publisher, along with other useful resources. Instructors also have access to the generic worksheet templates illustrated in the text.

Feedback from colleagues and their students, as well as from my own students, has shaped the content, style, and tone of this book. I would like to acknowledge the support of my deans and department chairs present and former, including Donavan Outten, Teresa Collins-Jones, Rita Jensen, Michelle Green, Jack O'Regan, Daniel Mynatt, Carol Karnes, David Reinhart, Fred Switzer, Tilman Sheets, Jo Ann Dauzat, and Donna Austin. Present and former colleagues with whom I have frequently discussed the teaching and learning of statistics include Kimberly Barchard, Kate Andrews, Kelly Gatewood, Mike Marrapodi, Shoshana Dayanim, Rick Frederick, Barry Tuchfeld, Susan Marcus, Hank Lehrer, Xavier Retnam, Mike Winiski, Jerry Tobacyk, Frances Kelley, and Mary Margaret Livingston.

Through several lively and informative interchanges with Dr. Rick Jerz during the writing of this text, I learned that Excel uses unusual methods for calculating percentiles and percentile ranks, and thus of quartiles as well. I have used Rick's correct method in this book, and show how to find correct percentiles and percentile ranks in Excel using formulas and cumulative percentages. In addition to his thorough review for this final version, Dr. Lê Xuân Hy used draft versions of this text with his classes. His feedback, along with that of his students, was immeasurably helpful in improving the accuracy and quality of this text. It was through interactions with Dr. Hy that I learned of some of the limitations of Excel's NORMSDIST function as discussed in Chapters 5 and 6. I have also used draft versions of this text in my own classes, and the predecessor to this text was used extensively in classrooms and online, so it is safe to say that this book is both classroom tested and instructor approved.

The following individuals served as external reviewers of this book. Their insights and suggestions improved the quality, accuracy, and coverage of this book.

- Kathleen S. Andrews, Argosy University
- Christine Browning, Crichton College
- Lê Xuân Hy, Seattle University
- Rick Jerz, St. Ambrose University
- Karl Kelley, North Central College
- Hank Lehrer, Purdue University
- Luke Rosielle, Gannon University

No published book is ever the work of a single individual, and I am grateful to Peter Davis of Pearson for believing in this project and for being an early and tireless advocate. I am also deeply indebted to Jeff Marshall at Pearson for his support and leadership in making this book a reality.

Finally, I am very appreciative of the support of my family, and especially that of my wife and business partner Shirley Pace, who tolerates my fascination with statistics and spreadsheets with good humor and grace.

About the Author

Larry A. Pace, Ph.D., is an award-winning professor of statistics, management, and psychology. He is currently a professor of psychology in the College of Undergraduate Studies at Argosy University Online, where he teaches undergraduate and graduate courses in statistics and quantitative research methods. Previously, he was a professor of psychology and chair of the behavioral sciences department at Anderson University in Anderson, SC. Dr. Pace has taught behavioral and business statistics and research methods courses for Argosy University, Anderson University, Clemson University, Keiser University, Ashford University, Capella University, Austin Peay State University, Louisiana Tech University, and Rensselaer Polytechnic Institute. He has written 15 books and more than 80 articles, chapters, and reviews, in addition to hundreds of online tutorials and reviews.

He earned the Ph.D. in psychological measurement with a content major in industrial/organizational psychology from the University of Georgia. Dr. Pace has served on the faculties of Argosy University, Anderson University, Clemson University, Louisiana Tech University, Louisiana State University in Shreveport, the University of Tennessee, Rochester Institute of Technology, and Rensselaer Polytechnic Institute. He was a visiting scholar in Cornell University's Johnson Graduate School of Management and the New York State School of Industrial and Labor Relations. He worked for Furman University as an instructional development consultant, for Xerox Corporation as an internal consultant and organizational effectiveness manager, and for a private consulting firm as an organizational development consultant. Among Dr. Pace's consulting clients have been AT&T, Compaq Computer Corporation, International Paper, Lucent Technologies, and Xerox Corporation.

Dr. Pace resides in Anderson, SC, with his wife and business partner Shirley Pace. The Paces are active community volunteers. They have four grown children and one grandson. When he is not busy teaching, doing research, or helping others with their research projects, Dr. Pace enjoys reading and writing about statistics, building spreadsheet models for statistical tests, figuring out things on the computer, cooking on the grill, exploring nature, playing several musical instruments (none of them particularly well), and tending a vegetable garden.

Brief Contents

Table of Contents

1   A Statistician's View of Excel 2007

In this chapter, you will learn about the features of Microsoft Excel, including the new Excel 2007 interface, working with cells and ranges, and setting up a data structure. You will learn how to navigate through a workbook file, how to identify and correct errors, how to size worksheet columns, and how to do math in Excel. At the end of this chapter, you will find a discussion of some very important terms for data management and statistics, and a brief overview of the remainder of the book.

Spreadsheets like Microsoft Excel are useful for handling, manipulating, storing, and exploring data, as well as basic statistical analyses. It is important to note that Excel is not perfect as a statistics tool. For example, critics have pointed out the inefficiency of several of Excel's computational algorithms. Some of the built-in statistical distributions do not work in extreme cases, and in a relatively few cases, unusual data can lead to computational errors. Microsoft is aware of such problems, and has fixed many of the statistical shortcomings of the program over the years, though not all of them. There are still problems in unusual cases. For example, the NORMSDIST function described in Chapters 5 – 7 does not work properly for z scores of extreme positive and negative values. As discussed in Chapter 9, the CHIINV function in Excel 2007 does not work in the extreme tails of the chi-square distribution. As mentioned in the preface and discussed more thoroughly in Chapter 2, the PERCENTILE and PERCENTRANK functions produce unexpected results. You should avoid these functions and use the methods delineated in this text to find correct percentiles and percentile ranks. Despite these limitations, Excel works well with the kinds of data most academics and professionals collect and analyze on a regular basis, and because of its wide availability, transparency, flexibility, and ease of use, Excel has become popular as an analytical and teaching tool.

Most computers today come with a spreadsheet program already installed. For users who do not already have one, spreadsheets are inexpensive (some are free). The flexibility of the spreadsheet makes it useful for many applications not available in a standard statistical package. Because Excel is not a statistics package, researchers perform sophisticated statistical analyses with dedicated statistics packages such as SPSS, SAS, or Minitab, or with programs and languages developed specifically for statistical or numerical computation, such as R and MATLAB. Some statistical purists refuse to use Microsoft Excel for statistics for the reasons stated in the previous paragraphs, but pragmatic researchers and practitioners in a variety of fields including business, social work, and, increasingly, psychology and the other behavioral sciences, find, despite its limitations, that Excel is too useful and too readily available to ignore. As a reflection of this trend, several recent statistics authors use spreadsheets as the primary or only computational tool (see for example Aczel & Sounderpandian, 2009; Bakeman & Robinson, 2005; Dretzke, 2009; Patterson & Basham, 2006).

About This Book

You will learn about descriptive and inferential statistics by reading this book and working through the examples and exercises. Although reading this book will not teach you everything there is to know about a spreadsheet program, you will also know quite a bit about the data management and statistical features of Excel 2007 by the time you are finished. This book about how to use a widely available and easy-to-use technology for basic descriptive and inferential statistics will be of assistance to students, teachers, professionals, and researchers. Interactive worksheet templates, workbooks containing the Excel files for most of the examples and many of the exercises in this book, and many other statistics resources are freely available to adopters of this text.

If you would like to learn more about the many other things besides statistics you can do with Excel 2007 and with Office 2007 in general, an excellent print source is *Office 2007: The Missing Manual* by Grover, MacDonald, and Vander Veer (2007). For the technically minded, Excel provides opportunities for advanced applications through programming and add-ins. However, to keep things as simple as possible, no macros or third-party add-ins are used in this book.

Readers who have used a dedicated statistics program like SPSS or Minitab will recognize the data views of SPSS and Minitab as spreadsheets. However, unlike programs that separate the variable and data views from the output, Excel combines the data view, the variable view, and the output view into a single problem space. In addition to its low cost and wide availability, Excel's unified problem space makes it useful for learning and teaching basic statistics. The student can see the data, the formulas, and the results all in the same place, and can instantly see the effects of data modifications on the results. Used in this way, Excel functions more like a statistics language or environment such as R than a dedicated statistics package. The user is one step closer to the data and the results than with SPSS, for example, which produces voluminous output in a "black box" fashion for typical users who do not write their own syntax and rely only on the point-and-click interface.

In this book, a shortcut approach is used to refer to Excel 2007's menu-driven structure. For example, you may read instructions to find the **AutoSum** tool in the **Editing** group of the **Home** ribbon. A more direct way to summarize these steps is **Home** > **Editing** > **AutoSum**. THE BOTTOM LINE text boxes appear throughout this book to summarize key points. To make them easy to locate, these boxes have solid borders and shading, and are in Bold Calibri font. Readers interested in reading a bulleted outline and those looking for a quick refresher for a given section or procedure will find these quick summaries helpful. In this book, **Boldface** type indicates a menu item the user clicks on or locates in the Excel interface. **Boldface** combined with angle brackets, such as <**Enter**> or <**Ctrl**> + **T** indicates the user should press one or a combination of keys. Function keys such as **F1** or **F4** are shown in **boldface** without brackets. **Boldface** type also refers to the titles of the tabs such as **Home**, **Insert**, and **Data**, as well as to the names of the associated groups such as the **Workbook Views**, **Show/Hide**, **Zoom**, **Window**, and **Macros** groups on the **View** ribbon.

Using a Spreadsheet

A spreadsheet fulfils purposes for quantitative information similar to the functions a word processor serves for text. With a spreadsheet, one can organize, store, update, analyze, summarize, present, and evaluate quantitative information. The electronic spreadsheet, and not the word processing program, was the first "killer app" for the personal computer. Even if you have never used a spreadsheet program, you will find Excel 2007 to be straightforward. Learning a spreadsheet program is somewhat harder than learning a word processing program like Microsoft Word or a presentation program like Microsoft PowerPoint. By contrast, a spreadsheet is easier to learn than a dedicated statistics package such as SPSS or a relational database program like Microsoft Access.

To find out more about Excel or to obtain a free trial version of Excel 2007, visit the Excel 2007 home page here:

http://office.microsoft.com/en-us/excel/default.aspx

The Excel User Interface

The 2007 version of Microsoft Excel introduced a new file format and a completely redesigned user interface (see Figure 1.1). If you have used previous versions of Excel, all of the functionality you are accustomed to is still there, although occasionally in new—and sometimes unexpected—places. In the upper left corner of the Excel 2007 interface is the round "Office Button" (see Figure 1.2). The most common commands are there, tucked away until you need them. This is where you print, save, and open workbook files. When you click the Office Button, you can access recent workbooks, customization options for the Quick Access Toolbar, and an array of other Excel options. Find these additional Excel options by clicking on a button at the bottom of the Office Button dialog (Figure 1.3). Excel options are discussed in more detail in the sections on customizing the Status Bar and installing the Analysis ToolPak. In addition to the Office Button, Microsoft introduced the "ribbon" with Office 2007. The ribbon replaced the Standard Toolbar in earlier versions. Figure 1.1 shows the ribbon, which provides a "super menu" that lets you get to everything Excel can do, using a tab-and-group hierarchy. On the ribbon, tabs organize groups, and groups organize related functions, tools, commands, and options. The groups appear in separate boxes on the ribbon. To illustrate, clicking on the **Home** tab reveals the **Home** ribbon with **Clipboard**, **Font**, **Alignment**, **Number**, **Styles**, **Cells**, and **Editing** groups. Placing the pointer over a group causes it to change appearance subtly (the background color is lightened). Holding the cursor over a particular icon in a specific group brings up a box with a description of the command, for instance the Office Button description shown in Figure 1.2. Many of these boxes are illustrated, and many of them display keyboard shortcuts for accessing the given command. If a particular command is currently unavailable, it will be "grayed out." To see an example of this, click on the **Review** tab in a new workbook. See in the **Comments** group that the options for deleting and selecting comments are not active because there are no comments in the worksheet.

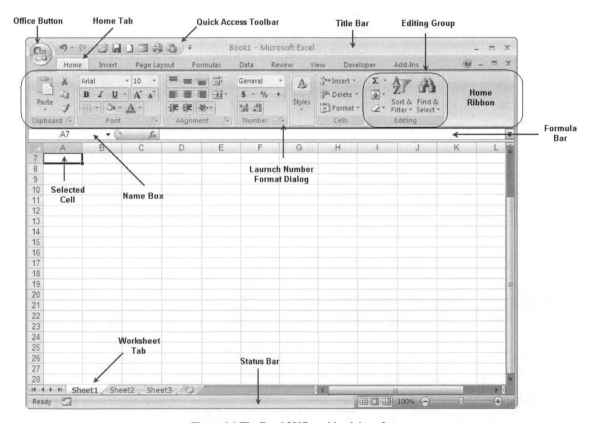

Figure 1.1 The Excel 2007 workbook interface

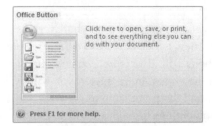

Figure 1.2 The Office Button

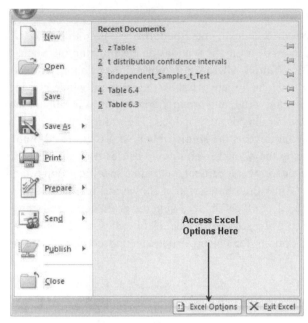

Figure 1.3 Office Button Dialog Box

The icons and labels in the available groups expand or contract to make optimum use of the available screen real estate. Figure 1.4 shows how the Excel **Home** ribbon appears at two different monitor resolutions (800 × 600 versus 1024 × 768). With smaller screen sizes, all of Excel's features are still available, but Excel reduces the size and detail of the labels and icons on the ribbon. For example, compare the appearance of the **Styles** group in the two screens. With smaller screen sizes, you will often need to click on dropdown arrows to access the available options. In the bottom right corner of many of the groups is a little "Launch Dialog" button represented as a square with a diagonal arrow (see the labeled icon in the **Number** group in Figure 1.1). When you click this button, you will launch a dialog or a task pane with additional features or customization options. Holding the cursor over the button will reveal an illustrated description of these features.

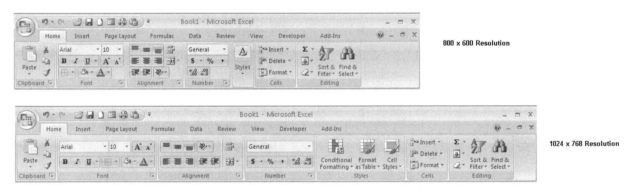

Figure 1.4 The Home ribbon at two different screen resolutions

When you add elements such as tables, charts, or pictures to your worksheet, a specific **Tools** menu will appear in the title bar above the ribbon tabs, and a new tab or tabs like **Format** for pictures and **Design** for tables will appear on the ribbon. These new tabs and ribbons will always be available, though not always visible. To see them again when they are not visible, simply select the object. In Chapter 2, you will examine in detail some of the useful things you can do with tables. Charts, graphs, and the pivot table tool are the subjects of Chapter 3, and you will learn to use **Chart Tools** providing customization options through additional groups.

Unlike the previous Standard Toolbar, the ribbon is not completely customizable. New tabs and groups will be added to the ribbon only when you install add-ins or add elements such as tables or charts. You cannot resize or move the ribbon, though you can minimize it. However, you also cannot accidentally delete or "lose" the ribbon the way you could the Standard Toolbar.

If you prefer a larger working area, you can minimize the ribbon by double clicking on any of the tabs such as **Home**, **Insert**, or **Page Layout**. After you minimize the ribbon, only the tabs will appear. When you click on a tab, the ribbon will reappear, "floating" atop the worksheet. The ribbon will vanish when you return to the work area. If you want to maximize the ribbon again, double click on any of the tabs. You can also minimize and maximize the ribbon by right clicking on the Office Button and then selecting or deselecting "Minimize the Ribbon."

THE BOTTOM LINE

- The Office Button provides access to printing, opening, and saving workbook files.
- The Office Button also provides a button at the bottom of the dialog to access Excel Options.
- The ribbon replaces the Standard Toolbar of previous versions.
- The ribbon provides a tab-and-group hierarchy allowing access to all the features available in Excel.
- Icons and labels in the available groups on the ribbon will shrink or expand as the screen resolution changes.
- Many groups have an additional "Launch Dialog" button at the bottom right corner.
- All options are available even when the Excel screen size is reduced, but you may need to click on a dropdown arrow to see the options.
- You can minimize the ribbon by double-clicking on any ribbon tab. Double-clicking on any tab restores the ribbon.
- When a command is not currently available, it will be "grayed out."

The Anatomy of a Worksheet

Excel 2007 holds a large amount of information. Earlier versions were limited to 256 columns and 65,536 rows per worksheet, but Excel 2007 includes 16,384 columns and 1,048,576 rows per worksheet. This is slightly more than 1,000 times more cells per individual worksheet than Excel 2003. An Excel workbook file can have multiple "plies" or individual worksheets. One navigates through these worksheets by clicking on the worksheet tabs at the bottom of the workbook interface (see Figure 1.5). By default, you can have up to 255 worksheets in a single workbook file. You can have even more if you have enough system resources.

If you find the worksheet tab labels "Sheet1, Sheet2, and Sheet3" unhelpful, you can double-click on a tab and rename it to something more useful. You can also right-click on the tab to rename the worksheet, as well as provide a color-coding scheme, much like physical notebook binder tabs. You can rearrange the order of the sheets by clicking on a tab and dragging it to a new position. You can add more worksheets when you need them by clicking on the last tab, as shown in Figure 1.5. If there are more sheets than can be displayed at one time, use the worksheet scroll buttons to the left of the worksheet tabs to navigate through the entire workbook. You can also simply right-click on any of these arrows to reveal a list of all the sheets in the workbook. From this list, you can click on any worksheet name to change the active sheet (Figure 1.5).

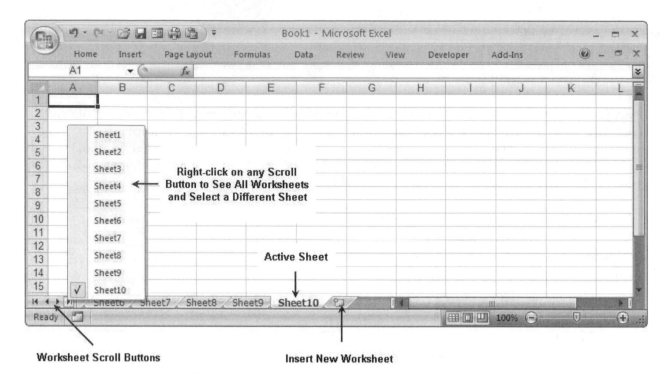

Figure 1.5 Navigating the workbook

The work area of a spreadsheet consists of *rows* and *columns* located beneath the column letters and to the right of the row numbers. The intersection of a row and a column is a *cell*. The columns of the worksheet are labeled with letters from left to right, beginning with A – Z, then AA – AZ, then BA – BZ, and so on, all the way up to XFD in Excel 2007. Excel numbers the rows from top to bottom beginning with 1. To find the address or "reference" of a particular cell, refer to the column letter(s) first and the row number second in locating, navigating to, or naming a cell or a range of cells. Figure 1.5 shows cell A1 is the upper left cell of the worksheet work area. The reference A1 appears in the Name Box. The dark borders and the highlighted row and column labels show A1 is the active cell.

Working with Worksheet Cells

A worksheet cell can contain any combination of the following kinds of information:

- Numbers (such as 12, 3.14, or the current date).
- Text (such as "Question_1," "Date," or "Name"–obviously without the quotes).
- Formulas (such as 1 + 1). To tell Excel it should add 1 and 1, you start with an = sign, as discussed later in this chapter in the section "Doing Math in Excel."
- Built-in functions (such as AVERAGE, STDEV, or FREQUENCY).
- Pointers to other cells and ranges in the same worksheet or another worksheet (such as =A132 or =Sheet2! B2). These pointers display in the current cell the contents of the cell to which one is pointing. You can even refer to cells or ranges in a different workbook file by enclosing the workbook name in brackets ([ ]) before the individual sheet name.

Enter numbers and text by selecting a cell and then typing directly into the cell. You can also select the cell and click in the Formula Bar to enter or format information. Excel recognizes numerical entries and right-justifies them by default. Excel also recognizes text and left-justifies it by default. If you want Excel to recognize a number as a text entry, you can precede the number with a single quote ('). Excel will give you an error warning (a little green triangle in the upper left corner of the cell) to let you know you have stored a number as text, which is precisely what you want to do on occasion, such as using 2010, 2011, and 2012 as column headings for three consecutive years. If you store these as text, the labels will keep the numbers from accidentally being included in your calculations and throwing off your results. When you format a number as text, Excel left-justifies the entry (see Figure 1.6).

When you enter numbers, remember a single cell should have a single number in it. Text entries in cells should be limited to small amounts of text used as labels for the values in adjacent cells or for column headings. Although you can make Excel cells large enough to contain substantial amounts of text, and can even force the program to wrap text in the cell to two or more lines, Excel is not a very good word processor. When you need to insert longer text entries, consider using a text box (**Insert** > **Text** > **Text Box**) that will float atop your worksheet. You can format cells and their contents by changing the font size and font face, the color, the cell background and border formatting, the alignment, number formatting, and other characteristics. Excel provides predefined Cell Styles accessible from the **Home** ribbon in the **Cells** group (**Home** > **Cells** > **Cell Styles**).

You can center a label across two or more columns by using the merge feature of Excel. Assume you would like "Successive Years" to be centered across columns A, B, and C (Figure 1.6). The text entry is in cell A1. Select cells A1:C1, and then click **Home** > **Alignment** > **Merge & Center**. After you click the **Merge & Center** icon, the three cells will be merged into a single cell, and the titled will be centered in the merged cell. To unmerge the cells, click in cell A1, and click **Merge & Center** again.

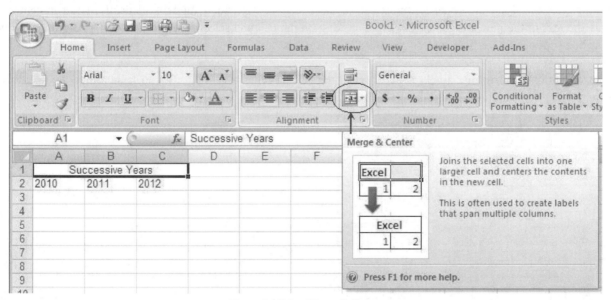

Figure 1.6 Using Merge & Center

If you prefer not to merge cells, you can still center text across a selection of cells by first selecting the cells and then clicking on the arrow at the bottom right corner of the **Alignment** group to launch the **Format: Cells; Alignment** dialog (see the arrow beneath the **Merge & Center** icon in Figure 1.6). You can also simply select the cells, click the right mouse button, and then click on **Format Cells**. On the Alignment tab of the resulting **Format Cells** dialog box, select **Horizontal**, **Center Across Selection**, and then click **OK** (see Figure 1.7). Although this alters the appearance of the text across two or more cells, the actual text entry remains in a single cell of the worksheet.

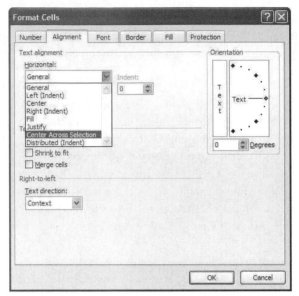

Figure 1.7 Centering text across multiple cells without merging cells

You can also merge cells vertically or both vertically and horizontally, but be aware that doing so will cause the loss of the entries in all but the upper left-most cell of the selection. After merging cells vertically, you can center or rotate the text in the new merged cell by right-clicking on the cell and selecting **Format Cells** > **Alignment**. Find the various options for vertical centering in the **Alignment** tab.

As just mentioned, to format a cell or cells, select the cell or cells, then right click to launch a context-sensitive menu (Figure 1.8) and then select **Format Cells**.

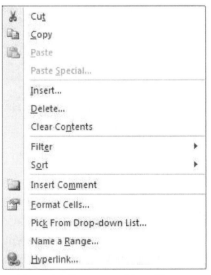

Figure 1.8 Context-sensitive cell menu

Remember you can also get to cell formatting options after selecting one or more cells by clicking on the "Launch Dialog" boxes at the bottom right of the **Font**, **Alignment**, and **Number** groups in the **Home** ribbon (see Figure 1.1).

In addition to putting information in specific worksheet cells, you can also add elements not attached to any specific cell. In addition to the previously mentioned text boxes, these elements include charts and graphs, pictures, clip art or other graphics, drawings, word art, equations, and other objects. All these objects float on top of your workbook file and can be moved, sized, copied, and deleted.

You can also copy, delete, and move cell contents. You can move a cell's contents to another location by cutting and then pasting, or you can select the cell, move the cursor to the highlighted cell border (the cursor becomes a four-way arrow), and then simply click and drag the cell and drop it in its new location. You can use the Format Painter (**Home** > **Clipboard** > **Format Painter**) to copy the formatting from one cell to another cell or cells. Standard Windows keyboard shortcut commands, such as <**Ctrl**> + **C** for copy, <**Ctrl**> + **X** for cut, and <**Ctrl**> + **V** for paste, also work in Excel. You can find the associated command icons for these operations in the **Clipboard** group of the **Insert** ribbon.

Although you can simply type information into cells in a haphazard fashion, you will ultimately find it most helpful to organize the information. Place related information in tabular fashion in columns and rows so you can apply formulas, functions, and tools most efficiently.

THE BOTTOM LINE

- The intersection of a row and a column is called a cell.
- Cells are referenced by the column letter(s) first and the row number second, as in cell D32.
- Cells can contain any combination of numbers (dates are also stored as numbers), text, functions, formulas, and pointers to other cells or other worksheets.
- Numbers are right aligned by default.
- Text is left aligned by default.
- Formulas and functions appear in the Formula Bar when the cell is selected.
- Cells and cell contents can be formatted in many ways.
- Cell contents can be copied, moved, and deleted.
- Cells can be merged and unmerged, and text can be centered across a selection of cells without having to merge the cells.
- You can add other elements not attached to specific cells of the worksheet. These elements include text boxes, graphics, equations, and other objects. These elements can also be copied, moved, and deleted.

Working with Ranges and Names

It is possible to work with more than one cell at a time. A series of consecutive cells is a ***range***. One kind of range is a set of consecutive values in a single column or a single row. This one-dimensional list of values is a one-dimensional ***array*** or ***vector***. To refer to an array, you use a colon to separate the references of the first cell in the array and the last cell of the array. Look ahead to Figure 1.18 at the end of this chapter. Notice the label and data values for Test1 are in Column B, starting in Row 1 and ending in Row 6. Refer to this array with the reference B1:B6. It typically does not hurt to include the label in the range with the values, because Excel will ignore the label when calculating statistics, and will use it when reporting them if you ask for a label.

When you refer to the same range repeatedly, and when you want to clarify the purpose of formulas and functions, you can use a shortcut called a ***named range***. Look ahead to the data in Table 1.1. You could give the name "Test1" to the associated values for the test. A very easy way to name a range is to select the range with your mouse, to click in the Name Box (Figure 1.1), and then to type the desired name directly in the Name Box. Press <**Enter**> to apply the name to the selected cell or range. It is okay to reuse the column label for the name of the range, so you can type in "Test1" (without the quotes) after selecting the range. Remember to press <**Enter**> to save the named range. After naming a range, you can include the range in functions and formulas by typing in the name rather than the cell references. You can click the dropdown arrow to the right of the Name Box to see all the named ranges and to select and return to any of them, even from another worksheet tab.

Named ranges have another advantage. If you decide to change a selected range, for example by adding or deleting records, you only need confirm that the named range includes the new information and edit the name to include the new information if it does not. After this, any formulas or functions referring to this range will still work properly, and will include the updated information.

Ranges can also include two or more columns and two or more rows. A tabular range with two or more columns and rows is a *matrix* or a *table*. As with an array, you refer to a matrix by referring to the first and last cells in the matrix. For example, go to Figure 1.18 and look at all the data. You could refer to the range A1:D6 and select the entire data table. It is also possible to name a matrix. You might want to call this range "Scores." Later in this book, you will learn about using a powerful kind of named object simply called a table.

When you create a table or chart or add a picture, Excel names it automatically, and you can select the object via the Name Box and the Name Manager. If you need to modify or delete a name, click on the **Formulas** tab to access the Name Manager (**Formulas** > **Defined Names** > **Name Manager**). You can also use the Name Manager to create names, though the shortcut of typing the desired name for cells and ranges directly into the Name Box is faster. For those interested in more advanced applications of names, in addition to naming ranges of cells, you can give names to single cells, to constants, and even to formulas. It is possible to use the OFFSET function to create a *dynamic range*, a device used in some of the statistics templates developed for this book. You will not see named formulas in the Name Box, but you can see and edit them via the Name Manager. Excel also automatically names certain objects added to the workbook, as discussed below.

In addition to their many other advantages, named ranges make it possible to write formulas others can more easily understand when they are using spreadsheets you create. This is very helpful for the computation of statistics and for building Excel formulas similar to the equations in statistics books. Range names can contain letters, numbers, and underscores, and must start with a letter. The names cannot contain spaces or special characters.

Here is an important caveat about naming a range. You should not attempt to name a range something conflicting with Excel's own conventions for naming cells. For example, you might think quite logically Q1 would be a good name for Question 1 in a survey, and Q2 would be a good name for Question 2. The problem is Excel already reserves Q1 and Q2 as labels for specific cells in the worksheet, namely, the intersection of column Q and rows 1 and 2. You will confuse Excel (and yourself) if you try to name a range with a cell reference, so this is something to avoid. If you type a cell reference such as Q1 in the Name Box, Excel will simply move the active cell to Q1 when you press <**Enter**>. This is a great way to move around in your worksheet, but not a good way to name ranges.

As noted before, Excel 2007 provides 16,384 columns, and by default uses letters for column labels, up to column XFD. This means many range names that work properly in early versions of Excel, such as "day1," "day2," and "day3," will conflict with cell references for actual worksheet cells using the references DAY1, DAY2, and DAY3. One way to avoid this with three letter names followed by a number is to use the names "day_1," "day_2," and "day_3." You may also simply prefer to use at least four letters in your range names and prevent this confusion altogether. Another way to avoid this problem is to switch to R1C1 cell referencing. This referencing uses numbers to represent both rows and columns, so cell A1 now becomes R1C1, and cell XFD101048576 (the bottom right cell of the worksheet) becomes R1048576C16384. The interested reader should consult the Excel help files for more information. Because the majority of Excel users do not use R1C1 referencing, we will not address it further. Other than the restrictions that the names cannot include spaces, cannot conflict with normal cell references, and must contain only letters, numbers, and underscores and begin with a letter, there are no additional limitations to named ranges.

THE BOTTOM LINE

- You can create and store a name for a cell, a range of cells, a constant, or a formula.
- The easiest way to name a cell or a range is to select it and then click in the Name Box, type the desired name, and press **<Enter>**.
- Selecting the name in the Name Box selects the particular named cell, range, or object.
- Names can be used in place of cell references in formulas and functions.
- Excel names tables and charts as special named objects in the workbook file. These names also appear in the Name Box
- It is possible to create dynamic ranges using the OFFSET function (this is not discussed further in this text).
- Names can be also be defined, edited, and deleted by selecting **Formulas > Defined Names > Name Manager**.

Relative and Absolute References

A cell or range reference can be *relative* or *absolute*. The default reference in Excel, such as the reference to cell A1, is a relative reference. If you copy or move a formula, function, or cell pointer from cell A1 to a different cell, any relative cell references to A1 or other cells will be indexed or incremented by Excel to refer to their new location(s) in the worksheet. You very often want to copy a formula from one cell to another or to a range and have the formula instantly update to refer to the new cell locations. Sometimes, however, this is exactly what you do not want to happen, because you want the reference a particular cell or range to be absolute.

To illustrate the distinction between absolute and relative cell references, let us refer to a cell, perhaps cell A12, which contains the function to calculate the mean of an array of numbers (see Figure 1.9). Now suppose you want to write a formula to calculate a deviation score for each number in a new column by subtracting the mean from the value in the adjacent cell. You can write a formula in cell B1 to calculate the deviation score for the first value by typing in = A1–A12, and when you press **<Enter>**, the formula will work perfectly. But the formula cannot be copied and pasted to cell B2 and still work properly, because the default indexing will change the formula to = A2–A13 and because cell A13 is empty, the deviation score will not be correct (Figure 1.10). To avoid this problem, change the reference to A12 to an absolute one by going back to cell B1 and changing the formula to = A1–A12. The dollar signs indicate an absolute reference to column A and row 12. Now when you copy and paste the formula from cell B1 to cell B2, the formula will change to = A2–A12, indexing the first reference and keeping the second reference constant. You can simply type in the required $ signs to change either the row or column (or both) references from relative to absolute.

Figure 1.9 Average of the 11 values is in cell A12

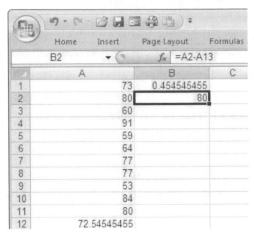

Figure 1.10 Relative reference increments due to new location (cell B2), and pasted function calculates deviation score incorrectly

Below, the corrected formula for cell B2 is shown in the Formula Bar (see Figure 1.11). The second deviation score is now also correct. Pasting this same formula into cells B3:B11 will result in the correct calculation of all the deviation scores.

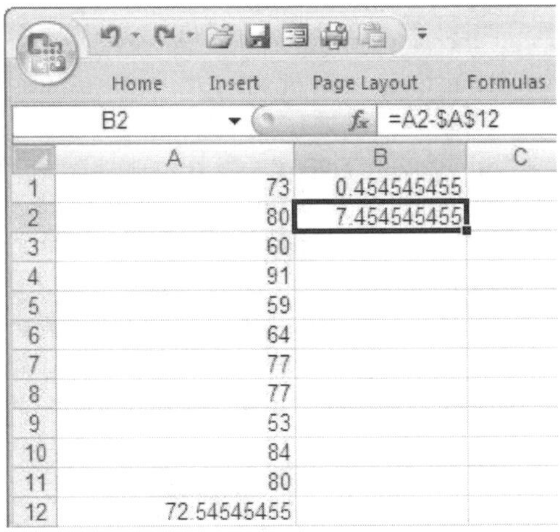

Figure 1.11 Absolute reference allows the correct calculation of the deviation score

You may use a convenient keyboard shortcut to change an address from relative to absolute and back again. Select a cell with a formula uses a relative reference, say cell B1 as discussed above. Then click in the Formula Bar, select the cell reference you want to make absolute (which is cell A12). Press the **F4** key. Excel adds the $ signs, changing the entry to A12. Pressing **F4** again changes the entry to A$12, changing it to a relative column reference combined with an absolute row reference. Pressing **F4** once more changes the reference to $A12, with an absolute column and relative row reference, and pressing **F4** one last time changes both references back to relative ones. Thus the **F4** key acts like a toggle with four states. The more you use Excel, the more you will appreciate the flexibility of relative and absolute references. When you use named ranges, those ranges will always make use of absolute references.

As mentioned previously, when you need to point to a cell or range in a different worksheet in the same workbook, you use an absolute or relative reference including the worksheet title followed by an exclamation point (!), such as

= Sheet2! A32 or = Sheet3! B7

It is even possible in a function or formula to refer to a cell or range in a different workbook file. When this is desired, the pointer should use square brackets to surround the name of the file, as illustrated below:

= [Book2] Sheet3! A1:$A99

When you refer to another workbook file, the pointer will not work automatically as do the ones within the same workbook. If you use a reference like the one above, when you press <**Enter**>, Excel will prompt you for the location of the other workbook file, and will you will have to navigate to it for each such reference.

When you modify the structure of your worksheet, for example by adding or deleting rows or columns, the absolute cell references will update to refer to their new locations in the modified worksheet. They will still work "as advertised" from their new absolute locations.

THE BOTTOM LINE

- The default cell reference in Excel is relative, such as A1.
- Absolute references are indicated by the $ symbol, such as A1.
- Column, row, and both column and row references can be absolute, as in A1, $A1, and A$1.
- The **F4** key is a shortcut to changing cell references from relative to absolute and back.
- Relative references index or increment when cell contents containing cell references are copied to new locations.
- Absolute references do not index or increment.
- Absolute references are updated when the worksheet structure is modified.
- References to other worksheet tabs include the worksheet tab title and an exclamation point (!).
- You can include a pointer or reference to another workbook file by inserting the file name in square brackets, e.g. ([filename]), but these pointers will not work automatically.

Setting Up a Data Structure

You can enter information into a cell of a worksheet in two different ways. You already saw one of these: Just type information directly into the cells of the worksheet or select the cell and then click to type in the Formula Bar. As a useful alternative, you can also use Excel's default data form, which is a timesaver when you have a large amount of data entry to do. Assume you have three test scores for each of five individuals (see Table 1.1) and want to enter this information into your worksheet for further analysis. Before you enter the data, set up a data structure with a row of column headings (variable names). Detailed instructions for setting up the data structure and entering the data follow. If you are new to Excel, you will want to open an Excel workbook file and follow along, trying to duplicate the screens you see in this book.

Table 1.1 Example data

Name	Test1	Test2	Test3
Lyle	88	92	89
Jorge	78	82	78
Kim	34	87	62
Frances	76	82	32
Tomeca	66	88	64

Set up the data structure by typing the column headings in Row 1, as shown in Figure 1.12. Use only letters, numbers, and underscores in your column headings, and keep the headings as brief as possible. Begin the heading with a letter. If you are planning to use the headings in another program such as SPSS, you should not use spaces in your headings. If you desire visual separation in your headings, you can use an underscore, as in Test_1. A bottom border (found under **Home** > **Font**) provides additional visual separation between the column headings and the data entries, though its use is entirely optional.

As previously discussed, to enter the data in the cells beneath the column headings, you can simply point to the cell with the mouse and click to select the cell or use the arrow keys to navigate from cell to cell. Begin typing, and information is displayed in the cell and the Formula Bar window simultaneously. As soon as you press <**Enter**> or <**Tab**> or simply select another cell, the information you typed into the cell or the Formula Bar will appear in both places. If you are entering formulas, functions, or cell pointers, after you enter the information, the Formula Bar will display the Formula View while the cell will display the result of its application (Value View).

	A	B	C	D
1	Name	Test1	Test2	Test3
2				
3				
4				

Figure 1.12 Data structure with column headings

To use a data form for data entry rather than having to type entries directly into worksheet cells or the Formula Bar, add the **Form** command to the Quick Access Toolbar. Click on **Office Button** > **Excel Options**. If you are having trouble locating **Excel Options**, look back to Figure 1.3. In the resulting dialog, click on **Customize**, and then use the dropdown menu to select **Commands Not in the Ribbon**. Scroll to **Form** and then click on **Add** (Figure 1.13). Click **OK**. The **Data Form** icon appears in the Quick Access Toolbar (Figure 1.14). After setting up the data structure, you can click in cell A2 to select it and then click on the **Data Form** icon. Accept the default to use the first row headers as your data labels and click **OK** (Figure 1.15). This form gives you the option of searching for and editing data entries as well as adding and deleting entries. In the form, you can click in a field to select it or use the <**Tab**> key to advance through the fields.

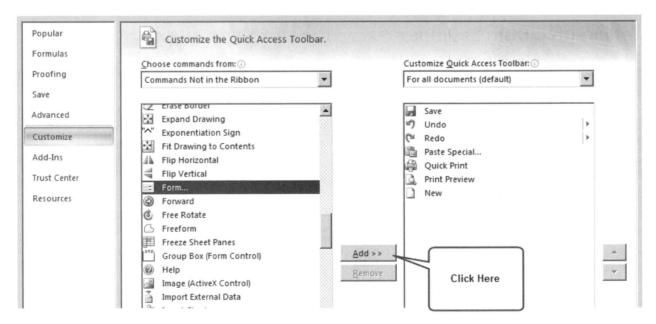

Figure 1.13 Adding the Data Form icon to the Quick Access Toolbar

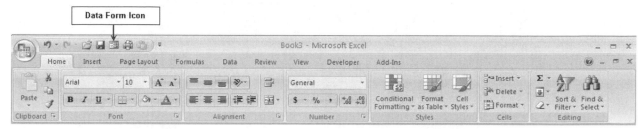

Figure 1.14 Data Form icon now appears on the Quick Access Toolbar

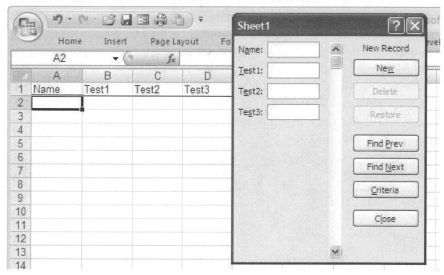

Figure 1.15 Default data form ready for inputting a new record

---

THE BOTTOM LINE

- Column headings should be as brief as possible.
- Headings should contain only letters, numbers, and underscores. You should begin each heading with a letter. If you plan to use the headings in SPSS or another program, do not use spaces in your headings.
- You can enter information directly into a cell, into the Formula Bar, or through a Data Form.

Identifying Errors and Sizing Columns

Sometimes you might inadvertently instruct Excel to do something it is incapable of doing, for example by misspelling the name of a function or entering an invalid range name. If this is the case, Excel will display #NAME? in the affected cell(s). If you try to divide by zero, Excel will give you a #DIV/0 error indicator. Other error indicators in Excel include #N/A, #NULL, #NUM, #REF, and #VALUE. When you receive these error indicators, you should consult the Excel help files for explanations and solutions.

On other occasions, the information in a cell could be perfectly acceptable, but may require too much space to display correctly in the narrow default column width of 8.43 characters. When this is the case, the information displays as ####### (see Figure 1.16 for an example). This is very easy to fix. You can select one or more columns by clicking in the row of column labels (A, B, C, D, etc.). Clicking and dragging will select adjacent columns. You can also select nonadjacent columns by holding down <**Ctrl**> and clicking on each column letter. After selecting a column or columns, click the right mouse button and select "Column Width." Entering a larger number will expand the column, and entering a smaller number will shrink it. It is also possible to format column width by selecting **Home** > **Cells** > **Format**.

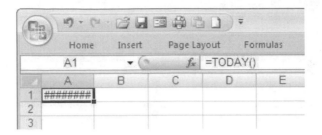

Figure 1.16 Default column is not wide enough to display the result of the Today() function

More directly, you can simply click and drag the right column border to the right or left to expand or shrink the column width. Move the cursor into the row of column labels (A, B, C, etc.) and see when the pointer is near the right border of a column, the cursor shape changes from a downward pointing arrow (for clicking and selecting the entire column) to a vertical line with double-pointing (left-right) arrows (Figure 1.17). At this point, you can hold down the left mouse button and shrink or expand the column width by dragging the mouse to the left or right. When you use this technique, Excel displays to the right and slightly above the left-right arrow the current column width in its own character units and in pixels.

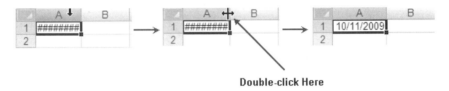

Double-click Here

Figure 1.17 Cursor changes to double-pointing arrow

If you double click the left mouse button when the cursor is the vertical line with the double-pointing arrow, the column will automatically resize to fit the contents of the widest cell entry in the column. This AutoFit feature has no effect if the column is already exactly wide enough for its contents. It only "auto-widens" and "auto-shrinks" when either there is not enough room for the contents or there is more room than necessary to display the contents. AutoFit also works when you type numbers or dates directly into a cell or when you reformat them. If the typed or formatted entry is too wide, Excel will widen the column accordingly when you press <**Enter**>. If you change a number or shrink the column width, Excel will display as many of the number's decimals as it can. If you type a larger number than the column can accommodate, Excel will report the number in scientific notation. However, the AutoFit feature does not automatically resize columns when you type in text or apply a function or formula to a cell. If you have a column with blank cells to the right, for example a column with a long title but narrower typical entries, you can also size the column to the width of the content in the active cell by selecting **Home** > **Cells** > **Format** > **AutoFit Column Width**.

Observe in the upper left corner of the worksheet area (to the left of A and above 1) the little rectangle with a triangle in it directly beneath the Name Box (see Figure 1.18). If you click this rectangle, you will select the entire worksheet. After you select the entire sheet, you can right-click to copy it, delete it, clear its contents, or format the entire sheet's cell contents, for example by changing fonts or number formats. When you select the entire worksheet, you can also use the trick just mentioned to resize all the columns of the worksheet at once by double-clicking on any column border. This device also works to resize the heights of the rows in the worksheet. Practice with column and row formatting will make your worksheets more attractive, and will make it easier for you to use these worksheets in other programs such as SPSS.

⊿	A	B	C	D
1	Name	Test1	Test2	Test3
2	Lyle	88	92	89
3	Jorge	78	82	78
4	Kim	34	87	62
5	Frances	76	82	32
6	Tomeca	66	88	64

Figure 1.18 Completed data entry

Examine the completed worksheet with all the data entered (see Figure 1.18). In the next chapter, you will finish setting up an effective data structure and will learn about using Excel for basic descriptive statistics.

THE BOTTOM LINE

- Excel displays various cell-content error indicator messages that begin with the pound sign (#). Consult the Excel help files for an explanation of error indicators.
- The ######## indicator means the default column (8.43 characters) or a column of any width is too narrow to display the cell's contents properly.
- Column widths can be changed by several methods, including double-clicking on the right cell border to expand or contract the column to fit the widest cell entry. This is called AutoFit.
- AutoFit also works when you type or format numbers and dates to expand the column width. AutoFit does not automatically resize columns when you type text.
- You can also use AutoFit to size a column to an individual cell's content by selecting the cell and then selecting **Home** > **Cells** > **Format** > **AutoFit Column Width**.
- You can select multiple columns by clicking and dragging in the column labels (A, B, C, etc.). You can select nonadjacent columns by <**Ctrl**> + click.
- You can select the entire worksheet by clicking in the rectangle above row 1 and to the left of column A. This allows you to format all the columns and rows at once.

Doing Math in Excel

Excel provides the following basic mathematical operations. Simply type the arguments and operators into the cell where you want the result to appear. You can freely mix these mathematical operators with each other and with functions and formulas. Arguments can be actual values, cell references, or names:

- Addition (indicated by the + sign), as in = 2 + 3 or = B1 + B2 or = Price + Tax.
- Subtraction (indicated by the – sign), as in = 6 – 4 or = C22 – C23 or = Maximum – Minimum.
- Division (indicated by the / sign), as in = 66 / 2 or =D19 / A12 or = MSB / MSW.
- Multiplication (indicated by the * sign), as in = 2 * 2 or = B1 * B7 or = X * Y.
- Exponentiation (indicated by the ^ sign), as in = 2 ^ 8 or = A21 ^ A22.

Excel also provides operators for negation (such as the negative sign in front of –4.3) and percent. The standard order of operations in Excel is parentheses, exponentiation, multiplication, division, addition, and subtraction (PEMDAS). You can force the operations into any desired order by the use of parentheses. You will want to examine the many mathematical, financial, and logical functions available in Excel, but in this book we will stay with the basics described above and the additional statistical functions and tools introduced throughout the text.

Mathematical operations are performed by entering values or cell references (either cell addresses or range names) as the "arguments." As indicated above, to add 2 and 2 in Excel, you select an empty cell where you want the result to appear, type = 2 + 2, and then press <**Enter**> or <**Tab**>, or simply select another cell. To subtract the value in cell B2 from the value in cell B3, you select an empty cell, then type = B3 – B2 and press <**Enter**>. To find the square of the value in the cell you have named X, you type in = X ^ 2 in an empty cell and press <**Enter**>.

Excel also has other useful functions you can mix with the mathematical operators above. Some of the most useful for statisticians are:

- Absolute value, found by the ABS function, as in ABS(A1) or ABS(B132).
- Counting the numbers in a range, performed by the COUNT function, as in COUNT(B2:B13) or COUNT(Test1).
- Factorial, $N! = N \times (N-1) \times (N-2) \times \ldots \times 1$, found by FACT($N$). Note 0! = 1 by definition.
- Maximum value, found by the MAX function, as in = MAX(Test1) or = MAX(A1:A13).
- Mean, found by the AVERAGE function, as in = AVERAGE(Test1) or = AVERAGE(A1:A24).
- Minimum value, found by the MIN function, as in = MIN(Test1) or = MIN(A1:A13).
- Square root, calculated by the SQRT function, as in = SQRT(Sheet2!B132) or = SQRT(81).
- Sum of squares, performed by the =DEVSQ function, such as = DEVSQ(Test1).
- Summation, performed by the SUM function, as in = SUM(Test1) or = SUM(A1:A11).

In the examples above, you can place in the parentheses the actual data values separated by commas, cell references separated by commas or colons (for consecutive ranges), or a range name. Excel updates these built-in functions dynamically so if any value in the dataset is changed, all formulas or functions referring to that value will reevaluate and instantly display the new result.

A Date with a Helpful Function

In addition to statistical functions, there are other helpful functions in Excel. For example, people often include dates in their spreadsheets. To Excel, a date is a special kind of number, and dates are stored as numbers by the program and then formatted as dates. Excel has several built-in date formats. There is no further discussion of the technical aspects of dates here, but Excel can perform operations on dates, just as it can with other kinds of numbers. The interested reader should consult the Excel help files.

A very useful Excel function is the one called TODAY() shown earlier in Figure 1.16. If you simply type =TODAY(), leaving the parentheses blank, in any empty cell, Excel will display the current date. The date will change to the current date whenever you open the workbook. You may need to increase the column width to display the results correctly. Double-clicking on the sizing icon, as discussed previously, instantly widens the column. The results are shown in Figure 1.19 below.

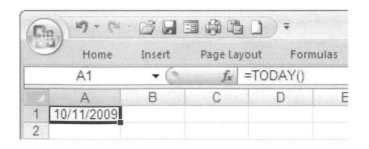

Figure 1.19 Using the TODAY() function to insert the current date in a worksheet

THE BOTTOM LINE

- Excel provides basic arithmetic operators for addition (+), subtraction (–), multiplication (*), division (/), and exponentiation (^).
- Excel also provides operators for negation (–) and percent (%).
- The order of operations in Excel is parentheses, exponentiation, multiplication, division, addition, and subtraction.
- The order of operations can be forced by the use of parentheses.
- Other useful functions include ABS, COUNT, DEVSQ, FACT, MIN, MAX, SUM, AVERAGE, and SQRT.
- A list of other statistical functions appears in Appendix A.
- Dates are stored as numbers in Excel.
- The TODAY() function returns the current date.

Important Terms and a Look Ahead

Before we proceed, let us define some important terms to make sure you understand them in the context of data management and statistical analysis. Knowing these definitions will help you learn the concepts and examples in this book.

Data points and datasets—people who studied Latin know that the word *data* is the plural of *datum*. These people are likely to say, "The data are symmetrical." Though this is correct, it also sounds a little stilted to most modern ears, and many people would say, "Data is collected" without hesitation. Instead of a Latin lesson, we are more interested in understanding how to structure data and datasets. A single data value is a ***data point***. An entire collection of data points is a ***dataset***. Depending on our assumptions or the nature of the data, the dataset may be a sample or a population. We can display data in rows, columns, or tables. We can have data values that are text labels (or numbers representing these text labels), data that are numbers, or both. Numbers can be integers or they can have decimals. Using cell formatting features can change the way Excel displays the numbers, but does not change the value stored in the program. If you wish, you can use functions such as ROUND for rounding or TRUNC for truncation to change the actual stored value.

Descriptive and inferential statistics—the branch of statistics dealing with summarizing, organizing, and presenting data in a meaningful way is ***descriptive*** (for describing) statistics. Descriptive statistics include both summary statistical indexes and tabular and graphical representations of data that help us see and understand the patterns in these data. Descriptive statistics are the subject of Chapters 2 – 5. ***Inferential statistics*** is the branch concerned with making estimates or inferences about population parameters from sample data. Our exploration of inferential statistics begins with confidence intervals in Chapter 6 and continues through Chapters 7 – 12.

Population and Parameter—a ***population*** is the entire collection of objects or individuals of interest. Populations can be large or small, so the defining characteristic is not the number of objects or individuals. Instead, the population is the group about which we want to make inferences, estimates, or generalizations. When we have the luxury of knowing the entire population, we have no need to sample. A ***parameter*** is a measurable characteristic of a population. We generally use Greek letters to represent population parameters and Latin letters to represent sample statistics. Appendix B provides information about how to format these Greek and Latin letters.

Sample and Statistic—a ***sample*** is a subset of the population of interest. There are various methods for taking samples, ranging from simple random sampling to sophisticated techniques involving clusters or strata. Regardless of how we select the sample, a key goal is to ensure that the sample is representative of the population. A ***statistic*** is a measurable characteristic of a sample. Our default assumption regarding our data will be that the data are a sample. This is important, because it affects the way we calculate and interpret our statistics.

Variable—a variable is a quantity or characteristic that takes on different values. We can classify variables in different ways, according to the scale of measurement, whether the variable is qualitative or quantitative, and whether the variable is discrete or continuous. We can also classify variables as independent or dependent. We contrast variables with constants. A constant takes on only a single value. Two of the most commonly used (and useful) constants in statistics and in mathematics generally are the quantity pi (π) and the quantity e (the base of the natural logarithms).

Measurement Scales—some variables are **nominal** (name only), also known as qualitative variables. Examples include race, sex, and marital status. Other variables are **ordinal** (implying order). Ordinal variables provide information regarding rank or position in the dataset, but do not provide information about the sizes of differences between these ranks. Obvious examples include finishing positions in a race or beauty contest. We also sometimes collect data as ranks or convert other data to ranks. For example, a professor could time students' completion of a test by writing down the starting time and the time each student turns in his or her test, but if the professor stacks the tests in order as she receives them, she will have a ranking from fastest to slowest completion times. This ranking will not tell us the difference in time between ranks 1 and 2 or between 2 and 3, but it will give us the correct order of finishing. **Interval** variables provide information about quantities of differences, but do not provide a true zero point. The most common example is temperature on the Fahrenheit or Celsius scales. On both these scales, the zero point is arbitrary, and thus we cannot say 100 degrees is twice as hot as 50 degrees. A less obvious, and perhaps more interesting, example is women's dress sizes (Lind, Marchal, & Wathen, 2008). For a size 8 dress, the measurements are bust (32 in.), waist (24 in.), and hips (35 in.) while for a size 10, the measurements are 34, 26, and 37, respectively, and for size 12, 36, 28, and 39. The intervals between the sizes are the same (2 inches for each measurement), but there is no true zero point. A dress size of 0 would not have measurements of 0. In fact, in this example, a size 0 would have the measurements 24, 16, and 27. Because there is no true zero point, we could not say a size 24 dress is twice as big as a size 12, or that a size 6 is half the size of a size 12. **Ratio** measurements occur on a scale with a true zero point. Physical measurements like height and weight are ratio measurements, as are measures of age or distance. So is the measurement of time, because there is a true zero point. We can say with assurance that 2 hours is twice as long as 1 hour. Money is also a ratio measurement, as zero dollars represents no money. To be clear, just because there is a zero point, this does not mean that negative numbers cannot represent negative quantities in ratio measurements. For example, money less than zero is called debt. Owing money represents less money than having no money. Similarly, a running back may gain or lose yards on a particular football play, or you can gain or lose weight.

Qualitative versus Quantitative Variables—qualitative variables correspond to nominal measures. They represent differences in quality, and not in amount. Some people call these **attribute** variables. We can describe qualitative differences in hair and eye color, religious or political preferences, and whether the person prefers paper or plastic bags at the grocery checkout. Quantitative variables correspond to differences in amount. Thus ordinal, interval, and ratio measures all are "quantitative," though many statisticians place ordinal measures in the qualitative category because ranks cannot give us the size or quantity of a difference between two objects.

You should note that although there are four scales of measurement, statistical techniques fall into three major categories, based on the types of data used. Nominal data can only be counted, so frequencies or percentages in categories provide us the only way to summarize and analyze such data. The chi-square tests in Chapter 11 are based on frequencies. Ordinal data allow us to consider inequalities or ranks. A set of statistical procedures called **nonparametric** or order statistics (Chapter 12) make use of ranks. Scale data (including interval and ratio measurements) allow us to use generally more powerful statistical techniques by calculating indexes and tests based on mathematical operations. These tests are often called **parametric** procedures because they estimate or make inferences about population parameters. Parametric procedures include t tests, analyses of variance, and correlation and regression (Chapters 7 – 10).

Discrete and Continuous Variables—*discrete variables* can take on only clearly separated values. The number of children in a family, the number of bedrooms in a house, the number of times you miss your statistics class, and the number of times a person has been married are all examples. Discrete variables do not have to result in integers, however. A person's shoe size might be 9, 9.5, or 10, but it cannot be 9.8749231. In Chapter 4 of this book, you will learn about two important discrete probability distributions, the binomial and the Poisson distributions. ***Continuous variables*** can take on any value within a specified range. The only limitation is the precision of the measuring instrument. Examples include physical measurements and time. Consider the air pressure in your car's tires in pounds per square inch, or the actual weight of that "16 oz." steak you just ordered. In statistics, we are very interested in several continuous probability distributions, including the normal distribution, the *t* distribution, the *F* distribution, and the chi-square distribution. You will learn more about these continuous distributions in this book, beginning with the discussion of the standard normal distribution in Chapter 5.

Independent and Dependent Variables—in statistics, we are concerned with independent and dependent variables. The independent variable is the "cause" and the dependent variable is the "effect." If we study the relationship between room temperature and students' ability to concentrate, the room temperature is the independent variable and concentration is the dependent variable. The dependent variable is the outcome we are trying to predict or explain. We commonly call the independent variable X and the dependent variable Y. Both must have at least two levels for us to study the relationship or association between the variables. We would at least have to have a "cold" and a "hot" room and at least "high" and "low" concentration to make any meaningful comparisons and to draw any meaningful conclusions. We will discuss independent and dependent variables throughout this book. In some cases, we do not have experimental control, and we might then refer to the "independent" variable as a predictor or explanatory variable and to the "dependent" variable as a criterion or response variable. We will discuss this distinction more fully in Chapter 10, which is about correlation and regression.

Measurement—we have already mentioned scales of measurement. Let us define measurement as the assignment of numbers to objects to represent quantities or qualities of attributes. In nominal measurement, we might use numbers as convenient labels for categories, such as 1 (*red*), 2 (*blue*), 3 (*green*), 4 (*brown*), 5 (*yellow*), and 6 (*orange*) when we describe the colors of M&M candies. The numbers imply nothing other than differences in colors. With ordinal, interval, and ratio measurements, the numbers assigned to objects provide increasingly more information about the attribute we are measuring. It is important to note that we are measuring the attribute and not the object itself.

Equipped with this new terminology, we can move ahead to our examination of descriptive statistics in Chapter 2.

Chapter 1 Exercises

1. Use Excel to find the answers to the following simple problems. Simply type the necessary data and enter the required formula or function in the blank cells of an Excel worksheet. Try using cell references instead of the actual values in your formulas and functions to make them reusable.
    a. Find the square root of 325351.
    b. What is 621 + 2443 + 12232 + 1232?
    c. What is 33 to the fourth power?
    d. What is 999 divided by 222?

2. Open a new workbook file and enter =TODAY() in cell A1. Observe the result. Adjust the column width if necessary to see the information correctly.

3. Use Excel to find the answers to the following problems.
    a. What is the square root of 10000?
    b. What is $(12 + 3) / 4$?
    c. What is $122 + \sqrt{49}$?
    d. Find 10!

4. For the following numbers, $X = \{106, 125, 121, 130, 99, 87, 102, 107, 111\}$, place the data in a single column in Excel. Use formulas with relative and absolute addressing to calculate the following:
    a. The mean value.
    b. The deviation of each raw score from the mean.
    c. The square of the deviation score.
    d. The absolute value of each deviation score.

5. Using the data from Figure 1.9, $X = \{73, 80, 60, 91, 59, 64, 77, 77, 53, 84, 80\}$, place the data in a single column in Excel. Use formulas with relative and absolute addressing to calculate the following:
    a. The mean value.
    b. The deviation of each raw score from the mean.
    c. The square of the deviation score.
    d. The absolute value of each deviation score.

6. For the data in #5 above, use Excel functions and formulas to sum the squared deviation scores you calculated above. Use the DEVSQ function with the raw data and compare the two answers.

7. For the data in #5 above, use Excel functions to find the following values:
    a. The minimum value.
    b. The maximum value.
    c. The square root of each value.
    d. The square of each value.

8. Explain the differences between relative and absolute cell references.

9. What is a named range? What are the advantages of named ranges? What is an important caution about named ranges?

10. Define the following terms: descriptive statistics, sample, statistic, variable, and measurement.

2   Tables and Descriptive Statistics

In this chapter, we conclude the discussion we began in Chapter 1 about data structuring. We then explore the basic table features and descriptive statistical functions of Excel. Chapter 2 topics include:

- The table feature (an enhancement of the Data List introduced in Excel 2003).
- Additional statistical functions and tools of Excel.
- The Status Bar.
- Installing the Analysis ToolPak and using the Descriptive Statistics tool.
- Describing the descriptive statistics.
- Using Excel formulas and tools to find percentiles and percentile ranks.

You will learn how to format data as a table and how to use simple formulas and various built-in functions to find descriptive statistics. Next, you will learn how to find the most common descriptive statistics for one or more variables at once using the Descriptive Statistics tool in the Analysis ToolPak. Last, you will learn how to find accurate percentiles and percentile ranks in Excel.

Working with Structured Data

As discussed in Chapter 1, it is best practice to enter a row of column headings that provide labels for the fields (variables) in your worksheet. Look back at the column headings in Figure 1.18. These labels provide information about the data in the worksheet. Although you may be tempted to enter long labels for the columns and use spaces in your headings, you should generally avoid this for statistical applications. To keep your workbook manageable, and for the labels to be most effective, you should anticipate you may also use the labels for range names. Thus you should keep the labels relatively short. As a reminder, the labels should begin with a letter, and should contain only letters, numbers, and underscores. The labels should contain no spaces. Following these conventions for labeling your variables makes it possible for programs like Minitab and SPSS to import the row of column headings from Excel as variable names. Many Excel users create a "data dictionary" or a "codebook" by placing the column headings in a separate worksheet along with more descriptive labels and information about the variables. This corresponds to the "variable view" in SPSS and other statistics packages.

With Excel 2003, Microsoft introduced an innovative feature called the Data List that made it simpler to work with structured data. This enhanced feature is simply a "Table" in Excel 2007. Although it is possible to sort and filter data without using tables, tables make it both easier and safer to use these procedures. Sorting one column without a data list or table destroys the relationship between the fields and records in other columns (many users including the author of this book have learned this lesson the hard way by ruining more than one dataset). Using the table keeps all the fields and records together when the records are sorted on one or more fields. We will discuss the table feature in more detail after examining Excel's built-in functions and tools.

THE BOTTOM LINE

- The Table feature is an enhancement of the Excel 2003 Data List.
- To be most effective, tables should be based on the data structuring procedure outlined previously, and should include a row of column headings.
- If you like, you can create a "data dictionary" or "codebook" in a separate worksheet in your workbook.

Built-In Functions and Tools

Let us begin our exploration with a versatile tool called AutoSum. Create a worksheet from the data in Figure 1.18, or retrieve your saved workbook file. Add an empty column labeled "PersonAvg" for the individual averages, and an empty row labeled "TestAvg" for the test averages (see Figure 2.1). Select the entire range of data including the empty row beneath and empty column to the right to the data. Look carefully at the Status Bar beneath the worksheet tabs at the bottom of the Excel interface. Excel has already supplied the count, the sum, and the average of the selected range (Figure 2.1). You can customize the Status Bar, as discussed later in this chapter.

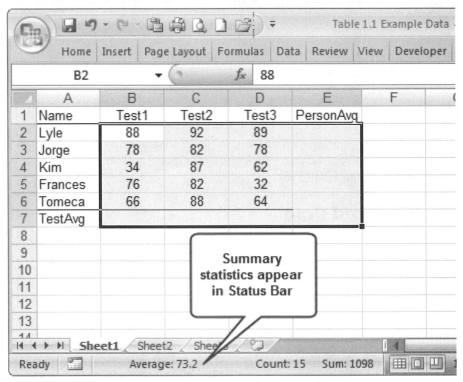

Figure 2.1 Summary statistics for the selected range

To compute the averages for all three tests and all five people, continue with the AutoSum feature (see Figure 2.2).

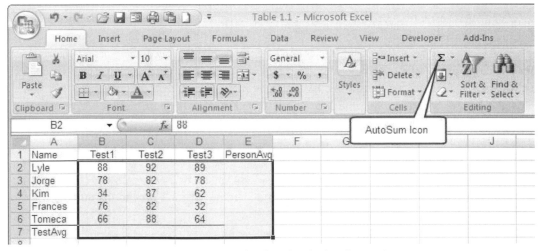

Figure 2.2 Preparation for using the AutoSum tool

From the **Home** ribbon, locate the **Editing** group. Then, click on the dropdown arrow beside the **AutoSum** icon (**Home** > **Editing** > **AutoSum**). From the dropdown list, select **Average,** and all the averages will be calculated at the same time (see Figure 2.2). After calculating them, you should format the averages to a single decimal place. You can change the number format of a selected cell or cells by clicking on the Launch Dialog button at the bottom right of the **Number** group, or by clicking on the dropdown arrow next to the word General (the default format) in the **Number** group and selecting **Number** (see Figure 2.3). You can also format decimals by selecting the Increase/Decrease Decimal tools (**Home** > **Number** > **Increase Decimal**) or (**Home** > **Number** > **Decrease Decimal**) (Figure 2.4). Finally, in the context-sensitive menu appearing when you right-click in a cell, you can also select **Format** > **Cells** > **Number** and change the number of decimal places to whatever you like. In general, the average should be reported with at least one more significant digit than the raw data, so for integers, the average should have at least one decimal place.

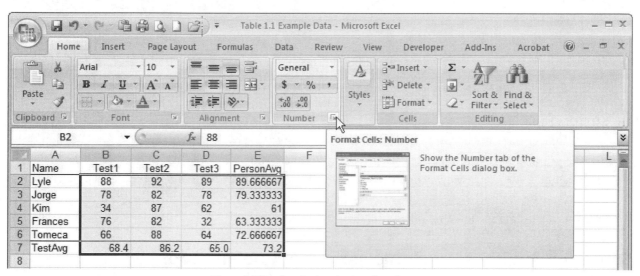

Figure 2.3 Results of using the AutoSum feature

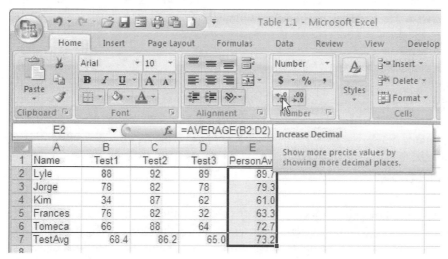

Figure 2.4 Using the Increase Decimal icon

The Formula View

As you have seen, when you enter a function or a formula in a cell or in the Formula Bar, the function or formula displays in the Formula Bar while the result of applying the function or formula appears in the cell itself. This is the normal behavior of Excel. You can click on any cell with a formula, function, or cell pointer in it, and immediately see the cell's function or formula in the Formula Bar. To view all the formulas in the cells of your worksheet at once, you can press the <Ctrl> key and then the grave accent key (`). This key is located at the top left of the keyboard under the tilde (~) to the left of the 1 key on most keyboards. Alternatively, you can choose the "Show Formulas" tool from the **Formulas** ribbon (**Formulas** > **Formula Auditing** > **Show Formulas**). With either approach, the formulas appear as in Figure 2.5, which shows that Excel used the AVERAGE function with relative cell references to compute all the means at once. Pressing <Ctrl> + ` or clicking on **Show Formulas** again returns the worksheet to the normal Value View.

	A	B	C	D	E
1	Name	Test1	Test2	Test3	PersonAvg
2	Lyle	88	92	89	=AVERAGE(B2:D2)
3	Jorge	78	82	78	=AVERAGE(B3:D3)
4	Kim	34	87	62	=AVERAGE(B4:D4)
5	Frances	76	82	32	=AVERAGE(B5:D5)
6	Tomeca	66	88	64	=AVERAGE(B6:D6)
7	TestAvg	=AVERAGE(B2:B6)	=AVERAGE(C2:C6)	=AVERAGE(D2:D6)	=AVERAGE(B7:D7)
8					

Figure 2.5 The Formula View. Press <Ctrl> + ` to toggle between Value and Formula Views

THE BOTTOM LINE

- The default view of a worksheet is the Value View in which values display in the worksheet area and the formula or function for the active cell displays in the Formula Bar.
- To change to the Formula View in order to see all the functions and formulas in a worksheet at the same time, enter <**Ctrl**> + `.
- Entering <**Ctrl**> + ` a second time will return to the Value View.

Summary Statistics Available From the AutoSum Tool

Clicking directly on the AutoSum icon causes Excel to add up the values in the selected range. You can also click the adjacent dropdown arrow to select any of these additional statistics:

- Sum
- Average
- Count
- Minimum
- Maximum
- More Functions (this gives access to the complete function library)

Setting up a Table

To set up a table, let us return to the worksheet you created from the data in Figure 1.18. If necessary, remove the row of test averages and the column of person averages. Select the desired range of data including the row of column headings, or simply click in the upper left cell of the contiguous data, and then click on **Insert** > **Tables** > **Table** (or enter <**Ctrl**> + **T**) (Figure 2.6). You can also select **Home** > **Styles** > **Format as Table** to create a table with a format from the gallery of styles.

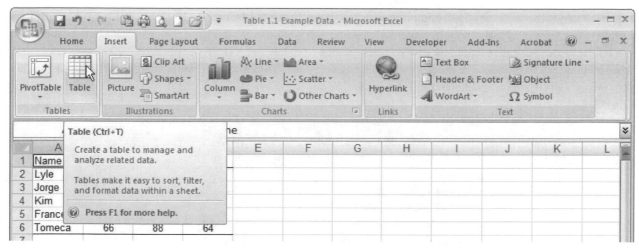

Figure 2.6 Creating a table

Figure 2.7 shows the completed table with default formatting. When you create a table and select it, the **Table Tools** will appear in the Title Bar along with an associated **Design** tab to access a new ribbon. Excel automatically names "objects," and will give the table object you just created the name "Table1." Locate the name in the **Properties** group of the **Design** ribbon in Figure 2.7). You can see the name and access the table from anywhere in the workbook, even from a different worksheet, by clicking on the dropdown arrow at the right end of the Name Box, and selecting Table1. When you select another worksheet or select a cell outside the table, the **Table Tools** menu and the **Design** tab will disappear from view and will not be visible again until you click inside the table or select the table from the Name Box.

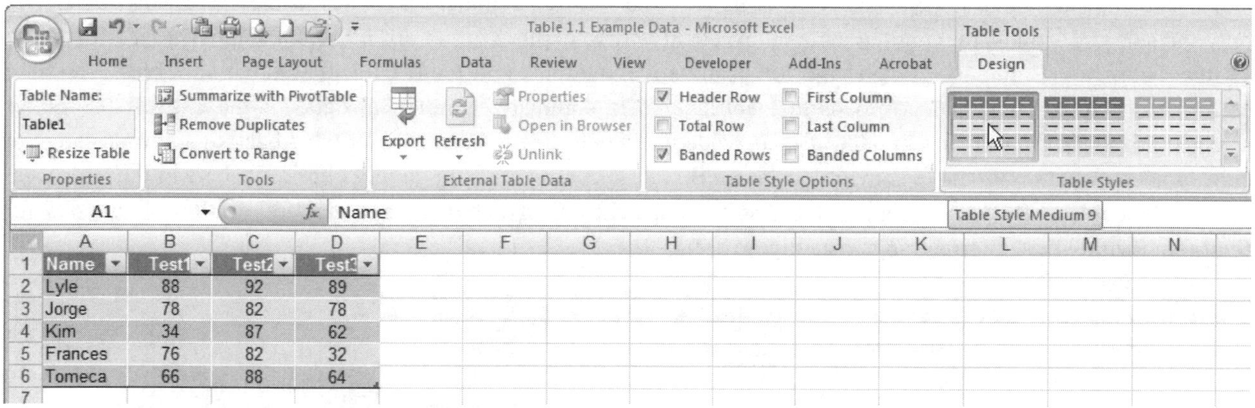

Figure 2.7 Table with default formatting and Table Tools' Design ribbon

You can click on the dropdown arrow to the right of any table heading (Figure 2.7) to access a variety of features including sorting alphabetically, numerically, or by color. You can apply filters by text values, numeric values, or by colors. You can click in the checkboxes to select the records to display. The records removed from view remain in the table, and appear again when you check "Select All." Finally, you can add a Total Row to summarize your data quickly, as discussed in the next section.

The Total Row

As you saw earlier, the Status Bar at the bottom of the workbook interface automatically displays various summary statistics for the selected data. It is also helpful to add a Total Row to the table to provide access to the summary statistics and any other built-in functions for each variable (column) in the table. To add a Total Row, click anywhere inside the table. On the **Design** ribbon, select **Total Row** (**Table Tools** > **Design** > **Table Style Options** > **Total Row**) (Figure 2.7). By default, Excel will assume you want to sum the last column of data in the table. You can add statistics for other columns, and you can modify or delete the function applied to the last column or any other column(s). Access these features by clicking any cell in the Total row. A dropdown arrow will appear, giving you a variety of choices for that column (Figure 2.8).

	A	B	C	D	E
1	Name	Test1	Test2	Test3	
2	Lyle	88	92	89	
3	Jorge	78	82	78	
4	Kim	34	87	62	
5	Frances	76	82	32	
6	Tomeca	66	88	64	
7	Total	68.4	86.2	65	
8				None	
9				Average	
10				Count	
11				Count Numbers	
12				Max	
13				Min	
14				Sum	
15				StdDev	
				Var	
				More Functions.	

Figure 2.8 Summary statistics available from the Total Row

When you filter the data in your table, Excel updates the selected summary statistics in the Total Row to refer to only the selected values, making the table an excellent way to explore group differences. In statistics, it is useful to set the Total Row summary to **Average** for quantitative variables and **Count** for qualitative variables. This is a convenient way to count categories or text entries and to summarize numerical data for the entire table or for selected groups of data. As a reminder, if you decide you would like to convert your table back to a normal range of cells, you can click on the table name in the Name Box to select the table (or simply click anywhere in the table). On the **Table Tools** > **Design** ribbon, in the **Tools** group, click **Convert to Range** and follow the instructions for returning the table to a normal range (see Figure 2.9).

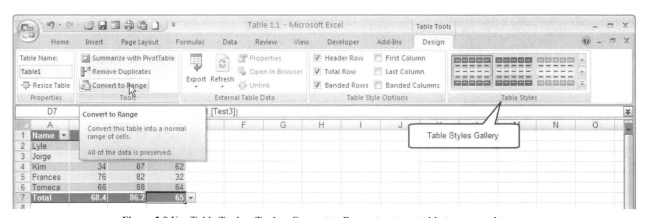

Figure 2.9 Use Table Tools > Tools > Convert to Range to return table to a normal range

Excel has a built-in set of table styles, and the user can easily change the table formatting from the **Table Tools** group (see Figure 2.9). Tables with appropriately labeled column headers have an additional advantage. Examine Figure 2.10, which shows the data from Table 2.1 (discussed later in this chapter) formatted as a table. When the table is too big to fit on a single screen, the row of column headings replaces the default column labels A, B, C. This makes it easier to know which column of data you are working with in a large table.

	State	Region	Wage2001	Wage2002	PctChg
19	Georgia	South	35,136	35,734	1.7
20	Pennsylvania	Northeast	34,978	35,808	2.4
21	Rhode Island	Northeast	33,603	34,810	3.6
22	Arizona	West	33,411	34,036	1.9
23	Ohio	Midwest	33,283	34,214	2.8
24	Oregon	West	33,204	33,684	1.4
25	Nevada	West	33,121	33,993	2.6
26	Missouri	Midwest	32,421	33,118	2.1
27	North Carolina	South	32,024	32,689	2.1
28	Indiana	Midwest	31,779	32,603	2.6
29	Florida	South	31,553	32,426	2.8
30	Wisconsin	Midwest	31,540	32,464	2.9
31	Tennessee	South	31,520	32,531	3.2
32	Hawaii	West	31,253	32,671	4.5
33	Vermont	Northeast	30,238	31,041	2.7
34	Kansas	Midwest	30,153	30,825	2.2
35	Alabama	South	30,102	31,163	3.5
36	Utah	West	30,077	30,585	1.7
37	Kentucky	South	30,021	30,904	2.9
38	South Carolina	South	29,255	30,003	2.6
39	Louisiana	South	29,131	30,115	3.4
40	Iowa	Midwest	28,837	29,668	2.9
41	Maine	Northeast	28,815	29,736	3.2
42	New Mexico	West	28,702	29,431	2.5
43	Nebraska	Midwest	28,377	29,448	3.8
44	Wyoming	West	28,043	28,975	3.3
45	Oklahoma	South	28,016	28,654	2.3
46	West Virginia	South	27,981	28,612	2.3
47	Idaho	West	27,768	28,163	1.4
48	Arkansas	South	27,260	28,074	3.0
49	Mississippi	South	25,923	26,665	2.9
50	North Dakota	Midwest	25,707	26,550	3.3
51	South Dakota	Midwest	25,601	26,360	3.0
52	Montana	West	25,195	26,001	3.2

Figure 2.10 Table displays column headings instead of default column letters (partial data)

Customizing the Status Bar

Unlike the ribbon, you can customize the Status Bar (see Figure 2.11). To access the customization options, right click in the Status Bar or any of the currently displayed features such as the Ready mode indicator in the lower left-hand corner of the worksheet. Check or uncheck the various features you want displayed in the Status Bar, some of which apply to the worksheet, and some of which apply to only a selected range. For example, if you turn on the Caps Lock, the status indicator in the customization dialog will change from Off to On. If you click in front of Caps Lock, the Caps Lock indicator will now show on the Status Bar. Summary statistics such as Average, Count,

Minimum, Maximum, and Sum will show only when you select numerical data. It is not necessary to use either tables or named ranges for these statistics to be displayed and to change when you change the data selection.

Figure 2.11 Options for customizing the Status Bar

Additional Statistical Functions

As an alternative or an addition to using a Total Row or the Status Bar, you can also get to Excel's built-in statistical functions via the **Insert Function** command. This command is always available by clicking on the *fx* symbol to the left of the Formula Bar. You can also select the **Formulas** tab, locate the **Function Library** group, and then select **Insert Function** as shown in Figure 2.12. Click on the dropdown arrow next to **More Functions** icon (a pair of books) at the bottom right of the **Function Library** group and click on **Statistical** (**Formulas** > **Function Library** > **More Functions**). A partial list of the statistical functions available in Excel 2007 appears in Figure 2.13.

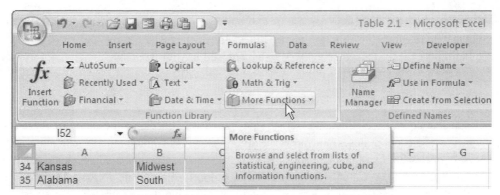

Figure 2.12 Function Library group reveals the More Functions icon

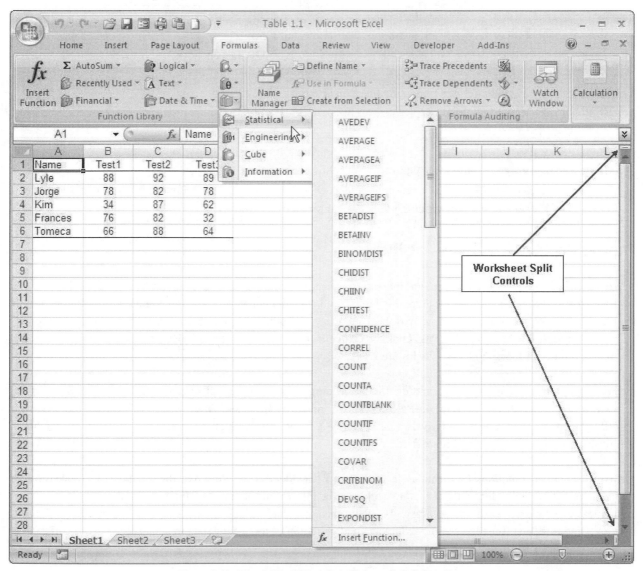

Figure 2.13 A partial list of Excel's built-in statistical functions

Clicking on the **Insert Function** icon or on any of the function names in the Function Library will launch a dialog box that allows you to enter arguments. Although there is a faster way to enter functions, selecting from menus and dialogs is helpful for learning the names of the functions and how to use them. With time and repetition, you will soon remember the names of the functions you use most often. The fastest way to enter a function is to type an "=" into a blank cell, and then enter the function name. For example, once you know the name of the AVERAGE function for calculating the mean, you can simply go to a blank cell in your worksheet, and type

$$= \text{AVERAGE}($$

Then, after the open left parenthesis, enter the actual values, cell references, or the name of the desired range of values. When you close the parentheses and press <**Enter**>, Excel will automatically calculate and display the average. Appendix A of this book contains a list of many of the most commonly used statistical functions in Excel. Throughout the book you will learn to type the name of the function for immediate access to it rather than to use the menu-driven interface. This will ultimately save you much time, and is worth the extra effort to learn.

THE BOTTOM LINE

- The AutoSum tool is located under **Home** > **Editing** > **AutoSum**. Clicking the icon produces the sum. The dropdown menu next to the icon gives access to the various additional functions.
- This tool allows the user to find the sum, average, count, minimum, and maximum values in a selected data range. Clicking **More Functions** opens the function library.
- Adding a Total Row to a table also provides access to various summary statistics for the columns of data in the table, as well as to the function Library.
- To add a Total Row, select the table name from the Name Box or select any cell in the table and then select **Table Tools** > **Design** > **Table Style Options** > **Total Row**.
- You can also gain access to the function library by clicking on the *fx* (**Insert Function** icon) at the left of the Formula Bar, or by selecting **Formulas** > **Function Library** > **Insert Function**.

Installing the Analysis ToolPak

Many Excel add-ins and macros provide increased or specialized statistical functionality. In order to keep things both as simple and as general as possible, this book avoids macros entirely, and is concerned with only one add-in, the Analysis ToolPak provided by Microsoft. The Analysis ToolPak comes with Excel, but is not installed by default. To install the Analysis ToolPak, click the **Office Button**, and then click the **Excel Options** button located at the bottom center of the dialog box (see Figure 2.14).

From Excel Options, click **Add-ins**, and then in the **Manage** box, select **Excel Add-ins**. Click **Go**. In the **Add-Ins available** box, click the **Analysis ToolPak** checkbox, and then click **OK**. After you have installed the Analysis ToolPak, there will be a **Data Analysis** tool available via the **Analysis** group under the **Data** ribbon (**Data** > **Analysis** > **Data Analysis**). See Figure 2.15.

Unlike the built-in functions or formulas in the cells of a worksheet, add-ins like the Analysis ToolPak produce static output. Changing data values in the worksheet results in any associated formulas and functions updating dynamically. However, with the Analysis ToolPak, changing data values does not update the Analysis ToolPak results. Therefore, you must run the procedure again after adding or modifying data to achieve updated results.

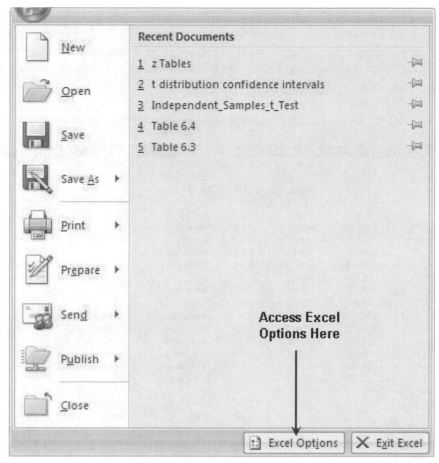

Figure 2.14 Accessing Excel options

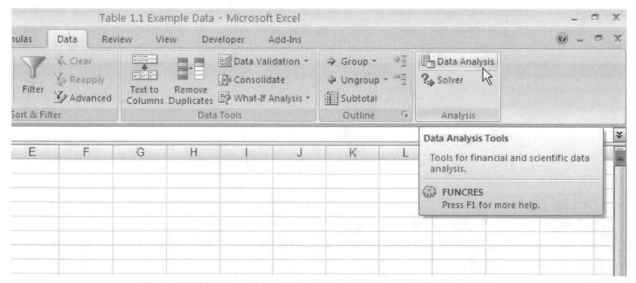

Figure 2.15 Analysis group and Data Analysis tool appear on the Data ribbon

Example Data

Table 2.1 shows the average wages reported by the U.S. Bureau of Labor Statistics for all covered workers in the 50 states and the District of Columbia) for the years 2001 and 2002 (source: http://www.bls.gov/cew/state2002.txt).

When you type the data into your own worksheet, you should structure the data as discussed previously, with a row for each state (record) and a column with an appropriate heading for each variable (see Figure 2.16). To build the worksheet structure, after selecting the range of all 51 entries for 2001 wages (and including the text label in the range), give the selected range the name "Wage2001" (without the quotes of course) by typing the name into the Name Box. You can do the same for the 2002 wages and the other fields in the worksheet.

Table 2.1 Average wages for all covered workers by state or district, 2001 and 2002

State	Region	Wage2001	Wage2002	PctChg	State	Region	Wage2001	Wage2002	PctChg
Alabama	South	30,102	31,163	3.525	Montana	West	25,195	26,001	3.199
Alaska	West	36,170	37,134	2.665	Nebraska	Midwest	28,377	29,448	3.774
Arizona	West	33,411	34,036	1.871	Nevada	West	33,121	33,993	2.633
Arkansas	South	27,260	28,074	2.986	New Hampshire	Northeast	35,481	36,176	1.959
California	West	41,327	41,419	0.223	New Jersey	Northeast	44,320	45,182	1.945
Colorado	West	37,952	38,005	0.140	New Mexico	West	28,702	29,431	2.540
Connecticut	Northeast	46,993	46,852	-0.300	New York	Northeast	46,727	46,328	-0.854
Delaware	South	38,427	39,684	3.271	North Carolina	South	32,024	32,689	2.077
District of Columbia	South	55,908	57,914	3.588	North Dakota	Midwest	25,707	26,550	3.279
Florida	South	31,553	32,426	2.767	Ohio	Midwest	33,283	34,214	2.797
Georgia	South	35,136	35,734	1.702	Oklahoma	South	28,016	28,654	2.277
Hawaii	West	31,253	32,671	4.537	Oregon	West	33,204	33,684	1.446
Idaho	West	27,768	28,163	1.423	Pennsylvania	Northeast	34,978	35,808	2.373
Illinois	Midwest	39,083	39,688	1.548	Rhode Island	Northeast	33,603	34,810	3.592
Indiana	Midwest	31,779	32,603	2.593	South Carolina	South	29,255	30,003	2.557
Iowa	Midwest	28,837	29,668	2.882	South Dakota	Midwest	25,601	26,360	2.965
Kansas	Midwest	30,153	30,825	2.229	Tennessee	South	31,520	32,531	3.207
Kentucky	South	30,021	30,904	2.941	Texas	South	36,045	36,248	0.563
Louisiana	South	29,131	30,115	3.378	Utah	West	30,077	30,585	1.689
Maine	Northeast	28,815	29,736	3.196	Vermont	Northeast	30,238	31,041	2.656
Maryland	South	38,253	39,382	2.951	Virginia	South	36,733	37,222	1.331
Massachusetts	Northeast	44,975	44,954	-0.047	Washington	West	37,459	38,242	2.090
Michigan	Midwest	37,391	38,135	1.990	West Virginia	South	27,981	28,612	2.255
Minnesota	Midwest	36,587	37,458	2.381	Wisconsin	Midwest	31,540	32,464	2.930
Mississippi	South	25,923	26,665	2.862	Wyoming	West	28,043	28,975	3.323
Missouri	Midwest	32,421	33,118	2.150					

As you learned in Chapter 1, you can enter the name of the desired range in an Excel function or formula rather than typing in the range of cell references. It makes much more sense to another user of your workbook to see this function:

$$= AVERAGE(Wage2001)$$

than it does to see this one:

$$= AVERAGE(C2:C52)$$

THE BOTTOM LINE
- The Analysis ToolPak provides many statistical tools.
- To install the Analysis ToolPak, click **Office Button > Excel Options > Add-ins > Manage Excel Add-ins > Go**.
- In the resulting Add-ins dialog, check the box in front of Analysis ToolPak and click **OK**.
- After installation, the Analysis ToolPak is available via **Data > Analysis > Data Analysis**.

Splitting a Worksheet

When your worksheets grow large, you can split the window (see the split between rows 11 and 47 in Figure 2.16) so you can look at different sections of the spreadsheet at the same time. You can split the worksheet horizontally, vertically, or both (Figure 2.17). To remove the split(s), simply drag the control back to its original position. In a sheet without splits, the horizontal split is found at the upper right corner of the worksheet's work area, and the vertical split is found at the lower right corner. Simply grab the split control (the horizontal or vertical bar) with your mouse cursor, and drag it to the position you desire. You can see these controls labeled in their original positions in Figure 2.12. If you cannot locate the split controls, or if they are not on your screen, you can also split a worksheet by using the View ribbon (**View** > **Window** > **Split**).

	A	B	C	D	E
1	State	Region	Wage2001	Wage2002	PctChg
2	District of Columbia	South	55,908	57,914	3.6
3	Connecticut	Northeast	46,993	46,852	-0.3
4	New York	Northeast	46,727	46,328	-0.9
5	Massachusetts	Northeast	44,975	44,954	0.0
6	New Jersey	Northeast	44,320	45,182	1.9
7	California	West	41,327	41,419	0.2
8	Illinois	Midwest	39,083	39,688	1.5
9	Delaware	South	38,427	39,684	3.3
10	Maryland	South	38,253	39,382	3.0
11	Colorado	West	37,952	38,005	0.1
47	Idaho	West	27,768	28,163	1.4
48	Arkansas	South	27,260	28,074	3.0
49	Mississippi	South	25,923	26,665	2.9
50	North Dakota	Midwest	25,707	26,550	3.3
51	South Dakota	Midwest	25,601	26,360	3.0
52	Montana	West	25,195	26,001	3.2
53					

Figure 2.16 Place the data for each field in a single column (partial data)

	A	B	A	B	C	D	E	F	G
1	State	Region	State	Region	Wage2001	Wage2002	PctChg		
2	District of Columbia	South	District of Columbia	South	55,908	57,914	3.6		
3	Connecticut	Northeast	Connecticut	Northeast	46,993	46,852	-0.3		
4	New York	Northeast	New York	Northeast	46,727	46,328	-0.9		
5	Massachusetts	Northeast	Massachusetts	Northeast	44,975	44,954	0.0		
6	New Jersey	Northeast	New Jersey	Northeast	44,320	45,182	1.9		
7	California	West	California	West	41,327	41,419	0.2		
47	Idaho	West	Idaho	West	27,768	28,163	1.4		
48	Arkansas	South	Arkansas	South	27,260	28,074	3.0		
49	Mississippi	South	Mississippi	South	25,923	26,665	2.9		
50	North Dakota	Midwest	North Dakota	Midwest	25,707	26,550	3.3		
51	South Dakota	Midwest	South Dakota	Midwest	25,601	26,360	3.0		
52	Montana	West	Montana	West	25,195	26,001	3.2		
53									
54									
55									
56									
57									
58									

Figure 2.17 Using horizontal and vertical splits to see more of the worksheet

Freezing Panes

If your worksheet is too large to fit in one screen, you may find it convenient to "freeze" the row of column headings and row labels. Then, when you scroll down in your worksheet, the column headings will stay on the screen. To do this, select **View** > **Window** > **Freeze Panes**. You can freeze the top row, the left column, or all the rows above and columns to the left of a selected cell.

THE BOTTOM LINE

- You can split a worksheet horizontally or vertically, or both.
- Drag the splits from their default location to the desired location.
- You can also split a worksheet by selecting **View** > **Window** > **Split**.
- You can freeze the top row, the left column, or the rows above and the columns to the left of a selected cell.
- Select **View** > **Window** > **Freeze Panes**.

Using Functions for Descriptive Statistics

Before discussing the Descriptive Statistics tool, let us explore some of the built-in statistical functions of Excel. The formulas below use named ranges for the sake of clarity. Various descriptive statistics can be computed and displayed by the use of simple formulas combined with Excel's built-in statistical functions. Excel functions determine and display measures of central tendency (mean, mode, and median), the variance and standard deviation, the minimum and maximum values, and many other summary statistics. A list of some of the most common and useful statistical functions in Excel appears in Appendix A. You might notice that Excel does not provide a "RANGE" function, so we must use a formula or the Descriptive Statistics tool to calculate the range.

Let us examine the use of a dialog box to paste a statistical function in Excel. We will calculate the average 2001 wage from Table 2.1. Remember we used the name "Wage2001" for the data. To use the AVERAGE function, select an empty cell in your worksheet, perhaps cell C53 (see Figure 2.18), and then click on *fx* next to the Formula Bar, or select **Formulas** > **Insert Function** (see Figure 2.19). In the resulting dialog box, scroll to the AVERAGE function and click **OK**.

	A	B	C	D	E
1	State	Region	Wage2001	Wage2002	PctChg
44	Wyoming	West	28,043	28,975	3.3
45	Oklahoma	South	28,016	28,654	2.3
46	West Virginia	South	27,981	28,612	2.3
47	Idaho	West	27,768	28,163	1.4
48	Arkansas	South	27,260	28,074	3.0
49	Mississippi	South	25,923	26,665	2.9
50	North Dakota	Midwest	25,707	26,550	3.3
51	South Dakota	Midwest	25,601	26,360	3.0
52	Montana	West	25,195	26,001	3.2
53					
54					

Figure 2.18 Select a cell for the output

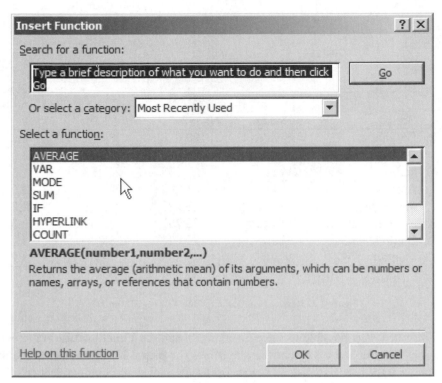

Figure 2.19 Insert Function dialog

You can then simply type the range name, Wage2001, in the Function Arguments dialog box. The formula result, 33,605, formatted without decimals because of the cell formatting in the selected cell, immediately appears in the lower right corner of the dialog box above the **Cancel** button (Figure 2.20). The more precise value stored in the cell appears in the middle of the box. Note the hyperlink in the bottom left corner of the dialog box for accessing the help file for the selected function.

When you click **OK**, the AVERAGE function will be pasted into the selected cell (Figure 2.21). Remember the result appears in the cell, while the function with its argument appears in the Formula Bar.

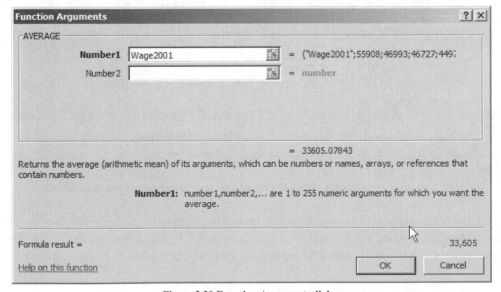

Figure 2.20 Function Arguments dialog

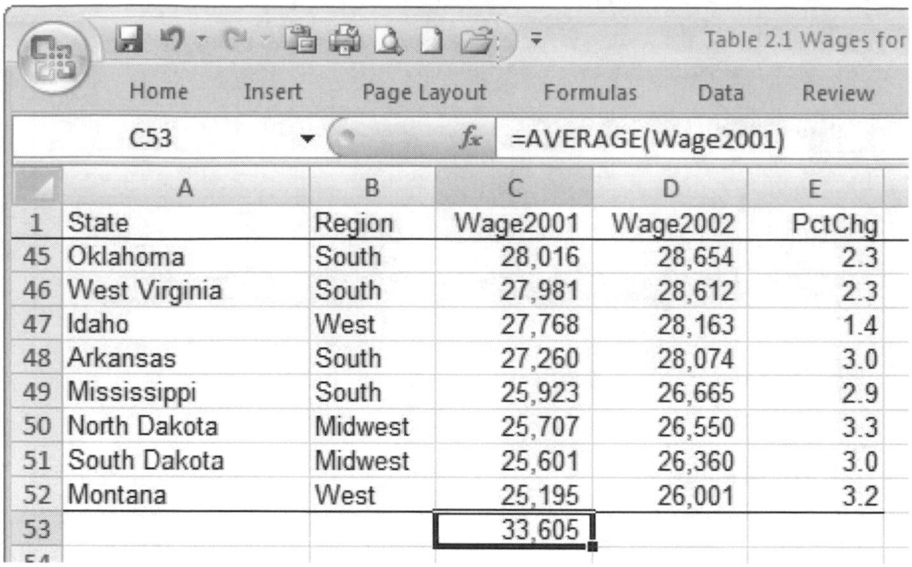

	A	B	C	D	E
1	State	Region	Wage2001	Wage2002	PctChg
45	Oklahoma	South	28,016	28,654	2.3
46	West Virginia	South	27,981	28,612	2.3
47	Idaho	West	27,768	28,163	1.4
48	Arkansas	South	27,260	28,074	3.0
49	Mississippi	South	25,923	26,665	2.9
50	North Dakota	Midwest	25,707	26,550	3.3
51	South Dakota	Midwest	25,601	26,360	3.0
52	Montana	West	25,195	26,001	3.2
53			33,605		

Figure 2.21 Result of application of the AVERAGE function

Although, as just illustrated, it is possible to enter functions though the **Function Library** group or other menu-driven approaches, it is more efficient to memorize the names (or keep a list nearby) and type them directly into blank cells where you want the results to display in your worksheet. You could simply select cell C53 and type

= AVERAGE(Wage2001)

and then press <**Enter**>. This direct approach is the one used throughout this book. One advantage of using the function library is that it is easy to access help for an unfamiliar function (see Figure 2.20). However, you can also get to the help menu for a function you just entered by clicking on the function name in the Formula Bar. You will then see a box with the information in the Formula bar and the function name as a hyperlink. Clicking on this link will launch the help file (Figure 2.22).

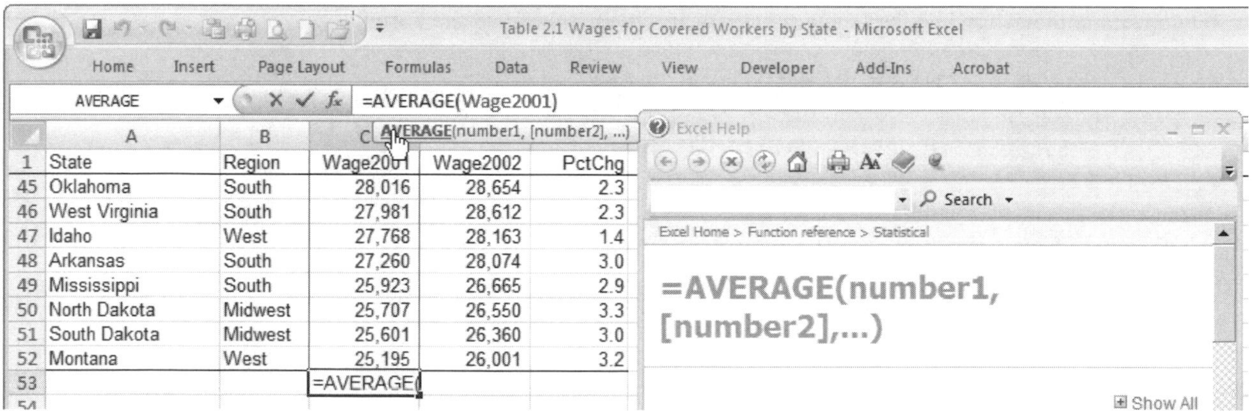

	A	B	C	D	E
1	State	Region	Wage2001	Wage2002	PctChg
45	Oklahoma	South	28,016	28,654	2.3
46	West Virginia	South	27,981	28,612	2.3
47	Idaho	West	27,768	28,163	1.4
48	Arkansas	South	27,260	28,074	3.0
49	Mississippi	South	25,923	26,665	2.9
50	North Dakota	Midwest	25,707	26,550	3.3
51	South Dakota	Midwest	25,601	26,360	3.0
52	Montana	West	25,195	26,001	3.2
53			=AVERAGE(		

Figure 2.22 Click on the link below the Formula Bar to activate the help menu

Table 2.2 shows the Formula View to demonstrate how to use Excel functions and simple formulas to calculate and display common descriptive statistics for both years' wages for all 50 states and the District of Columbia. The calculated values appear in Table 2.3. Named ranges make it clear which variables are being summarized.

Table 2.2 Examples of summary statistics (Formula View)

Statistic	2001 Wages	2002 Wages
Minimum	=MIN(Wage2001)	=MIN(Wage2002)
Maximum	=MAX(Wage2001)	=MAX(Wage2002)
Range	=MAX(Wage2001)-MIN(Wage2001)	=MAX(Wage2002)-MIN(Wage2002)
Count	=COUNT(Wage2001)	=COUNT(Wage2002)
Mean	=AVERAGE(Wage2001)	=AVERAGE(Wage2002)
Median	=MEDIAN(Wage2001)	=MEDIAN(Wage2002)
Variance	=VAR(Wage2001)	=VAR(Wage2002)
Standard Deviation	=STDEV(Wage2001)	=STDEV(Wage2002)

Table 2.3 Statistics (Value View) after cell formatting

Statistic	2001 Wages	2002 Wages
Minimum	25195	26001
Maximum	55908	57914
Range	30713	31913
Count	51	51
Mean	33605.08	34348.57
Median	32024	32689
Variance	39234361.67	38627114.77
Standard Deviation	6263.73	6215.07

After finding the mean and standard deviation, you can use the STANDARDIZE function in Excel to produce z scores for each value of X. Supply the actual values or the cell references for the raw data, the mean, and the standard deviation, and the STANDARDIZE function will calculate the z score for each observation. The subject of z scores and the standard normal distribution is so crucial to statistics that Chapter 5 is devoted to the topic.

Descriptive Statistics in the Analysis ToolPak

You saw above how to use simple formulas and built-in functions to find descriptive statistics. The Analysis ToolPak further simplifies and streamlines the computation of the most commonly used descriptive statistics. The Descriptive Statistics tool calculates and displays descriptive statistics for one or more variables. To access this tool, select **Data** > **Analysis** > **Data Analysis**. If you do not see the **Data Analysis** icon on the **Data** ribbon, you must first install the Analysis ToolPak as explained earlier in this chapter.

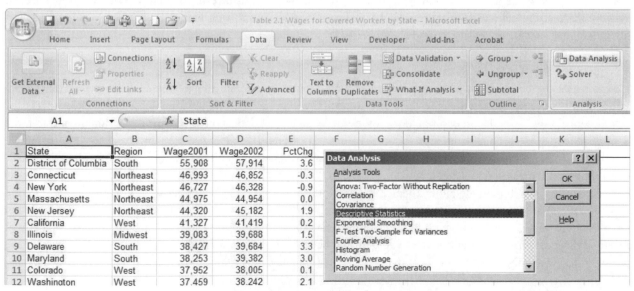

Figure 2.23 Accessing the Data Analysis tools

In the Data Analysis dialog box, scroll to Descriptive Statistics and click **OK**. Figure 2.24 shows the Descriptive Statistics dialog box. Click in the Input Range field and enter the desired range or range name. If the dialog box is in your way, you can move it by clicking in the title bar and dragging it to another location. You can also minimize the dialog box by clicking the little "minimize dialog" icon resembling a miniature spreadsheet at the right of the field and selecting the desired range with the mouse or arrow keys. After entering the range, when you press <**Enter**> or click on the "maximize dialog" icon, the dialog box will return to full size. You can minimize and restore the box when entering the output range as well.

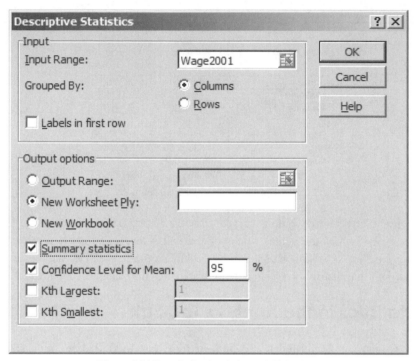

Figure 2.24 Descriptive Statistics tool dialog box

Because there are headings in the first row and the headings were included in the selected input range, you should check the box in front of "Labels in first row." If you check labels and you do not have labels, Excel will obediently use the first data value as a label, and your analyses will be incorrect as a result. If you do not have or use labels, Excel will label the output *Column1*, *Column2*, *Column3*, and so on for each included variable. Meaningful labels obviously make the output easier to read and interpret.

You must check at least the box in front of "Summary statistics" (Figure 2.23) for this tool to work. It is also a good idea to check the box in front of "Confidence Level for Mean." The default for a 95% confidence interval is what you usually want, but you can easily change it to a different value, such as 99% or 90%. What Excel labels the "Confidence Level" is the maximum error of estimate added to and subtracted from the sample mean for a confidence interval for the population mean. The separate CONFIDENCE function in Excel makes use of the standard normal (z) distribution, while the confidence interval reported by the Descriptive Statistics tool uses the t distribution on the assumption the data are a sample and the population parameters are unknown. We will discuss confidence intervals in more detail in Chapter 6. The summary output (after widening some columns and formatting some numbers) appears in Table 2.4 The #N/A displayed for the mode in Table 2.4 indicates the current data do not have a modal value, that is, no value in the dataset occurs more than once. When data are multimodal, Excel will locate and report on the first and lowest value of the mode, so you should always check to see whether there are more modes. One good way to do with is to build a simple frequency distribution, as discussed later in this chapter.

Table 2.4 Summary output from Descriptive Statistics tool

Wage2001		Wage2002	
Mean	33605.08	Mean	34348.57
Standard Error	877.10	Standard Error	870.28
Median	32024	Median	32689
Mode	#N/A	Mode	#N/A
Standard Deviation	6263.73	Standard Deviation	6215.07
Sample Variance	39234361.67	Sample Variance	38627114.77
Kurtosis	2.26	Kurtosis	3.03
Skewness	1.32	Skewness	1.42
Range	30713	Range	31913
Minimum	25195	Minimum	26001
Maximum	55908	Maximum	57914
Sum	1713859	Sum	1751777
Count	51	Count	51
Confidence Level(95.0%)	1761.70	Confidence Level(95.0%)	1748.02

Describing the Descriptive Statistics

Following are brief explanations of the descriptive statistics calculated and displayed by the Descriptive Statistics tool. As mentioned, this tool assumes the data are a sample from a larger population, and thus reports estimates of the population parameters.

1. The *mean* is the arithmetic average of the numeric values in the selected range. This function is implemented directly in Excel as AVERAGE(Range), where you replace "Range" with numerical values separated by commas, a range of cell references such as C5:C52, or the name of a range, such as Wage2001.

$$\overline{X} = \frac{\sum X}{n}$$

2. The *standard error* is the standard error of the mean, calculated as follows, using the sample standard deviation and the sample size. There is no intrinsic Excel function for the standard error of the mean. We will discuss this value further in Chapter 6.

$$s_{\overline{X}} = \frac{s_X}{\sqrt{n}}$$

3. The *median* is the 50th percentile. The median separates the top half of the scores from the bottom half. It is the observed (always the case for odd-numbered n) or hypothetical (often the case for even-numbered n) value found at the location

$$\frac{n+1}{2}$$

in the ordered (sorted from lowest to highest) dataset. The Excel function MEDIAN(Range) finds the median. If the number of data points is odd, the median is the middle value in the dataset. If the number of data points is even, Excel reports the average of the two middle values in the ordered dataset as the median, which may be an observed or hypothetical value.

4. The *mode* is the most frequently occurring value in a dataset. Data may have no modal value (see Table 2.4 for an example), a single mode, or more than one mode. The Excel function is MODE(Range). If the data have multiple modes, Excel will report as the mode the value it encounters first in the data. If you want to ensure you have the lowest or first instance of the mode, you should sort the data before applying the mode function or using the Descriptive Statistics tool.

5. The sample *standard deviation* is calculated as

$$s_X = \sqrt{\frac{\sum (X - \bar{X})^2}{n-1}}$$

The Excel function for the above index is STDEV(Range). This is the estimate of the population standard deviation. Although some authors claim this is an unbiased estimate of the population standard deviation, that is not precisely true. However, it is a sufficiently unbiased estimate for most purposes.

6. The *sample variance* is the square of the standard deviation. The Excel function is VAR(Range). This is the unbiased estimate of the population variance.

$$s_X^2 = \frac{\sum (X - \bar{X})^2}{n-1}$$

7. *Kurtosis* is an index of the "peakedness" or flatness of the data distribution. Excel returns an estimate of the "relative" kurtosis. The normal distribution by definition has zero relative kurtosis. Values greater than zero indicate relatively peaked (leptokurtic) distributions, and negative kurtosis indicates relatively flatter (platykurtic) distributions. Kurtosis in Excel is calculated as

$$\left(\frac{n(n+1)}{(n-1)(n-2)(n-3)} \sum \left(\frac{X - \bar{X}}{s_X} \right)^4 \right) - \frac{3(n-1)^2}{(n-2)(n-3)}$$

The intrinsic Excel function is KURT(Range).

8. *Skewness* is a measure of the symmetry of the data distribution. Excel returns an estimate of the population skewness. Data may be positively skewed, negatively skewed, or symmetrical (unskewed). The normal distribution has zero skew. Skewness in Excel is calculated as

$$\frac{n}{(n-1)(n-2)} \sum \left(\frac{X - \bar{X}}{s_X} \right)^3$$

The intrinsic Excel function is SKEW(Range).

9. The *range* is the difference between the maximum and the minimum values. There is no intrinsic function for the range in Excel, but entering any blank cell and typing the following simple formula

$$= \text{MAX(Range)} - \text{MIN(Range)}$$

will calculate and display this value.

10. The *maximum* is the largest value in the distribution. The Excel function is MAX(Range).

11. The *minimum* is the smallest value in the distribution. The Excel function is MIN(Range).

12. The *sum* is the total of all the raw data values. The Excel function is SUM(Range).

13. The *count* is the number of all the raw data values, or *n*. The Excel function is COUNT(Range).

14. As discussed briefly above, the *confidence level* Excel reports is the "maximum error of estimate," which is one-half the width of a confidence interval for the population mean at the specified level of confidence. This value uses the *t* distribution rather than the normal distribution, on the assumption the population standard deviation is unknown. The margin of error is calculated using a two-tailed *t* value at $n - 1$ degrees of freedom and the desired alpha level (usually .05 or .01):

$$t_{\alpha/2}(s_{\bar{X}})$$

The $(1 - \alpha)(100\%)$ confidence interval for the population mean is:

$$\bar{X} - t_{\alpha/2}(s_{\bar{X}}) \leq \mu \leq \bar{X} + t_{\alpha/2}(s_{\bar{X}})$$

This is the confidence interval reported by SPSS and other statistics packages. As a reminder, while the Descriptive Statistics tool uses the *t* distribution for confidence intervals, Excel's separate CONFIDENCE function uses the standard normal distribution. For more information about confidence intervals, refer to Chapter 6.

A Note on Samples, Populations, and Terminology

The variance of a population is by definition the average squared deviation from the population mean:

$$\sigma_X^2 = \frac{\sum_{i=1}^{N}(X - \mu)^2}{N}$$

Excel provides two different functions for the variance and the standard deviation. One of these is the commonly used estimator of the population parameter. As discussed above, Excel makes the default assumption one's data are a sample rather than a population. The STDEV and VAR functions use an $n - 1$ correction in the denominator of the equation for the variance. To produce accurate estimates of the population parameters, these functions use the following formula for the variance (the standard deviation is simply the square root of the variance):

$$s^2 = \frac{\sum(X - \bar{X})^2}{n-1}$$

To access the sample variance directly, type

$$= \text{VAR(Range)}$$

and for the sample standard deviation,

$$= \text{STDEV(Range)}$$

As discussed above, these are the values reported by the Analysis ToolPak and by most statistical packages. The second function treats the data as a population, and the mean as the population parameter, μ. These functions use N as the denominator in the definitional formula shown earlier and repeated below:

$$\sigma^2 = \frac{\sum (X - \mu)^2}{N}$$

In Excel the population variance is reported by

$$- \text{VARP(Range)}$$

and the population standard deviation by

$$= \text{STDEVP(Range)}$$

It is easy to remember the differences between these functions because P stands for "population."

You should know that some statistics authors use slightly different definitions, calling the following value the "sample variance," stressing that the variance is the average squared deviation (see, for example, Hays & Winkler, 1970, p. 274).

$$s_x^2 = \frac{\sum (X - \bar{X})^2}{n}$$

This usage necessitates another term for the unbiased estimate of the population variance $\hat{s}_x^2$ (read "s-hat squared"). Hays and Winkler (1970, p. 279) refer to this as a "modified" sample variance.

$$\hat{s}_x^2 = \frac{\sum (X - \bar{X})^2}{n - 1}$$

The reader should be aware of such nuances in terminology from author to author.

Excel also has functions called STDEVA and STDEVPA. These functions are useful for calculating the sample or population standard deviation when the data range contains text in addition to numerical values, or contains logical values such as True or False. True is evaluated as 1, and False is evaluated as 0. Numbers and logical values are included, but other text values are ignored in the calculations.

THE BOTTOM LINE

- Summary statistics can be found by using functions and formulas or by use of the Analysis ToolPak.
- The Descriptive Statistics tool is available by selecting **Data > Analysis > Data Analysis > Descriptive Statistics**.
- This tool provides various descriptive statistics and can calculate a margin of error for the population mean estimated from the sample data.
- These statistics assume the data are a sample, not a population.

- The confidence level reported by the Descriptive Statistics tool is based on the *t* distribution, while Excel's separate CONFIDENCE function uses the standard normal (*z*) distribution.

Frequency Distributions

A frequency distribution or frequency table is a listing of the possible values of X along with the number of times that value (or range of values) occurs in the dataset. When you report the frequencies of individual X values, you create a **simple frequency distribution**. When you report the frequencies in intervals, you create a **grouped frequency distribution**. The FREQUENCY function and the Histogram tool in the Analysis ToolPak can generate simple and grouped frequency distributions. We examine both approaches below.

Simple Frequency Distributions

Assume you asked 24 randomly selected students at Paragon State University how many hours they study each week on average. You collect the following information (see Table 2.5).

Table 2.5 Weekly study hours for 24 PSU students (hypothetical data)

5	5	3
2	8	4
6	2	2
2	7	4
5	3	4
4	5	3
2	6	2
5	5	5

Enter the data in a single column in Excel, with an appropriate label (see Figure 2.25). The raw data are in Column A. In Column B, type the possible individual X values, which are known in Excel terminology as "bins."

For a simple frequency distribution, each individual value is a bin. In Column C, Excel displays the frequency of each X value in the dataset. The frequency distribution in Column C was created by use of the FREQUENCY function and an **array formula**. To enter the array formula, one selects the entire range in which the frequency distribution will appear (in this case, the range C2 to C8), clicks in the Formula Bar window, and then enters the formula, which points to the "data array" (cells A2:A25) and the "bins array" (cells B2:B8). Finally, press <**Ctrl**> + <**Shift**> + <**Enter**> to place the results of the formula in the output range (see Figure 2.26 for the Formula View revealing the array formula). If your array formula does not work, the most common mistake is hitting just the <**Enter**> key instead of <**Ctrl**> + <**Shift**> + <**Enter**>. You cannot enter the array formula separately in each cell, or type the braces around the formula to make it work. It must be entered as described above. Entering an array formula takes both practice and confidence, but is worth the effort, as you will find array formulas useful in a variety of situations.

	A	B	C	D
1	Hours	X	f	
2	5	2	6	
3	2	3	3	
4	6	4	4	
5	2	5	7	
6	5	6	2	
7	4	7	1	
8	2	8	1	
9	5			
10	5			
11	8			
12	2			
13	7			
14	3			

Figure 2.25 Simple frequency distribution in Excel

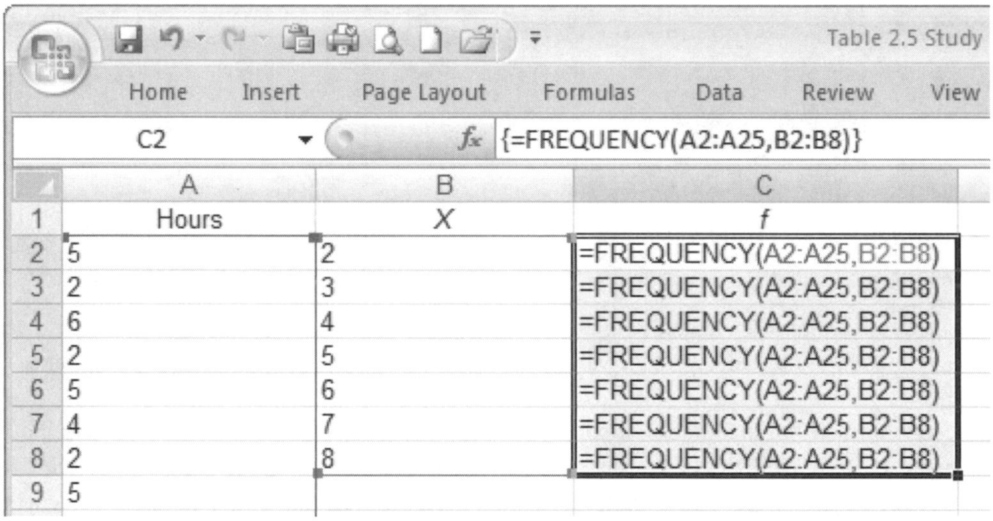

Table 2.5 Study

Home   Insert   Page Layout   Formulas   Data   Review   View

C2 f_x {=FREQUENCY(A2:A25,B2:B8)}

	A	B	C
1	Hours	X	f
2	5	2	=FREQUENCY(A2:A25,B2:B8)
3	2	3	=FREQUENCY(A2:A25,B2:B8)
4	6	4	=FREQUENCY(A2:A25,B2:B8)
5	2	5	=FREQUENCY(A2:A25,B2:B8)
6	5	6	=FREQUENCY(A2:A25,B2:B8)
7	4	7	=FREQUENCY(A2:A25,B2:B8)
8	2	8	=FREQUENCY(A2:A25,B2:B8)
9	5		

Figure 2.26 Array formula creates a simple frequency distribution

It is also possible to create a simple frequency distribution without array formulas by using the Analysis ToolPak's Histogram tool. To create a frequency table using the Analysis ToolPak, select **Data** > **Analysis** > **Data Analysis** > **Histogram**. Identify the input range and the bins range as before, and the tool will create a simple frequency distribution (see Figure 2.27). When you use this tool, Excel will add a "catchall" category labeled "More," which in this case is empty, as we have included all the possible values of X.

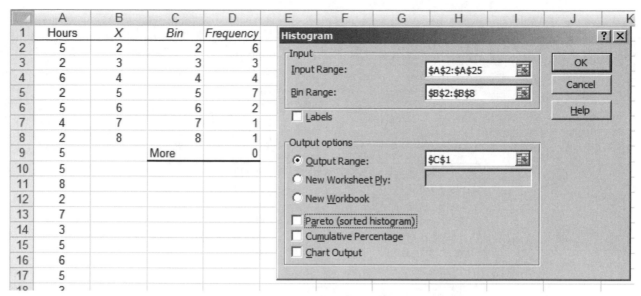

Figure 2.27. Using the Analysis ToolPak to produce a simple frequency distribution

Grouped Frequency Distributions

In addition to simple frequency distributions, you can use the Histogram tool to produce Pareto charts, cumulative percentage charts, and grouped frequency distributions and histograms. For grouped frequency distributions, the bins are the ***upper limits*** of class intervals. If you omit the bin range in the Histogram tool's dialog box, Excel will create bins (or class intervals) automatically. You may specify the bins for grouped frequency distributions by providing a column of the upper limits of the class intervals. Table 2.6 compares the grouped frequency distribution created by Excel (A) with a grouped frequency distribution with manually created bins (B). The data used for the grouped frequency distribution are the 2001 wages for the 50 states and the District of Columbia reported earlier in Table 2.1.

For grouped frequency distributions, the results are generally more meaningful when the user supplies the bins instead of allowing Excel to create its own class intervals. There is no exact science to determining the proper number of class intervals, but generally, there should around 10 (Howell, 2008), and certainly no more than 20 intervals (or bins). One rule of thumb for determining the minimum number of class intervals is to find the power to which 2 must be raised to equal or exceed the number of observations in the dataset. Another useful rule of thumb for determining the number of class intervals is to find the closest integer to $\sqrt{N}$. Using too few intervals makes the grouped frequency distribution less useful because the patterns or trends in the data are not clearly displayed. Similarly, using too many intervals makes the data appear flatter because most intervals will have few observations (Moore, McCabe, Duckworth, & Sclove, 2003). If you desire greater granularity, and a plot showing all the data, you might consider producing a dot plot instead of a grouped frequency distribution. Excel does not produce dot plots, but MegaStat and other Excel statistics add-ins do, as do SPSS, Minitab, and other statistics packages. You can also create a dot plot in Excel through some manipulation of the column chart in the Chart Tools.

Return to the data for average 2001 wages for the fifty states and Washington D.C. from Table 2.1. For those data, N = 51, and $2^5 = 32 < 51$, so five class intervals would probably be too few intervals, while a minimum of $2^6 = 64 > 51$ or six class intervals should be a good starting point according to one rule of thumb, and $\sqrt{51} = 7.1414$ would suggest about seven intervals according to the other rule of thumb. Of course, reason should prevail. Data often have natural breaks and traditional logical intervals. Class intervals of \$5,000 make a great deal of sense when dealing with money.

Examination of Table 2.6 reveals Excel may produce class intervals with fractional widths (A), while the user-supplied bin ranges (B) would be obviously more understandable to most users. Both the Excel-supplied and the user-supplied bins show the typical positively skewed distribution of income.

Table 2.6 Grouped frequency distributions

A. Bins supplied by Excel

Bin	Frequency
25195	1
29582.57143	14
33970.14286	17
38357.71429	11
42745.28571	3
47132.85714	4
51520.42857	0
More	1

B. Bins supplied by user

Bin	Frequency
30000	15
35000	18
40000	12
45000	3
50000	2
55000	0
60000	1

As discussed, you can use either the FREQUENCY function or the Histogram tool to produce the grouped frequency distribution. Excel uses the upper limit of the class interval to define the bin, and then uses this upper limit to label the frequency distribution when you use the Histogram tool. Frequency distributions are often presnted in graphic form in addition to tabular form. You will learn in Chapter 3 how to produce simple and grouped frequency polygons and histograms.

THE BOTTOM LINE

- You can create simple and grouped frequency distributions in Excel with the FREQUENCY function and an array formula.
- For the simple frequency distribution, the "bins" range is the sorted list of possible X values.
- For the grouped frequency distribution, the "bins" range is a column of upper limits for the selected class intervals.
- The number of class intervals for a grouped frequency distribution should be around 10, no more than 20, and somewhere around the square root of the sample size. Reason should prevail when you develop class intervals.
- You can also use the Histogram tool (**Data** > **Analysis** > **Data Analysis** > **Histogram**) to produce simple and grouped frequency distributions.
- If you omit the bins range when using the Histogram tool, Excel will provide its own class intervals.

Finding Percentiles and Percentile Ranks

In addition to simple and grouped frequency distributions, another way to help determine the "location" of a particular score is to compare the raw score to a percentile. Percentiles divide an ordered dataset into hundredths, and a *percentile score* is the score at or below which a given percent of the cases lie (Welkowitz, Cohen, & Ewen, 2006). Saying a score is at the 5th percentile indicates only 5% of the cases were the same or lower, while 95% of the cases were higher than the given raw score. Closely related to the percentile is the *percentile rank*, which is the percent of cases in the specific reference group (or dataset) scoring at or below the given score. We will discuss both percentiles and percentile ranks.

Excel provides a built-in function called PERCENTILE, but this function does not work properly in many cases. There is a "Rank and Percentile" tool in the Analysis ToolPak as well, but you should also avoid it, too, as it produces incorrect ranks and percentiles. To be safe, you should use the location formulas shown here (or use a dedicated statistics package such as SPSS) to find correct percentiles. Although the concept of a percentile is a simple one, the determination of actual percentile scores is not always quite so simple. Consider the following hypothetical test scores for 36 students.

Table 2.7 Hypothetical test scores for 36 students

52	69	73	81
59	70	73	81
62	70	74	82
67	72	74	82
67	72	75	83
67	72	75	85
67	72	76	85
67	72	78	87
69	73	80	90

Recall the location of the median. We find this value, also known as the 50th percentile, at the location $(n + 1) / 2$ in the ordered dataset. Let us expand our location definition for the median as follows

$$l_{50} = (n+1)\left(\frac{50}{100}\right)$$

where l_{50} is the **location** (and not the value) of the median in the dataset sorted from smallest to largest. Remember the median may not be an observed value in the dataset when the number of observations is even. When n is an even number, the median is the average of the two middle values in the ordered dataset. Thus with 36 observations, the median is located at the position $37 / 2 = 18.5$ in the ordered dataset. Thus, we calculate the median as the average of the 18th and 19th values. Another way to conceive of this is that we go to the 18th value and then go halfway from the 18th to the 19th value. This same "distance-based" logic applies to percentiles in general when the percentile is not an observed value in the dataset. For our purposes, we will adopt the definition of percentile advanced by the National Institute of Standards. The reader should note there are other definitions, and that these definitions may lead to different values from the ones we determine here. We will define the 0th percentile as the minimum value in the dataset, and the 100th percentile as the maximum value. We can now define the location of any other percentile between 0 and 100 as

$$l_p = (n+1)\left(\frac{p}{100}\right)$$

for values $0 < p < 100$. When the location is not an integer, we will separate the value of the location l into k, the integer, and d, the decimal part. Then we can find the value of the percentile as follows. The percentile score, $X(p)$, is found from the location formula as the value of the observation at position k plus the d times the distance between the values at positions k and $k + 1$:

$$X(p) = X_k + d\left(X_{k+1} - X_k\right)$$

Let us illustrate with the 36 hypothetical test scores in Table 2.7. First, we will find the median. We find that the 18th and 19th values are both 73, so we report 73 as the median. Excel's MEDIAN function and the PERCENTILE function both report this value correctly. However, the PERCENTILE function can produce unexpected results for other values, as shown below.

Let us also find the 25th percentile and the 75% percentile. These are the first and third **quartiles** (dividing the dataset into fourths. To find the 25th percentile, use the general location formula for percentiles.

$$l_{25} = (n+1)\left(\frac{25}{100}\right) = 37(.25) = 9.25$$

Applying the location formula to find the 25th percentile, we go to the 9th value in the ordered dataset, and then go .25 of the distance between the 9th and 10th values. Once again, we find that these two values are the same in our example data, so the 25th percentile is 69.

However, locating the 75th percentile is not quite so simple:

$$l_{75} = (n+1)\left(\frac{75}{100}\right) = 37(.75) = 27.75$$

We go to the 27th value in the ordered dataset, and then go 0.75 of the distance between the 27th and the 28th values.

$$X(75) = X_{27} + .75(X_{28} - X_{27}) = 80 + .75(81 - 80) = 80.75$$

This is the correct value for the 75th percentile, according to our definitions. However, Excel's PERCENTILE function returns the unexpected value of 80.25, which is also the value returned by Excel's QUARTILE function. Excel clearly uses a different procedure from the one presented here (and in most statistics texts) to determine the locations (and thus the values) of percentiles. Some research verified that Excel uses the following formula to locate the value of a percentile.

$$l_p = 1 + (n-1)\left(\frac{p}{100}\right)$$

Excel's location formula will correctly identify the location of the median, but will potentially identify different locations from those our formula finds for all other percentiles. Note other programs besides Excel use this definition of the location of percentiles, for instance the statistical programming language R.

To develop a general formula for determining the correct value of a percentile using our definition, we can use the INDEX function in Excel to find the data values at positions k and $k + 1$ in the dataset, and the MOD (for *modulo*) function to find the decimal part, d, of the location. Assume we are interested in locating the 10th percentile in our dataset. We can write an Excel formula to determine the "position" of the 10th percentile in the ordered dataset. To make our formula more flexible, assume we call the data range "scores," and store the value of the desired percentile, in this case, 10, in cell E1. Because there are 36 observations, the following formula will determine the desired location value for the 10th percentile, position 3.7 in the ordered dataset:

= (COUNT(scores) + 1) * (E1/100)

Assume we enter the location formula in cell E2. The following general formula[1] in cell E3 determines the value of the 10th percentile by locating the 3rd value in the ordered dataset, and then adding to that value 0.7 of the distance between the 3rd and 4th values (See Figure 2.28):

$$= INDEX(scores, E2) + MOD(E2, 1) * (INDEX(scores, E2 + 1) - INDEX(scores, E2))$$

The INDEX function locates the value at the integer part of 3.7, i.e., 3. The MOD function produces the remainder, 0.7, from dividing 3.7 by 1. Then the formula locates the 4th value and finds 0.7 of the distance between the 3rd and 4th values. A column of index numbers adjacent to the data values is not required, but makes it clear which values are identified and used by the formula. We can now use this worksheet model to find any desired percentile simply by changing the value in cell E1.

	A	B	C	D	E	F	G	H	I	J	K
						Table 2.7 Hypothetical Test Scores - M					
	Home	Insert		Page Layout	Formulas	Data	Review	View	Developer	Add-Ins	Acrobat
	E3				f_x	= INDEX(scores, E2)+MOD(E2, 1)*(INDEX(scores, E2 + 1)-INDEX(scores, E2))					
	A	B	C	D	E	F	G	H	I	J	K
1	Index	Scores			10	Desired Percentile					
2	1	52			3.7	Percentile Location					
3	2	59			65.5	Percentile Value					
4	3	62									
5	4	67									

Figure 2.28 General formula determines percentile values in an ordered dataset

Verify the accuracy of this formula by finding the values of the median, the 25th, and the 75th percentiles. The results are the same as those from our previous calculations. SPSS also produces the same values for the 25th, 50th, and 75th percentile scores as those produced by our calculations and the formula shown in Figure 2.28. When the formula identifies a location value higher than n, you should report the maximum value of X as that percentile score, which is the approach used by SPSS.

Now that we have examined the location and determination of percentile scores, let us turn to a related problem, the determination of percentile ranks. As mentioned earlier, the ***percentile rank*** of any given score is the percentage of scores at or below that score. To automate this determination, Excel provides the PERCENTRANK function, but like the PERCENTILE function, it produces incorrect results.

We define the percentile rank as follows, where cf_l is the cumulative frequency of the score immediately *lower* than X, and f_i is the frequency of scores at the value X. When there are multiple values of X, this definition assumes that half of the values are above X, and half are below.

$$PR_X = \frac{cf_l + .5(f_i)}{N} \times 100\%$$

Note that the percentile rank is not simply the cumulative percentage up to and including a particular score. To illustrate, let us find the percentile rank for a value of 70 in our 36 hypothetical test scores. Note that there are 10

---

[1] Dr. Rick Jerz developed this general formula for locating the correct values of percentiles using Excel, and it is presented here with his permission.

values lower than 70, and two 70s in our dataset. Although the cumulative percentage of scores up to and including 70 is 33.33% (12/36 × 100%), the percentile rank for 70 is 30.56%:

$$PR_{70} = \frac{cf_l + .5(f_i)}{N} \times 100\% = \frac{10 + .5(2)}{36} \times 100\% = 30.56\%$$

Using the FREQUENCY function to produce a frequency table allows us to write Excel formulas to determine the cumulative frequencies below each value of X and to find the correct percentile ranks for all 36 scores (Figure 2.29).

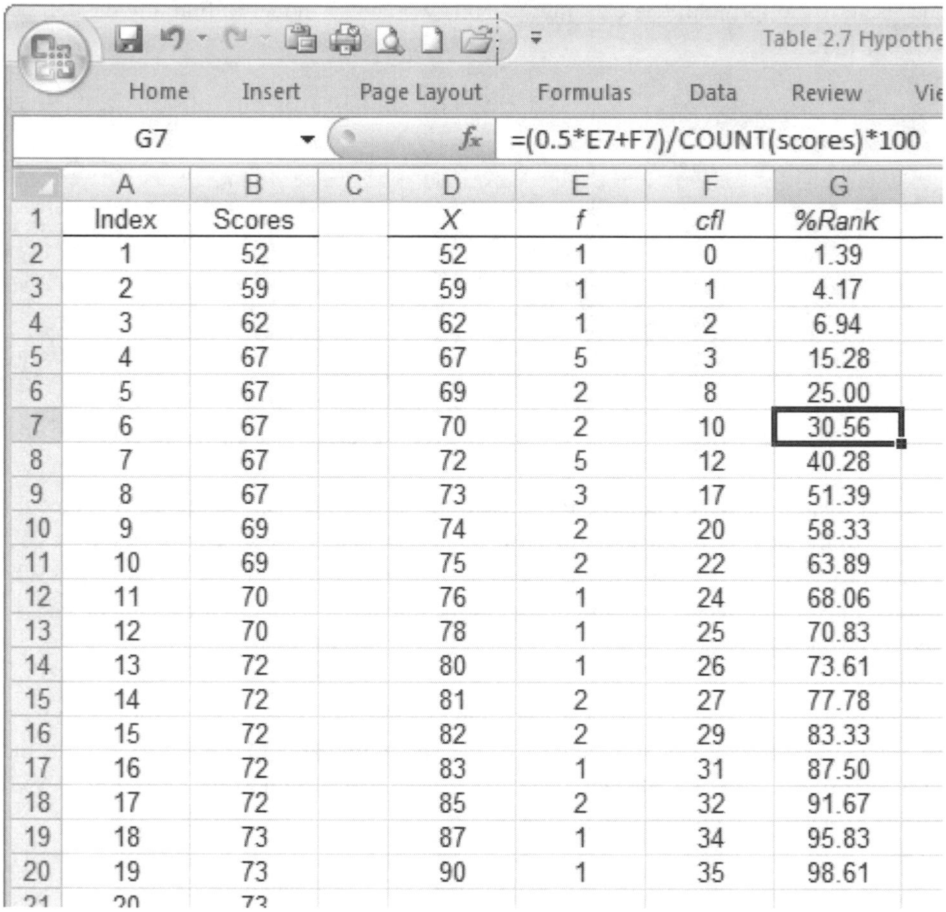

	A	B	C	D	E	F	G
1	Index	Scores		*X*	*f*	*cfl*	*%Rank*
2	1	52		52	1	0	1.39
3	2	59		59	1	1	4.17
4	3	62		62	1	2	6.94
5	4	67		67	5	3	15.28
6	5	67		69	2	8	25.00
7	6	67		70	2	10	30.56
8	7	67		72	5	12	40.28
9	8	67		73	3	17	51.39
10	9	69		74	2	20	58.33
11	10	69		75	2	22	63.89
12	11	70		76	1	24	68.06
13	12	70		78	1	25	70.83
14	13	72		80	1	26	73.61
15	14	72		81	2	27	77.78
16	15	72		82	2	29	83.33
17	16	72		83	1	31	87.50
18	17	72		85	2	32	91.67
19	18	73		87	1	34	95.83
20	19	73		90	1	35	98.61
21	20	73					

Figure 2.29 Using Excel formulas to find correct percentile ranks

THE BOTTOM LINE

- A ***percentile*** is the value at or below which a certain percentage of scores fall in the ordered dataset.
- Excel's PERCENTILE function produces incorrect values in many cases.
- You can use the standard method and formulas shown in this book to find correct values for percentiles.
- A ***percentile rank*** is the percentage of scores that fall at or below a given raw score in the ordered dataset.
- The PERCENTRANK function also produces incorrect values in many cases.
- You can use the cumulative percentage table method described in this text to identify correct percentile ranks.

Chapter 2 Exercises

1. For the data from Table 2.5, use the Descriptive Statistics tool to calculate the mean, mode, median, count, minimum, maximum, range, variance, and standard deviation of study hours.

2. Using the same data, create a table and use a Total row to find the summary statistics from exercise #1, above.

3. For the data from Table 2.7, use the Descriptive Statistics tool to find the mean, mode, median, count, minimum, maximum, range, variance, and standard deviation for the 36 hypothetical test scores.

4. Using the same data, use Excel's built-in functions to compute and compare the values of the standard deviation and variance treating the dataset as a sample and treating the dataset as a population. Why are these values different?

5. For the data from Table 2.1, use the Descriptive Statistics tool to calculate the mean, mode, median, count, minimum, maximum, range, variance, and standard deviation of the *PctChg* variable for the 51 records. What does the average percent change tell you about the wage level differences between 2001 and 2002?

6. Using the same data, create a table and then sort the data on the *PctChg* variable. Which states had wages that declined from 2001 to 2002? Which states had less than 1% wage growth? Which state had the highest wage growth?

7. Using the same dataset, what is the 25th percentile for 2001 wages? What is the 75th percentile? What is the 2001 percentile rank for Washington D.C.?

8. Using the same dataset, what is the 25th percentile for 2002 wages? What is the 75th percentile? What is the 2002 percentile rank for California?

9. Using the same dataset, create a grouped frequency distribution for the 2002 wages. Use the following values for your upper class limits (bins). Create frequency distributions using the FREQUENCY function and the Histogram tool and compare the results.

UpperLimit	Frequency
30000	
35000	
40000	
45000	
50000	
55000	
60000	

3   Charts, Graphs, and More Tables

In this chapter, you will learn how to create charts and graphs and how to use the PivotTable tool. Charts and graphs are easily constructed and modified in Excel. You can display these alongside the data for ease of visualization. The charts and graphs are dynamically linked to the data, and update automatically when the data are modified. For these reasons, Excel becomes a better tool to use than dedicated statistical software for basic statistics. This chapter covers the following:

- Pie charts
- Bar charts
- Histograms
- Line graphs
- Scatterplots
- Pivot tables

Excel provides options for adding three-dimensional effects and other creative formatting to your charts and graphs. For statistics, you should be careful not to overuse these embellishments. For example, 3-D column charts and pie charts distort the data and introduce a false third dimension. Simpler is definitely better, and you should control the appearance of your charts and graphs to make them most useful. For a discussion of common graphical distortions and some good recommendations for avoiding them, see Bennett, Briggs, and Triola (2009).

Presenting data graphically is a part of descriptive or exploratory statistics. Pie charts and bar charts are useful for summarizing frequencies and percentages in categories for nominal and ordinal data. Bar charts (also called bar graphs) are helpful for presenting quantitative information such as averages for separate categories. For interval and ratio data, histograms, line graphs, and scatterplots are appropriate. You will find the table feature and the PivotTable tool in Excel helpful for summarizing both qualitative and quantitative data.

Pie Charts

A pie chart divides a circle into relatively larger and smaller slices based on the relative frequencies or percentages of observations in different categories. The following summary data (Table 3.1) are from the dataset introduced in Chapter 2, the 2001 and 2002 wages for covered employees in the 50 states and the District of Columbia (see Table 2.1). The PivotTable tool discussed later in this chapter was used to count the number of states in each region.

Table 3.1 Data for pie and bar charts

Region	Count
Midwest	12
Northeast	9
South	17
West	13

To construct a pie chart in Excel 2007, select the data including the labels and then click on the **Insert** ribbon. Locate the **Charts** Group (see Figure 3.1).

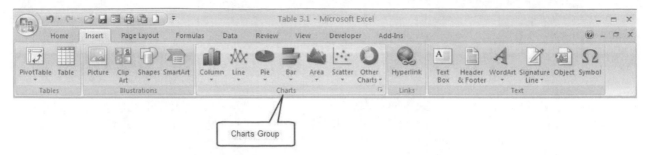

Figure 3.1 Charts group appears on the Insert ribbon

Now locate the **Pie** chart icon. Remember we will summarize these actions as **Insert** > **Charts** > **Pie.** Click on the **Pie** icon and choose the default plain 2-D pie chart (see Figure 3.2). Excel immediately creates a pie chart and places it in the worksheet.

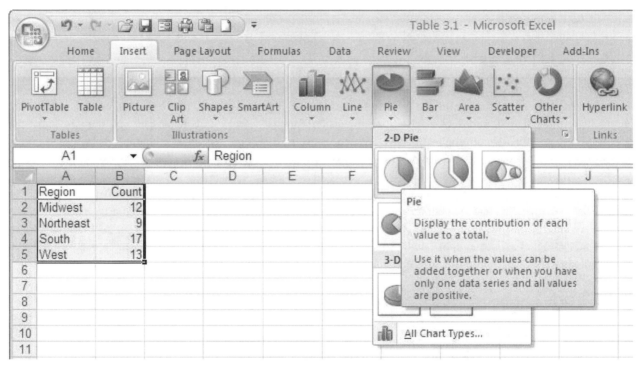

Figure 3.2 Select the 2-D Pie chart option

See the completed pie chart in Figure 3.3. Charts are graphic objects not attached to a cell or cells in the workbook. Like a table, the chart object is also named and is accessible from the Name Manager and the Name Box. You can move, copy, resize, and delete chart objects quite easily. It is also possible to copy and paste charts into Microsoft Word or PowerPoint for reports and presentations. Excel provides full-color formatting for these graphic objects.

When you create a chart or graph, Excel provides additional **Chart Tools** with ribbons tabs for **Design**, **Layout**, and **Format**. Excel comes with a gallery of chart styles on the **Design** ribbon (**Chart Tools** > **Design** > **Chart Styles**), and the **Layout** and **Format** ribbons provide options for customizing chart objects (see Figure 3.4). The **Chart Tools** will vanish when you click outside the chart, but will reappear when you click on the chart again. This is Excel's way of simplifying the user interface.

It should be apparent that it is very easy to create and modify charts in Excel. Around 30 years ago, it took graphic artists to create charts as attractive as these.

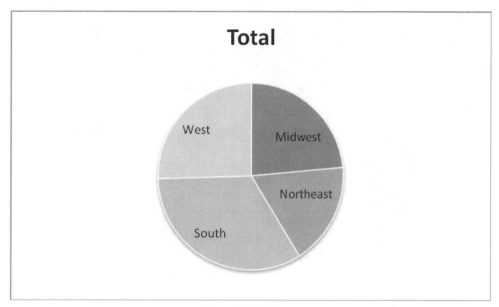

Figure 3.3 Pie chart

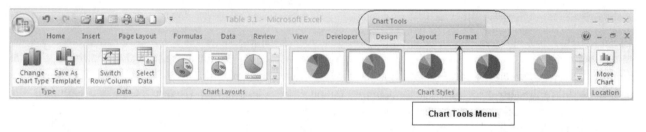

Figure 3.4 Chart Tools menu adds Design, Layout, and Format ribbons

Bar Charts

Let us use the same data and techniques to produce a bar chart. Although Excel has a chart type labeled "bar," it is horizontal in orientation and should generally be avoided. To generate a bar chart in Excel, follow the steps for the pie chart above, but select **Column** this time, and the upper-left option (the default 2-D Clustered Column chart) as the chart type. Once again, Excel immediately produces the chart you selected. Using the Design, Layout, and Format ribbons, you can modify the bar chart. For example, let us modify the bar colors. To do so, right-click on one of the bars and then select **Format Data Series**. Select the option "**Vary colors by point**" under the **Fill** menu (see Figure 3.5 for the result). You can experiment changing other chart features by right clicking on them and exploring their formatting options.

In addition to their use for displaying frequencies in categories, bar charts (or bar graphs) provide an excellent way to summarize other quantitative information, such as averages or totals, by categories.

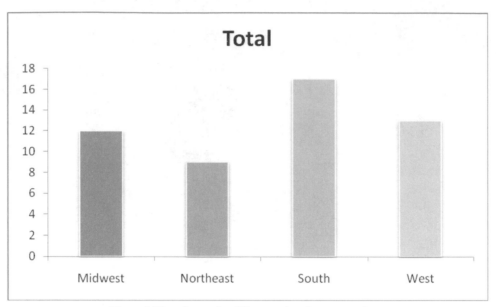

Figure 3.5 Bar chart using different colors for separate bars

Histograms

The *X* axis in a histogram represents a continuum of quantitative values, so the bars should touch. We will use the study hour data from Chapter 2 (see Table 2.5) to illustrate the histogram. We must use special formatting options to remove the gaps between the bars, so we begin the process of creating a histogram by starting with a column chart, just as we did in the above section. Use the **Column** option in the **Charts** group (**Insert** > **Charts** > **Column**), but select only the array of frequencies. Do not include the "bins" (the *X* values) in the adjacent column. We will use these as our category labels for the *X* axis after we create the chart. Excel by default will label the columns beginning with 1. Sometimes this is appropriate, but most often it is not.

After selecting the frequencies as your source data and producing your initial histogram, you will enter the cell references to the bins as your Category (*X*) axis labels (see Figure 3.6). Remember to reach the **Design** ribbon, you must select the histogram or click on its name in the Name Box. It is also easy to click on the default axis labels and then right-click to select the data. When you select the chart or click in it, its default name will appear in the Name Box and the **Chart Tools** menu will reappear.

To remove the unwanted gaps between the bars of your histogram, right-click on one of the bars and select **Format Data Series** (Figure 3.6). Change the gap size to zero under **Series Options**. You can pick any axis labels, numerical or text, you would like for your histogram or other chart object. The easiest way to do this is to right-click anywhere on the *X* axis labels and then choose **Select Data**. You can also click the **Select Data** icon in the **Design** ribbon. In either case, the Select Data Source dialog will allow you to edit and change the horizontal (category) axis labels to the appropriate values, as well as to add, edit, or remove the legend entries (see Figure 3.7). You can also use the **Format Data Series** option to change the appearance of the bars. Let us put a solid border around each bar and remove the default solid fill. We will also use the **Layout** ribbon under **Chart Tools** to customize the chart by adding axis titles and a chart title. The completed histogram after these modifications is displayed in Figure 3.8.

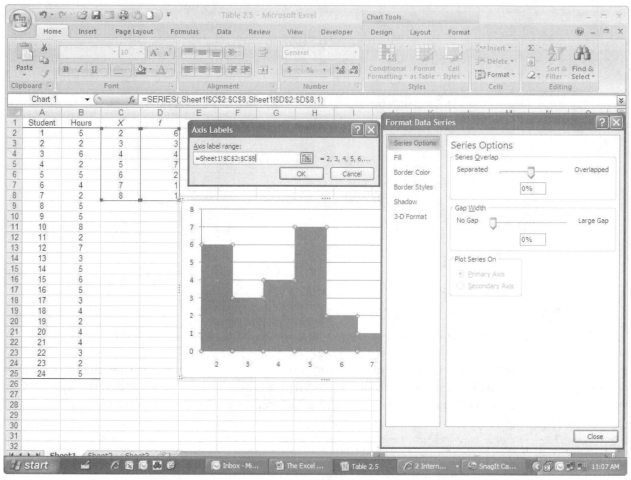

Figure 3.6 Adding correct *X*-axis category labels and removing gaps

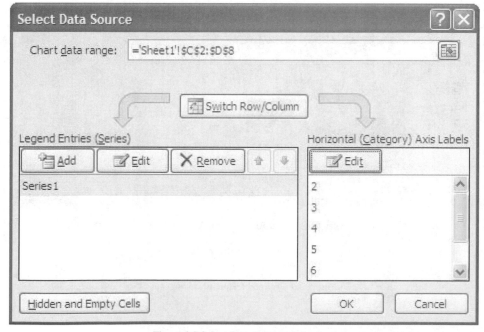

Figure 3.7 Select Data Source dialog box

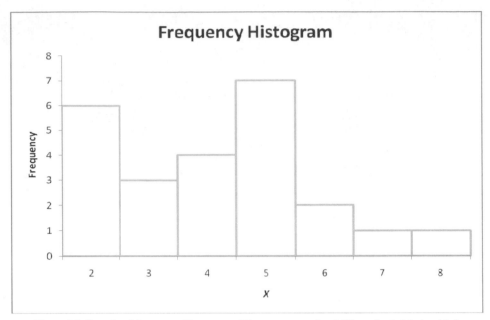

Figure 3.8 Completed frequency histogram with gaps removed and title and axis labels added

In addition to a simple frequency histogram, you can also produce a histogram from a grouped frequency distribution. The following histogram presents the grouped frequencies of average wages of covered workers from the year 2001 (see Table 2.1). Because the columns represent intervals, we can use the interval midpoint as the label for each column. You can easily modify the appearance of the bars and can display data values above the bars if you like (Figure 3.9). The best way to learn these additional features is to experiment with the **Chart Tools** menu, and you are encouraged to do so.

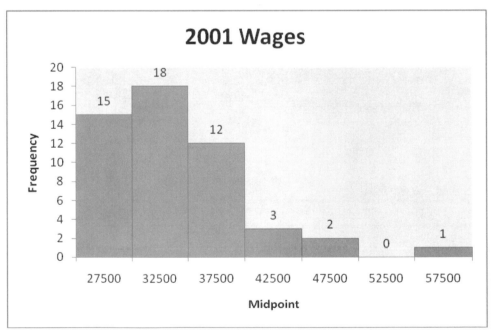

Figure 3.9 Grouped frequency histogram

Line Graphs

A frequency polygon is a special kind of line graph. The data used to produce a simple frequency distribution in Chapter 2 and our frequency distribution in Figure 3.8 are used once again to produce a frequency polygon. Select the data, omitting the X values, and then select the **Line** graph option from the **Insert** ribbon (**Insert** > **Charts** > **Line**) as shown in Figure 3.10. Select "Line with Markers" in the 2-D line graph menu. If you do happen to select the X values along with the frequencies, Excel will make a graph with two lines. Add the correct X axis category labels as with the histogram. The completed and formatted frequency polygon appears in Figure 3.11.

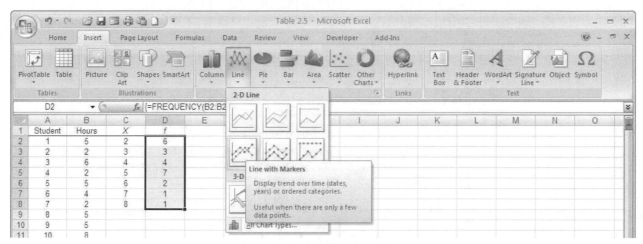

Figure 3.10 Producing a line graph in Excel

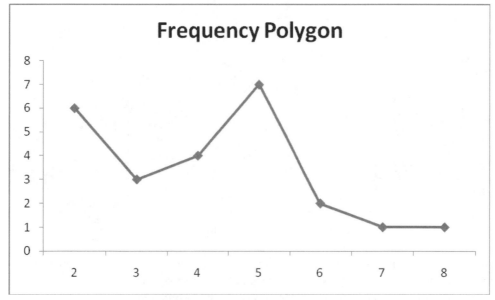

Figure 3.11 Completed frequency polygon

Scatterplots

A scatterplot provides a graphical view of pairs of measures on two variables, X and Y. Assume you were given the following data (Table 3.2) concerning the number of hours 20 students study each week (on average) and each student's GPA (grade point average). A scatterplot will help you to explore whether there seems to be a relationship between study hours and grades.

Table 3.2 Study hours and GPA

Student	Hours	GPA	Student	Hours	GPA
1	10	3.33	11	13	3.26
2	12	2.92	12	12	3.00
3	10	2.56	13	11	2.74
4	15	3.08	14	10	2.85
5	14	3.57	15	13	3.33
6	12	3.31	16	13	3.29
7	13	3.45	17	14	3.58
8	15	3.93	18	18	3.85
9	16	3.82	19	17	4.00
10	14	3.70	20	14	3.50

Place the data in three columns of an Excel worksheet, as shown in Figure 3.12. As before, select the data, click the **Insert** tab to open the **Insert** ribbon, and then in the **Charts** group, select **Scatter** as the chart type (see Figure 3.12). As before, the scatterplot is immediately produced. To add the trend line (see Figure 3.13, left-click on any element in the data series, right-click, and select **Add Trendline**. Select **Linear** as the line type.

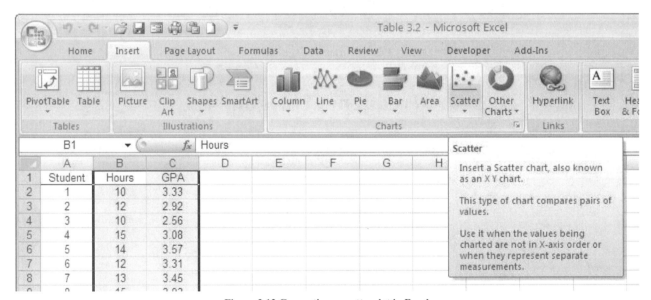

Figure 3.12 Generating a scatterplot in Excel

The scatterplot appears in Figure 3.13. As you have learned, you can remove the gridlines, add titles, and make other adjustments via the ribbons located under **Chart Tools**. You can also select an element, such as the X or Y axis, click the right mouse button, and select formatting options from the resulting menu.

We will return to this example in Chapter 10, where you will learn more about correlation and regression. You will learn how to test the significance of the relationship between study hours and grades, and how to determine the formula for the trend line.

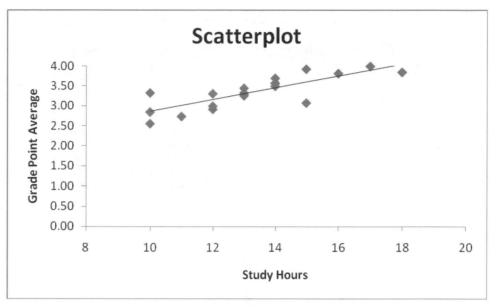

Figure 3.13 Completed scatterplot

THE BOTTOM LINE

- To insert a pie chart, bar chart, line graph, scatterplot, or other chart in Excel, select the relevant data then **Insert > Charts**. Then select the desired chart and options.
- For line graphs and histograms, the *X* axis labels should be added after the chart is created.
- Charts are not attached to specific cells in the worksheet.
- Charts can be moved, sized, formatted, copied, and deleted.
- When you create a chart in Excel, it is dynamically linked to the data.
- Charts are special named objects and as such are available via the Name Box and the Name Manager.
- When you create a chart, you have access to **Chart Tools** with **Design**, **Format**, and **Layout** ribbons.

Pivot Tables

The pivot table tool makes it possible to count and summarize text entries as well as numerical values. You can use the pivot table feature with or without a data table. To access this tool, select the **Insert** ribbon and then the **PivotTable** option in the Tables group (**Insert > Tables > PivotTable**). If your data are formatted as a table, you can select **Table Tools > Design > Tools > Summarize with PivotTable**. As with other graphic objects, you can choose from a gallery of predefined styles for your pivot table. Among many other things, this tool can be used to summarize nominal or ordinal data for pie charts and bar charts, as well as to produce histograms and frequency tables. This tool can also summarize quantitative data such as those in Table 3.5. For example, a pivot table could present the averages of the salaries for male and female CEOs in each of the industries.

The responses in Table 3.3 were provided by 40 college students who indicated that they like peanut M&Ms and expressed a color preference. To produce a pivot table in Excel, first place the data in a single column of an Excel worksheet, as shown in Figure 3.14. It this case it is very important to have a column heading. Otherwise, the pivot table tool will take the first entry as the label and reduce the number of observations by one. You might use the label "Color" for the column heading. You can also name the range if you like, but that is not necessary for the pivot table.

Table 3.3 Peanut M&M color preferences for 40 college students

Student	Preference	Student	Preference	Student	Preference	Student	Preference
1	Green	11	Blue	21	Red	31	Red
2	Blue	12	Green	22	Red	32	Green
3	Green	13	Brown	23	Green	33	Blue
4	Green	14	Green	24	Red	34	Blue
5	Red	15	Red	25	Yellow	35	Red
6	Green	16	Blue	26	Blue	36	Green
7	Blue	17	Blue	27	Blue	37	Blue
8	Blue	18	Brown	28	Blue	38	Blue
9	Yellow	19	Brown	29	Orange	39	Red
10	Green	20	Yellow	30	Blue	40	Orange

	A	B	C
1	Student	Color	
2	1	Green	
3	2	Blue	
4	3	Green	
5	4	Green	
6	5	Red	
7	6	Green	
8	7	Blue	
9	8	Blue	
10	9	Yellow	
11	10	Green	
12	11	Blue	
13	12	Green	

Figure 3.14 M&M color preferences of 40 college students (partial data)

The PivotTable tool is somewhat complex, so be patient as you learn to use it. To create the pivot table, select the entire data range including the column heading and then select **Insert** > **PivotTable** (see Figure 3.15). You will now see a **PivotTable Tools** menu with an **Options** ribbon and a **Design** ribbon. In the PivotTable Field List, click and drag the "Color" item to the Row Labels area, and then drag the "Color" item to the Values area (see Figure 3.16). Because the data are text entries, Excel will alphabetize the labels for lack of any other organizing principle. You can sort the data in your pivot table if you prefer a different arrangement.

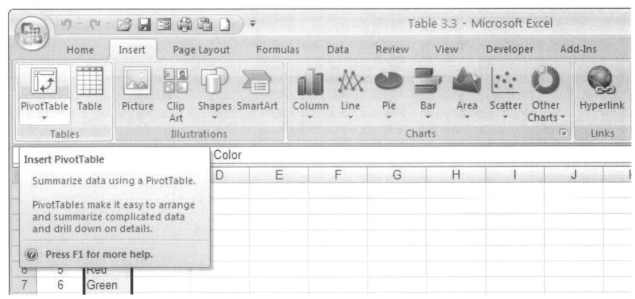

Figure 3.15 Generating a pivot table in Excel

When you enter numerical data into a pivot table rather than text labels, Excel will sum the numbers by default. You can change the field settings in the pivot table to count or average the values, or to display different summary statistics. In the **PivotTable Tools** > **Options** ribbon, click on **Field Settings** in the **Active Field** group to change these settings (see Figure 3.16). As a shortcut, right-click on the field directly in the pivot table and select **Value Field Settings** to see the available settings. The "PivotTable Field List" task pane also allows you to change the variable field settings in the Values area (see Figure 3.17). Once you have created your pivot table, you can click on **PivotTable Tools** > **Options** > **Tools** to create various kinds of charts.

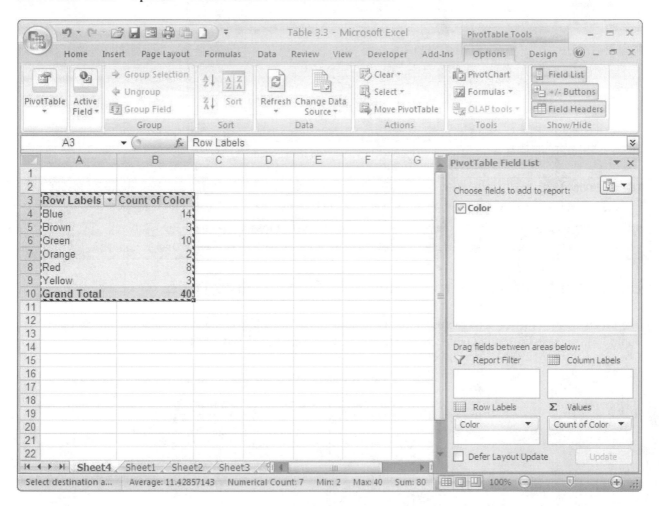

Figure 3.16 Pivot table in a new worksheet

The completed pivot table appears as Table 3.4. This feature of Excel is a time-saver when you have to summarize large amounts of categorical data, and will be useful for the chi-square tests discussed later in this book.

Table 3.4 Completed pivot table

Row Labels ▾	Count of Color
Blue	14
Brown	3
Green	10
Orange	2
Red	8
Yellow	3
Grand Total	**40**

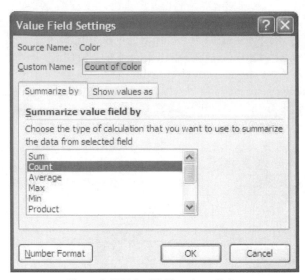

Figure 3.17 Value Field settings dialog

THE BOTTOM LINE

- Pivot tables can summarize both numerical and text entries for one or two variables (categories).
- To create a pivot table, select the relevant data and then select **Insert > Tables > PivotTable**.
- Creating a pivot table gives access to a **PivotTable Tools** group with **Options** and **Design** ribbons.

Using the Pivot Table to Summarize Quantitative Data

The following hypothetical data represent the sex, industry, age, and salary in thousands of dollars for 50 CEOs (see Table 3.5). You can use a pivot table to summarize the CEOs' ages by sex and industry.

Table 3.5 Hypothetical CEO data

Sex	Industry	Age	Salary	Sex	Industry	Age	Salary
1	1	53	145	0	2	51	368
1	2	33	262	0	1	48	659
1	3	45	208	0	2	45	396
1	3	36	192	0	2	37	300
1	2	62	324	0	1	50	343
1	3	58	214	0	2	50	536
1	2	61	254	0	2	50	543
1	3	56	205	0	1	53	298
1	2	44	203	0	2	70	1103
1	3	46	250	0	1	53	406
1	3	63	149	0	2	47	862
1	3	70	213	0	1	48	298
1	1	44	155	0	1	38	350
1	3	50	200	0	3	74	800
1	1	52	250	0	1	60	726
0	1	43	324	0	3	32	370
0	1	46	362	0	1	51	536
0	2	55	424	0	3	50	291
0	1	41	294	0	1	40	808
0	1	55	632	0	3	61	543
0	2	55	498	0	3	56	350
0	1	50	369	0	1	45	242
0	2	49	390	0	3	61	467
0	2	47	332	0	2	59	317
0	1	69	750	0	3	57	317

Place the data in four columns in an Excel worksheet (see Figure 3.18). Sex is coded 1 (*female*) and 0 = (*male*), and the industries are 1 (*manufacturing*), 2 (*retail*), and 3 (*service*). Use sex as the column field and industry as the row field. Then find the averages of the ages for male and female CEOs in each industry.

	A	B	C	D	E
1	Sex	Industry	Age	Salary	
2	1	1	53	145	
3	1	2	33	262	
4	1	3	45	208	
5	1	3	36	192	
6	1	2	62	324	
7	1	3	58	214	
8	1	2	61	254	
9	1	3	56	205	
10	1	2	44	203	
11	1	3	46	250	
39	0	1	38	350	
40	0	3	74	800	
41	0	1	60	726	
42	0	3	32	370	
43	0	1	51	536	
44	0	3	50	291	
45	0	1	40	808	
46	0	3	61	543	
47	0	3	56	350	
48	0	1	45	242	
49	0	3	61	467	
50	0	2	59	317	
51	0	3	57	317	

Figure 3.18 CEO Data in Excel worksheet (partial data)

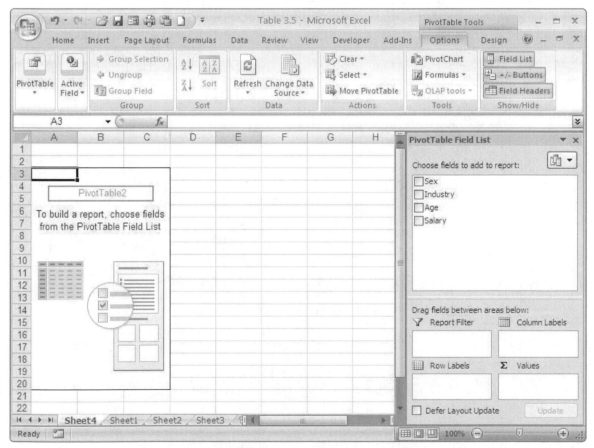

Figure 3.19 Preparation for the pivot table

To build the pivot table, select the entire dataset including the row of column headings, and then select **Insert** > **Tables** > **PivotTable**. Accept the defaults to place the pivot table in a new worksheet. In the PivotTable Field List, drag the "sex" item to the columns field and the "industry" item to the rows field as shown in Figure 3.19. By default, Excel will label the row entry "Row Labels" and the column entry "Column Labels." To change these, you can simply select the cell and type in the appropriate label such as "Industry" in cell A4, or you can select **PivotTable Tools** > **Design** > **Layout** > **Report Layout** > **Show in Tabular Form**. In either case, you will have a dropdown arrow at the right of the field label that allows you to filter the data (Figure 3.20). After modifying the field labels, you can then move the age field to the Values area and change the field settings to Average (see Figure 3.21). The finished pivot table after some number formatting appears in Figure 3.22. It is often best to use the PivotTable tool to summarize quantitative data, but then copy the summary information to a new location in the workbook so you can manipulate it more easily outside the pivot table framework.

	Sex ▾		
Industry ▾	0	1	Grand Total
1			
2			
3			
Grand Total			

Figure 3.20 Row and column fields identified

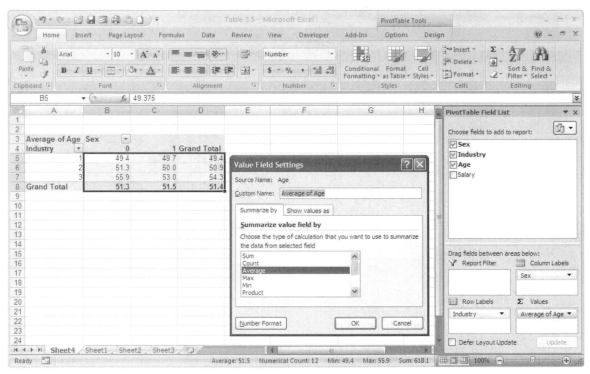

Figure 3.21 Changing PivotTable field settings

	A	B	C	D
1				
2				
3	Average of Age	Sex ▾		
4	Industry ▾	0	1	Grand Total
5	1	49.4	49.7	49.4
6	2	51.3	50.0	50.9
7	3	55.9	53.0	54.3
8	Grand Total	51.3	51.5	51.4
9				

Figure 3.22 Completed pivot table

The Charts Excel Does Not Readily Produce

There are many charts and plots commonly used in exploratory data analysis (Tukey, 1977) including boxplots, dot plots, and stem-and-leaf plots. You can easily create these charts and plots with dedicated statistics packages such as Minitab and SPSS. By contrast, Excel does not readily produce these charts. They require manipulation of the Chart tools, use of a third-party add-in, or macros. A cursory Internet search will reveal the workarounds available to construct these missing charts and plots in Excel.

As mentioned, Excel add-ins provide Excel with many of these missing graphical tools, along with enhanced statistical capabilities. Below is a boxplot of the ages of the 50 CEOs shown in Table 3.5. This boxplot was produced using the Excel add-in MegaStat (see Figure 3.23).

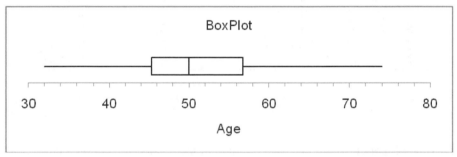

Figure 3.23 Boxplot provides a graphical display of the five-number summary

The same data appear in Figure 3.24 as a dot plot (also produced using MegaStat).

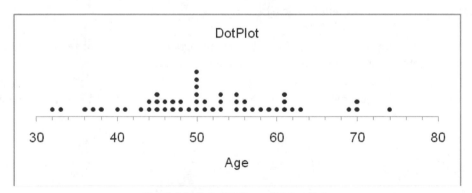

Figure 3.24 Dot plot shows all data points

Chapter 3 Exercises

1. Use the PivotTable tool to summarize the average 2002 wages for covered workers for each region shown in Table 2.1. *Hint*: You will have to change the Value Field Setting from *Sum* to *Average*.

2. Use the information you just generated to make a bar chart of the average 2002 wages by region.

3. Make a side-by-side (clustered) bar chart showing the 2001 and 2002 wages by region.

4. Use the PivotTable tool to summarize the average percent change in wages by region.

5. The following data were obtained from the Bureau of Labor Statistics, Current Population Survey. The data represent 2007 unemployment in percentage and 2007 weekly wages in dollars for people with various education levels. Produce a bar chart to show the percentage of unemployment by educational attainment.

Label	Education	Unemployment	WeeklyWage
0	No high-school diploma	7.1	428
1	High-school graduate	4.4	604
2	Some college, no degree	3.8	683
3	Associate degree	3.0	740
4	Bachelor's degree	2.2	987
5	Master's degree	1.8	1165
6	Professional Degree	1.3	1427
7	Doctoral Degree	1.4	1497

6. Using the same data as above, produce a bar chart to show the average weekly wages by educational attainment.

7. Using the same data as above, produce a scatterplot of the relationship between unemployment and weekly wage. Add a trendline to your plot.

8. Using the data in Table 3.5, produce a scatterplot of the relationship between age and salary. Produce separate scatterplots for male and female CEOs.

9. Using the same data, produce a grouped frequency histogram of the ages of the 50 CEOs. Determine an appropriate number of class intervals and appropriate interval limits.

10. Convert the grouped frequency histogram in exercise #9 above to a grouped frequency polygon.

4   Discrete Probability Distributions

In this chapter, you will learn how to work with two important discrete probability distributions, the binomial distribution and the Poisson distribution. Excel has built-in functions for finding probabilities associated with these distributions.

The Binomial Probability Distribution

Consider a random variable with only two possible outcomes. We can call one of these outcomes "success," and the other outcome "failure." In some cases, success is easy to define, but in many cases, the distinction between success and failure is arbitrary. To avoid the overworked example of a coin toss, let us use as our example a student's score on a multiple-choice test item. The student either gets the item right (1) or misses the item (0). Let us call the probability of success p and the probability of failure $q = 1 - p$.

We are interested in the number of successes, r, in a series of independent trials, N, in which the outcome of each trial is either a success or a failure, and in which the probability of success for each trial is the same. Returning to our example, let us assume a particular student did not study, and there were 10 multiple-choice items on a statistics quiz. To simplify matters, let us further assume the student has a .25 probability of getting each item right by guessing. We want to know the probability of the student getting 7 items right by guessing on all 10 items.

We can find the probability of r successes in N independent trials when the probability of a success for each trial is p from the following formula (Hays & Winkler, 1970):

$$P(r \text{ successes} \mid N, p) = \binom{N}{r} p^r q^{N-r}$$

The term $\binom{N}{r}$ (read "N choose r") is the "binomial coefficient," and is also abbreviated as nCr. It determines the number of combinations or ways you can select r things from a total of N things, ignoring the order of the r things. In this case, you are asking how many ways you could choose any 7 of the 10 quiz items. The binomial coefficient is evaluated as

$$\binom{N}{r} = \frac{N!}{r!(N-r)!} = \frac{10 \times 9 \times 8 \times \cancel{7} \times \cancel{6} \times \cancel{5} \times \cancel{4} \times \cancel{3} \times \cancel{2} \times \cancel{1}}{(\cancel{7} \times \cancel{6} \times \cancel{5} \times \cancel{4} \times \cancel{3} \times \cancel{2} \times \cancel{1})(3 \times 2 \times 1)} = \frac{10 \times 9 \times 8}{3 \times 2 \times 1} = 120$$

Cancellation of like terms makes it easier to evaluate the binomial coefficient, leaving you with less computational work to perform. In fact, Excel can do all the work for you. Enter a blank worksheet cell and type

= COMBIN(10,7)

and the answer, 120, appears instantly when you press <**Enter**>. In the current case, $p = .25$, $q = .75$, $N = 10$, and $r = 7$. Instead of the probability of exactly 7 questions right, we are really interested in the probability the student would get 7 *or more* items right by guessing, so we could evaluate the probability of 7, 8, 9, and 10 items and add those together. To avoid confusion, let us label the binomial probability with a capital P and the probability of success on a given trial with a lower case p. The probability of getting exactly 7 items right by guessing is about .003:

$$P = \binom{N}{r} p^r q^{N-r} = 120 \times .25^7 \times .75^3 \approx .003$$

We can find this binomial probability in Excel by use of the following formula

$$= \text{BINOMDIST}(7, 10, 0.25, \text{FALSE}) \approx .003$$

FALSE indicates we are seeking the exact probability of 7 successes out of 10 trials when the probability of success on a single trial is .25. Substitute 8, 9, and 10 for the 7 in the previous formula for those respective probabilities, and add them together for the probability of $7 - 10$ items correct.

A Template for Binomial Probabilities

The template in Figure 4.1 shows the binomial probabilities for $0 - 10$ items right if the probability of getting an individual item right by guessing is .25. Adding the probabilities for 7, 8, 9, and 10, we determine the student has about 4 in 1,000 chances of passing the test by guessing on every item. The generic template makes it easy to solve various problems using the binomial distribution. The user enters N and p and the template calculates all the probabilities automatically.

	A	B	C	D	E	F	G	H
1	N	p		Table of Binomial Probabilities				
2	10	0.25		Enter N in cell A2 and p in cell B2				
3								
4	r	p(exactly r)	p(at most r)	p(at least r)		Mean	2.5	
5	0	0.05631	0.05631	1.00000		Variance	1.875	
6	1	0.18771	0.24403	0.94369				
7	2	0.28157	0.52559	0.75597				
8	3	0.25028	0.77588	0.47441				
9	4	0.14600	0.92187	0.22412				
10	5	0.05840	0.98027	0.07813				
11	6	0.01622	0.99649	0.01973				
12	7	0.00309	0.99958	0.00351				
13	8	0.00039	0.99997	0.00042				
14	9	0.00003	1.00000	0.00003				
15	10	0.00000	1.00000	0.00000				
16								

Figure 4.1 Binomial probability template

If you would rather use the BINOMDIST function for the current example, you can find the probability of more than 6 successes in 10 trials, that is, 7, 8, 9, or 10 successes, by entering

$$= 1 - \text{BINOMDIST}(6, 10, 0.25, \text{TRUE}) \approx .004$$

TRUE indicates we are finding cumulative probabilities. This formula finds the cumulative probability of $0 - 6$ successes and subtracts that probability from 1, leaving us with the probability of 7, 8, 9, or 10 items correct.

The Mean and Variance of a Binomial Distribution

We can compute the mean of any discrete probability distribution by the following formula:

$$\mu = \sum \left[xp(x) \right]$$

The variance of a discrete probability distribution is found from this formula

$$\sigma^2 = \sum \left[(x - \mu)^2 \, p(x) \right]$$

We can use the formulas above to determine the mean and variance of the binomial distribution for $N = 10$ and $p = .25$ (Table 4.1).

Table 4.1 Calculating the mean and variance of a binomial distribution

r	$P(r)$	$rP(r)$	$(r-\mu)$	$(r-\mu)^2$	$(r-\mu)^2 P(r)$
0	0.056	0.000	-2.500	6.250	0.352
1	0.188	0.188	-1.500	2.250	0.422
2	0.282	0.563	-0.500	0.250	0.070
3	0.250	0.751	0.500	0.250	0.063
4	0.146	0.584	1.500	2.250	0.328
5	0.058	0.292	2.500	6.250	0.365
6	0.016	0.097	3.500	12.250	0.199
7	0.003	0.022	4.500	20.250	0.063
8	0.000	0.003	5.500	30.250	0.012
9	0.000	0.000	6.500	42.250	0.001
10	0.000	0.000	7.500	56.250	0.000
	Mean	2.500		Variance	1.875

For a binomial distribution, we can calculate the mean more simply as

$$\mu = Np$$

And the variance of a binomial distribution is more simply defined as

$$\sigma^2 = Npq$$

For our distribution of the number of successes in 10 trials with a probability of success of .25 on a given trial, the mean and variance are

$$\mu = Np = 10 \times .25 = 2.5$$

and

$$\sigma^2 = Npq = 10 \times .25 \times .75 = 1.875$$

Application of the Binomial Probability Distribution

Example 1. A Rasmussen poll conducted in February 2009 indicated public support for the economic recovery plan at the time was 37%. If the poll is representative, what is the probability that more than 5 and fewer than 9 people in a randomly selected sample of 15 people would be supportive of the recovery plan?

We are looking for the probability of 6, 7, or 8 people supporting the economic recovery plan if $p = .37$. The probability that 6, 7, or 8 people out of a random sample of 15 would support the plan is $p = .2008 + .1516 + .0890 = .4414$. The binomial probability template shown earlier makes solving this problem easier (see Figure 4.2).

	A	B	C	D	E	F	G
1	N	p		Table of Binomial Probabilities			
2	15	0.37		Enter N in cell A2 and p in cell B2			
3							
4	r	p(exactly r)	p(at most r)	p(at least r)		Mean	5.55
5	0	0.00098	0.00098	1.00000		Variance	3.4965
6	1	0.00861	0.00959	0.99902			
7	2	0.03540	0.04499	0.99041			
8	3	0.09010	0.13509	0.95501			
9	4	0.15874	0.29383	0.86491			
10	5	0.20510	0.49893	0.70617			
11	6	0.20076	0.69969	0.50107			
12	7	0.15160	0.85128	0.30031			
13	8	0.08903	0.94032	0.14872			
14	9	0.04067	0.98098	0.05968			
15	10	0.01433	0.99531	0.01902			
16	11	0.00383	0.99914	0.00469			
17	12	0.00075	0.99989	0.00086			
18	13	0.00010	0.99999	0.00011			
19	14	0.00001	1.00000	0.00001			
20	15	0.00000	1.00000	0.00000			

Figure 4.2 Using the template for the Example 1

We can also make use of the CUMULATIVE option and solve this problem by subtraction. The cumulative probability of up to 8 minus the cumulative probability of up to 5 will reveal the cumulative probability of 6 – 8:

$$= BINOMDIST(8, 15, 0.37, TRUE) – BINOMDIST(5, 15, 0.37, TRUE)$$

This formula returns the same answer we found by adding the separate probabilities, .4414.

Example 2. The binomial probability distribution has many useful applications. One of the most helpful is a simple nonparametric test called the sign test (Hays, 1973). Assume we have matched pairs of observations. We can determine the difference between the two observations, and determine the sign of the difference, positive or negative. If the two observations are distributed equally, the number of positive differences should be approximately the same as the number of negative differences.

In a study of 15 second graders' attitudes toward using computers in the classroom, the children responded to a facial hedonic scale like the following (Figure 4.3):

Figure 4.3 Facial hedonic scale

The children simply pointed to the face that represented their feelings when the teacher used the computer and when the student used the computer. We could conceive these non-numeric data as ordinal or perhaps even interval measures, but it is also very easy to see the differences for each child as simply positive, negative, or no difference. For purposes of our illustration, let us label the faces with the numbers 1 – 5. The hypothetical results are as follows. A positive difference means the student preferred to use the computer, while a negative difference means the student preferred to watch the teacher use the computer (Table 4.2).

Table 4.2 Student ratings of computer use

Pair	Student	Teacher	Difference
1	4	3	+
2	3	3	tie
3	5	2	+
4	3	2	+
5	4	5	-
6	4	1	+
7	4	1	+
8	4	1	+
9	5	1	+
10	4	3	+
11	5	3	+
12	4	2	+
13	3	4	-
14	2	1	+
15	5	4	+

Customary practice is to discard the tie, so we retain 14 differences, of which 12 have a positive sign, and 2 have a negative sign. Let us use the binomial distribution to determine the probability of 12 or more positive signs if the probability of a positive (or negative sign) for each child is .50. We can use the BINOMDIST function of Excel:

$$= 1 - \text{BINOMDIST}(11, 14, 0.5, \text{TRUE})$$

This formula finds the cumulative probability of 0 – 11 "successes" and subtracts that from 1 to determine the probability of 12, 13, or 14 successes when the probability of success on each "trial" is .5. We find the probability of observing 12 or more positive differences is approximately .0065 under the null hypothesis that the positive and negative signs are equally distributed. The binomial distribution template and the Status Bar can help solve this problem (Figure 4.4). Note the answer .0065 is already in cell D17, as the probability of at least 12 successes.

The sign test as presented here is a "one-tailed" test. We are testing the hypothesis that the number of signs would be equal to or higher than the number observed if the null hypothesis that the two outcomes have equal probability is true. In this case, the null hypothesis is that the student is equally likely to prefer watching the teacher use the computer and using the computer him or herself. The alternative hypothesis is that the student is more likely to prefer using the computer than watching the teacher use it. In Chapter 6, we will discuss hypothesis testing in more depth and will distinguish further between one- and two-tailed hypothesis tests.

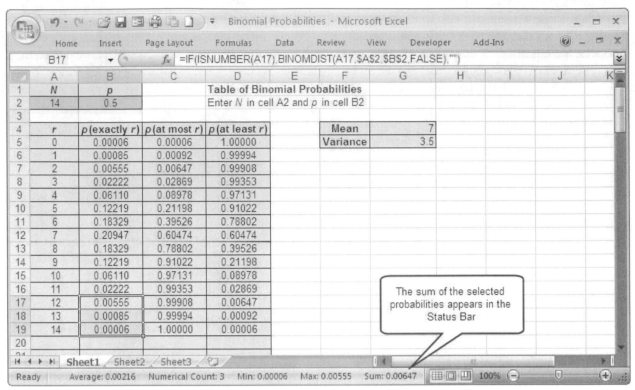

Figure 4.4 Using the binomial distribution template to solve the current problem

Normal Approximation to the Binomial Distribution

We will discuss the normal distribution in more depth in the next chapter. Even though the normal distribution is continuous and the binomial distribution is discrete, the probabilities associated with the two become very close when the sample size (number of trials) is large (Moore, 2004). As an example, assume 60% of American adults say they have purchased one or more items over the Internet. What is the probability that 1,520 or more individuals in a random sample of 2,500 adults would have made an Internet purchase? We can use the BINOMDIST function in Excel:

$$= 1 - \text{BINOMDIST}(1519, 2500, 0.6, \text{TRUE})$$

This will find the probability of 1,520 or more Internet shoppers in a sample of 2,500. The answer is approximately $p = .213$. To use the normal approximation, we can calculate a z score and look up the right-tailed probability of that particular z score in a table of the standard normal distribution. The mean is $Np = 2,500 \times .60$ or 1,500. The standard deviation is $\sqrt{Npq} = \sqrt{2500 \times 0.6 \times 0.4} = 24.4949$. Calculating a z score:

$$z = \frac{X - \mu}{s_X} = \frac{1520 - 1500}{24.4949} = 0.817$$

The area beyond $z = 0.817$ is found from a table or by the use of Excel's NORMSDIST function. We will discuss z scores and the NORMSDIST function in detail in Chapter 5. For now, let us evaluate our z score, using the same logic we did with the binomial distribution, that is, finding the area to the right of the z score by subtracting the area to the left of z from 1:

$$= 1 - \text{NORMSDIST}(0.817)$$

We find the probability to the right of $z = 0.817$ to be .207, which differs only slightly (.006) from the value calculated using the binomial probability formula. In this case, the normal approximation is very effective.

THE BOTTOM LINE

- The binomial distribution describes the probability of r successes in N trials when the probability of success on any trial is p.
- Excel's BINOMDIST function returns both exact probabilities and cumulative probabilities.
- The syntax for the BINOMDIST function is BINOMDIST(r, N, p, CUMULATIVE) where CUMULATIVE is FALSE for exact probabilities and TRUE for cumulative probabilities.
- Constructing tables of binomial probabilities assists in problem solving and decision making.
- The sign test is a simple nonparametric test based on the binomial probability distribution.
- The normal distribution serves as a good approximation of the binomial distribution as the number of trials becomes large.

The Poisson Probability Distribution

Another useful discrete probability distribution is the Poisson distribution (named after French mathematician S. Poisson, who derived it). Suppose we are interested in the occurrence of some relatively rare event over some interval. In addition to the obvious interval of elapsed time, the interval could be some measure of distance, area, or volume.

The Poisson distribution is a limiting form of the binomial distribution as N becomes larger, p becomes smaller, and Np remains constant (Walpole & Myers, 1972). Imagine a rare event with a probability of .001. We might be interested in determining the probability of a certain number of times the rare event would occur during 5,000 trials. It would be cumbersome to use the formulas for the binomial distribution with $N = 5,000$ and $p = .001$. However, remember the expected value of the binomial distribution is $Np = 5$. As long as Np is constant, we can use the Poisson distribution for very large N and very small p. When Np is not too small or large, say, it ranges from .01 to 50 (Aczel & Sounderpandian, 2009), we can approximate the binomial probability as

$$P(X = r \mid \lambda) = \frac{e^{-\lambda} \lambda^r}{r!}$$

Where X equals the number of occurrences of the event of interest, λ (lower case Greek lambda) is the "intensity" or mean of the process, and e is a mathematical constant, the base of the natural logarithms. The value of $\lambda = Np$ is the expected number of occurrences, or the "intensity" of the event. Returning to our example, if the expected number of occurrences is 5, what is the probability of 3 occurrences during the interval?

$$P(X = 3 \mid 5) = \frac{e^{-5} 5^3}{3!}$$

Excel provides functions EXP for e and FACT for factorials, so we could find the probability of observing 3 "successes" with the following formula:

$$= (EXP(-5) * 5\char`\^3) / FACT(3)$$

The value is approximately .1404. Obviously, calculating Poisson probabilities by hand, or even with Excel formulas, would become laborious, but Excel provides a built-in function, POISSON. Like the BINOMDIST function, it returns both exact and cumulative probabilities, denoted by the arguments FALSE (for exact probabilities) and TRUE (for cumulative probabilities). Note r can take on any integral value because there is no upper bound to the number of occurrences of an event in a given interval (Hays, 1973). An interesting property of the Poisson distribution is that both its mean and variance are equal to $Np = \lambda$. The interested reader should consult a theoretical statistics text for further explanation and proof of this equality, but a conceptual understanding is not too difficult to grasp. As N increases and p deceases while Np remains constant, $q = 1 - p$ approaches 1 as p approaches 0. Thus, the variance of the binomial distribution, Npq approaches Np, which is also the mean.

A Template for Poisson Probabilities

A template based on the Poisson distribution can help in problem solving and decision making (Figure 4.5). The template works in a fashion similar to the binomial probability template, and reports the exact probability of X successes, the cumulative probability of X, and the probability of at least X successes. In this case, the only input is the expected number of successes, Np (or λ) per interval. Because there is no upper limit on the number of "successes," formulas in the template simply accumulate the probabilities for $X > 25$.

Application of the Poisson Probability Distribution

The Poisson distribution has many interesting applications. The distribution can be used to model such diverse events as the distribution of data entry errors, the incidence of warranty claims, the number of customers waiting to be served in a restaurant, the number of accidents on a stretch of highway during a two-month period, and the number of people on hold to speak with a customer service representative. The following examples illustrate some problems you can solve with the Poisson distribution.

	A	B	C	D	E
1	Mean	5		Enter Np in cell B1	
2					
3	X	$p(X)$	p(at most X)	p(at least X)	
4	0	0.0067	0.0067	1.0000	
5	1	0.0337	0.0404	0.9933	
6	2	0.0842	0.1247	0.9596	
7	3	0.1404	0.2650	0.8753	
8	4	0.1755	0.4405	0.7350	
9	5	0.1755	0.6160	0.5595	
10	6	0.1462	0.7622	0.3840	
11	7	0.1044	0.8666	0.2378	
12	8	0.0653	0.9319	0.1334	
13	9	0.0363	0.9682	0.0681	
14	10	0.0181	0.9863	0.0318	
15	11	0.0082	0.9945	0.0137	
16	12	0.0034	0.9980	0.0055	
17	13	0.0013	0.9993	0.0020	
18	14	0.0005	0.9998	0.0007	
19	15	0.0002	0.9999	0.0002	
20	16	0.0000	1.0000	0.0001	
21	17	0.0000	1.0000	0.0000	
22	18	0.0000	1.0000	0.0000	
23	19	0.0000	1.0000	0.0000	
24	20	0.0000	1.0000	0.0000	
25	21	0.0000	1.0000	0.0000	
26	22	0.0000	1.0000	0.0000	
27	23	0.0000	1.0000	0.0000	
28	24	0.0000	1.0000	0.0000	
29	25	0.0000	1.0000	0.0000	
30	>25	0.0000	1.0000	0.0000	

Figure 4.5 Poisson probability template

Example 1. The number of people waiting in line for lunch at your favorite restaurant during the period 11:30 A.M. to 12:30 P.M. averages four customers. Assume the number of customers waiting is a Poisson process. What is the probability that if you visit the restaurant for lunch during this time, you will observe no one waiting in line? The POISSON function takes the following arguments:

$$POISSON(X, mean, CUMULATIVE)$$

where X is the observed number of occurrences, "mean" is the intensity or expected value of the Poisson process, and CUMULATIVE is replaced with TRUE or FALSE for cumulative or exact probabilities, respectively. In this situation, to find the probability of no occurrences, we enter

$$= POISSON(0, 4, FALSE)$$

The probability there will be no one in line is about .02, which means, of course, there is also a probability of about .98 that there will be one or more people waiting in line when you arrive at the restaurant. What is the probability that you will find more than four people waiting? Use the following formula:

$$= 1 - POISSON(4, 4, TRUE)$$

Press <**Enter**> to determine that the probability five or more people are waiting in line is approximately .37. Using the Poisson template provides the answers to both questions above:

	A	B	C	D	E
1	Mean	4		Enter *Np* in cell B1	
2					
3	*X*	*p*(*X*)	*p*(at most *X*)	*p*(at least *X*)	
4	0	0.0183	0.0183	1.0000	
5	1	0.0733	0.0916	0.9817	
6	2	0.1465	0.2381	0.9084	
7	3	0.1954	0.4335	0.7619	
8	4	0.1954	0.6288	0.5665	
9	5	0.1563	0.7851	0.3712	

Figure 4.6 Using the Poisson probability template for Example 1

Example 2. Many university-based researchers rely on unpaid student volunteers to enter experimental data. Suppose the average number of errors is two per page when students enter data from a lengthy questionnaire. What is the probability a student will make three or more errors on the next page he or she enters? What is the probability the student will make zero errors?

To find the probability the student will make three or more errors, we enter

$$= 1 - POISSON(2, 2, TRUE)$$

The formula will find the probability of three or more errors on the next page, which is approximately $p = .32$. To find the probability of zero errors, we enter

$$= POISSON(0, 2, FALSE)$$

The probability is approximately .14 that there will be no errors on the next page. As before, using the Excel template makes finding these values easy (see Figure 4.7).

	A	B	C	D
1	Mean	2		Enter *Np* in cell B1
2				
3	*X*	*p*(*X*)	*p*(at most *X*)	*p*(at least *X*)
4	0	0.1353	0.1353	1.0000
5	1	0.2707	0.4060	0.8647
6	2	0.2707	0.6767	0.5940
7	3	0.1804	0.8571	0.3233

Figure 4.7 Using the Poisson probability template for Example 2

THE BOTTOM LINE

- The Poisson distribution is a limiting form of the binomial distribution as *N* increases, *p* decreases, and *Np* remains constant.
- The Poisson distribution is used to model the occurrence of relatively rare events over intervals.
- The mean and variance of the Poisson distribution are both equal to $Np = \lambda$.
- Excel's POISSON function finds both exact and cumulative Poisson probabilities.
- The syntax for the POISSON function is POISSON(*X*, mean, CUMULATIVE) where CUMULATIVE is FALSE for exact probabilities and TRUE for cumulative probabilities.
- Creating a reusable Poisson distribution template assists in problem solving and decision making.

Chapter 4 Exercises

1. A statistics professor picks 5 students at random. In this class, the probability of the student being a male is .625. Use the binomial distribution.
    a. What is the probability all five students are males?
    b. What is the probability all five students are females? (*Hint*: You can find either the probability of zero males when *p* = .625, or you can find the probability of 5 females when the probability of being a female in the class is .375. The results will be identical.)
    c. What is the probability 3 or more of the students are males?

2. Use the COMBIN function or the binomial coefficient to determine how many groups of 5 students, disregarding order, a professor can select from a class of 25.

3. Sally has an average of 80% on her previous quizzes. Assume Sally has a probability of .80 of getting each item correct on her next 10-item quiz. Use the binomial distribution.
    a. What is the probability Sally will make 90 or 100 on her next quiz?
    b. What is the probability Sally will make a 60 or a 70 on her next quiz?
    c. What is the probability Sally will make between 0 and 50 on the quiz?

4. If 40% of voters in a community are opposed to a proposed tax increase, what is the probability that at most 5 of a sample of 15 randomly selected voters will favor the tax increase? Use the binomial distribution.

5. DuPont Corporation's 2008 Automotive Color Popularity survey indicated 20% of car purchasers prefer a white vehicle to any other color available. What is the probability 10 or more of the next 20 cars sold at Anderson AutoPlex will be white? Use the binomial distribution.

6. Fifteen children participated in a blind taste test for two versions of a new breakfast cereal. Children reported their preference by indicating which of two brands they preferred. The order of presentation of the

two cereals was counterbalanced. A plus sign indicates a preference for Brand A, a zero indicates a tie, and a negative sign indicates a preference for Brand B. Perform and interpret a sign test using the binomial distribution.

Child	Sign
1	+
2	+
3	+
4	+
5	+
6	+
7	+
8	+
9	+
10	+
11	+
12	0
13	+
14	-
15	+

7. The number of speeding tickets issued on a 10-mile stretch of Interstate highway averages 3 per month.
   a. Using the Poisson distribution, determine the probability of 5 tickets in a given month.
   b. Determine the probability of fewer than 3 tickets in a given month.
   c. What is the probability of more than 5 tickets in a given month?
   d. What is the probability of anywhere from 6 to 8 tickets in a given month?

8. A certain coastal area of the country is, on average, hit by 5 hurricanes per year. Use the Poisson distribution to determine the probability, in a given year, that
   a. No hurricane will hit this area.
   b. Fewer than 3 hurricanes will hit this area.
   c. More than 6 hurricanes will hit this area.
   d. Between 4 and 7 hurricanes will hit this area.

9. A restaurant has 15 tabletops. The average number of tabletops occupied in an hour is 10. Use the Poisson distribution to determine the probability, in a given hour, that
   a. 15 or fewer tables will be occupied.
   b. Exactly 10 tables will be occupied.
   c. Between 5 and 8 tables will be occupied.

10. A certain dangerous intersection results in 3 traffic accidents per week. Use the Poisson distribution to determine the probability, during a given week, that
   a. At most 2 accidents will occur.
   b. At least 2 accidents will occur.
   c. More than 2 accidents will occur.

5   Working with z Scores and the Standard Normal Distribution

Virtually every statistics book has a table of probabilities associated with the standard normal distribution. The use of such tables is not necessary if you have Microsoft Excel. In this chapter, you will learn how to use the STANDARDIZE function in Excel to produce z scores from raw data. You will review Chebyshev's Inequality and the Empirical Rule. You will learn how to use the NORMSDIST and NORMSINV functions and simple formulas to find areas to the left and right of given z scores in the standard normal distribution, the area between two z scores, the probability of a given z score, and the z score for a given probability. You will learn how to use the data filtering options of Excel to compare theoretical and empirical probabilities. Last, you will learn how to use the NORMINV function to find cutoff scores.

Learning about z scores and finding areas for intervals under the normal curve are foundational to the transition from descriptive to inferential statistics, and Chapter 5 will give you the tools you need to make that transition.

The z Score

A z score is a *combination statistic* that shows how far away from the mean of the distribution any particular score is, both in direction (the sign shows whether the raw score is higher than or lower than the mean) and in magnitude. We can define the z score for any value in a population as

$$z = \frac{X - \mu}{\sigma}$$

The z score is a standardized score representing the distance between the value and the mean in standard deviation units. For a population with a mean of 100 and a standard deviation of 15, the value 130 would have a z score of 2.00, indicating that a score of 130 is 2 standard deviation units above the mean:

$$z = \frac{X - \mu}{\sigma} = \frac{130 - 100}{15} = \frac{30}{15} = 2.00$$

In the absence of population parameters, we can calculate a z score for any raw score X by using sample statistics as estimators of the population values. We subtract the sample mean from the raw score and then divide that difference by the sample standard deviation.

$$z = \frac{X - \bar{X}}{s_X}$$

Estimating Percentiles Using z Scores

Recall the example from Chapter 2 used to illustrate percentiles for a hypothetical set of test scores (Table 2.7). Assume you scored 80 on the test. Looking back at Figure 2.31, you find that your percentile rank was 75%. When scores are normally distributed, the normal distribution gives us an easy way to estimate percentiles. Let us determine the *z* score for a raw score of 80. We would need the mean (73.694) and the standard deviation (7.985). You can find these values using the Descriptive Statistics tool or Excel's built-in AVERAGE and STDEV functions. To calculate your *z* score, subtract the mean from your raw score, and divide the resulting difference by the standard deviation. Your *z* score is 0.79.

$$z = \frac{X - \overline{X}}{s_X} = \frac{80 - 73.694}{7.985} = \frac{6.036}{7.985} = 0.79$$

Although the computations for a *z* score are straightforward, Excel provides a function called STANDARDIZE, which returns the *z* score for a given value of *X*, the mean, and the standard deviation of the dataset. To find your *z* score, you could simply type the following into the blank cell where you want the *z* score to appear, and then press **<Enter>**

= STANDARDIZE(80, 73.694, 7.985)

The value of *z* shows how many standard deviation units away from the mean the raw score is, and the sign of the *z* score shows whether the raw score is higher or lower than the mean. A *z* score of –3.00 indicates the raw score is 3 standard deviations below the mean. A *z* score of +2.47 indicates the raw score is 2.47 standard deviations above the mean. Thus, your *z* score means you scored 0.79 standard deviations above the mean. As with a percentile rank, you can use the *z* score as an indicator of the relative location of a given raw score in the distribution. The larger the *z* score is in absolute value, the farther away from the mean the raw score is.

Now let us determine what your percentile rank would be if the hypothetical test scores were normally distributed. To do this, use the NORMSDSIST function to evaluate the cumulative probability (the area from negative infinity up to the value) of your *z* score.[2] Enter a blank worksheet cell and type

= NORMSDIST(0.79)

Press **<Enter>**, and the resulting value, .785 (or the 78.5[th] percentile), is quite close to the 75th percentile you found earlier from the cumulative percentage table. In the standard normal distribution, 78.5% of the values are equal to or below .79 standard deviations above the mean. As sample data become more and more normally distributed, percentiles estimated from *z* scores will be closer and closer to the empirical ones.

Chebyshev's Inequality and the Empirical Rule

The *z* scores for any sample of data, whether the data are normally distributed or not, will by definition have a mean of 0 and a standard deviation of 1. Although a mean of zero is important in standardized scores, it has no relationship to the zero used in a ratio scale of measurement to represent the absence of the quantity being measured (Roscoe, 1975). As the sample becomes more normally distributed, the standard normal distribution becomes increasingly helpful in making decisions about probabilities. Standard scores are useful even when data are not normally distributed, because they still help us know how extreme a particular score is in any distribution.

---

[2] The NORMSDIST function in Excel 2007 works properly with values of *z* between approximately –12.2920 and +8.0269. Values lower than –12.2920 will show a cumulative probability of 0.0, and values higher than 8.0269 will show a cumulative probability of 1.0. For this reason, functions like NORMSINV and ZTEST that make use of the NORMSDIST function may return #NUM errors for extreme *z* scores or for functions or formulas based on those *z* scores.

Chebyshev's Inequality states in a distribution of any shape, no more than $1/k^2$ of the values will be more than k standard deviations away from the mean. Thus, no more than $1/2^2 = 1/4$ of the values will be more than ±2 standard deviations away from the mean. This means at least 3/4 or 75% of the values will be within ±2 standard deviations of the mean in any distribution. No more than 1/9 of the values will be more than ±3 standard deviations away from the mean. This means at least 8/9 or 89% of the values will be within ±3 standard deviations of the mean.

When the distribution of values is "mound-shaped" and symmetrical like the normal distribution, with most of the values close to the mean and with the relative frequencies tapering off in the tails of the distribution, you can apply the tighter standards of the *Empirical Rule*, also known as the "68 – 95 – 99.7 Rule."

- Approximately 68% of the values will be within ±1 standard deviation of the mean
- Approximately 95% of the values will be within ±2 standard deviations of the mean
- A vast majority (about 99.7%) of the values will be within ±3 standard deviations of the mean

The NORMSINV function

Excel's NORMSINV function can help us find even more precise limits than those stated by the Empirical Rule. For example, the critical values of z for a 95% confidence interval are $z = ±1.960$. We can use the NORMSINV function instead of tables to find these values. Because the standard normal distribution is symmetrical, when you find a value of z separating the upper 2.5% of the standard normal distribution from the lower 97.5%, the same value with a negative sign will separate the lower 2.5% from the upper 97.5%, leaving the desired 95% in the middle. Thus the area beyond (to the right of) the upper critical value and the area beyond (to the left of) the lower critical value in this instance will add up to 5%, and the area between these two critical values will be 95%. To find these critical values in Excel, you can simply type the following into a blank worksheet cell where you want the result to display

$$= NORMSINV(.975)$$

Press <**Enter**>, and Excel will return the value 1.959963985 ≈ 1.960. You can also type in

$$= NORMSINV(.025)$$

and receive the result –1.959963985. As long as you are centering the interval on the mean, these two values will always be the same in absolute value, differing only in sign. When you have found one critical value, you have automatically found the other. Remember when you are placing a $(1 – \alpha)(100\%)$ confidence interval to use $\alpha/2$ as the "argument" for the NORMSINV function. Thus to find critical values for a $(1 – .10)(100\%) = 90\%$ confidence interval, use the following syntax:

$$= NORMSINV(.95)$$

Verify that the critical values of z that separate the middle 90% of the standard normal distribution from the upper and lower 5% are $z = ±1.645$.

The Standard Normal Distribution

When we convert any normal distribution to z scores, we obtain the *standard normal distribution*. The standard normal distribution has a mean of 0 and a standard deviation of 1. The total area under the standard normal curve is also 1. We can convert any normal random variable X with a mean of μ and a standard deviation of σ to the standard normal distribution by a simple transformation:

$$z = \frac{X - \mu}{\sigma}$$

Using algebra, we can also find the inverse transformation of *z* to *X*:

$$X = \mu + z(\sigma)$$

As mentioned, when we do not know the population parameters, we use sample statistics to calculate *z*:

$$z = \frac{X - \bar{X}}{s}$$

and

$$X = \bar{X} + z(s)$$

As you have already seen, Excel provides a number of functions for working with standard (*z*) scores and the normal distribution. Because there are infinitely many possible normal distributions, it convenient to work with the standard normal distribution shown in Figure 5.1. Keep in mind that the curve is a theoretical abstraction. It is the result of the application of a mathematical formula:

$$f(z) = \frac{1}{\sqrt{2\pi}} e^{-z^2/2}$$

This formula has only one quantity that varies, which is the value of *z* itself. Everything else in the formula is a constant, including the values of π and of *e*, the base of the natural logarithms. Close examination of the equation indicates that the maximum density will be at *z* = 0 and that the distribution will be symmetrical because of the squared term. Although the normal distribution is theoretical, statisticians have found it very useful for a variety of applications.

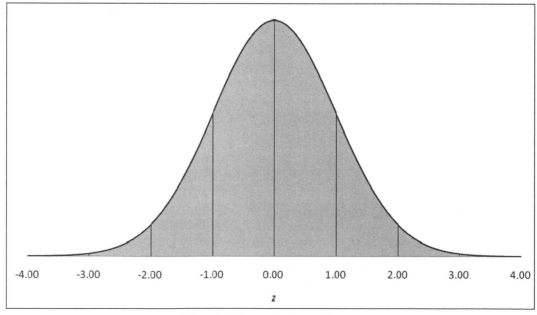

Figure 5.1 The standard normal curve

The Central Limit Theorem

One of the most important uses of the standard normal distribution is to make inferences about population means from sample data. The ***central limit theorem*** tells us that regardless of the shape of the parent distribution, the distribution of sample means approaches the normal distribution as the sample size increases. More precisely, the central limit theorem shows as n, the sample size, increases, the sampling distribution of means approaches a normal distribution with a mean of μ, the population mean, and a standard deviation of $\sigma/\sqrt{n}$, the "standard error of the mean," discussed earlier. In the absence of population parameters, we can use sample statistics, and we estimate the standard error of the mean for samples of size n as $s_X/\sqrt{n}$. As you have already seen, Excel calculates and reports this value when you use the Descriptive Statistics tool. The central limit theorem allows us to use the normal distribution, or an estimate of the normal distribution known as the t distribution, to make estimates and inferences about population means and the differences between population means using sample data. We will explore these inferential techniques in more detail beginning in Chapter 6.

THE BOTTOM LINE

- A z score is a combination statistic showing how many standard deviation units away from the mean a given raw score is, and in which direction (above or below the mean).

- By definition, z scores for any dataset will have a mean of 0 and a standard deviation of 1.

- We can use the limits of Chebyshev's Inequality to indicate how extreme a given score is in a distribution of any shape.

- When data are normally distributed, the limits of the Empirical Rule apply.

- Excel provides the STANDARDIZE function to calculate z scores.

- Excel provides the NORMSDIST function to find the probability of a given z score in the standard normal distribution.

- Excel provides the NORMSINV function to find the z score associated with a given probability.

Finding Areas under the Standard Normal Curve

Excel makes it easy to find the probabilities (or areas) associated with intervals under the standard normal curve, and thus eliminates the need for tabled values of the standard normal distribution. The built-in functions NORMSDIST and NORMSINV make it possible to "look up" a probability for any z score or to look up a z score (or scores) for any given probability. In statistics, we are generally interested in finding the areas for four kinds of intervals in the standard normal distribution (see Figure 5.2):

1. The area to the left of a given z score, a *left-tailed* probability,
2. The area to the right of a given z score, a *right-tailed* probability,
3. The area between two given z scores, an interval with upper and lower limits, or a *confidence interval*, and
4. The combined area to the left of one z score and the right of another z score, usually the same z score in absolute value and differing only in sign, (a *two-tailed* probability).

The normal distribution (theoretically) ranges from $-\infty$ to $+\infty$, and the curve never touches the X axis. Technically, a left-tailed probability has the limits $-\infty$ and z, and a right-tailed probability has the limits z and $+\infty$. This means any interval between $-\infty$ and $+\infty$ has a non-zero probability. But, as you have already learned, the majority of the area of the standard normal curve lies between ±3 standard deviations. As you have seen, Excel provides a function called NORMSDIST(z). We can use the NORMSDIST function instead of tables of z scores and their associated probabilities to find areas under the standard normal curve. The NORMSDIST function takes only one argument, the value of z. This function works with positive, zero, and negative z scores. The NORMSDIST function returns the cumulative (left-tailed) probability in the standard normal distribution from $-\infty$ up to *z*. Because the total area under the standard normal curve is 1, we can find the area to the right of any *z* score by subtraction. Examine Figure 5.2. Working with $z = \pm 1.96$, let us find the four kinds of areas identified above using Excel:

1. The area to the left of $z = -1.96$ is = NORMSDIST(-1.96) = .025.
2. The area to the right of $z = +1.96$ is = 1–NORMSDIST(1.96) = .025.
3. The area between $z = -1.96$ and $z = +1.96$ is = NORMSDIST(1.96) – NORMSDIST(-1.96) = .95. We can find this area by the formula above, or by finding the area to the left of $z = -1.96$ and the area to the right of $z = +1.96$, adding the two areas, and then subtracting that sum from 1. The answer is the same in either case.
4. The two-tailed probability to the left of $z = -1.96$ and to the right of $z = +1.96$ can be found by either addition or subtraction. A quick and reliable way to find this two-tailed probability is to use the following formula:

$$= 2 * (1–NORMSDIST(ABS(1.96)) = .05$$

This formula uses the ABS function and thus works for both positive and negative *z* scores. It finds the area to the right of $+z$, and then doubles that area to calculate the two-tailed probability. Another way to find this area is by subtraction. Remember to put the higher *z* score before the lower one in this formula:

$$=1 – (NORMSDIST(1.96) – NORMSDIST(-1.96)) = .05$$

By subtracting the area between the two *z* scores from 1, this general formula will find the combined area to the right of the higher *z* score and to the left of the lower *z* score. This formula will work with any two *z* scores, and not just ones with the same absolute value. Figure 5.2 shows the results of our calculations.

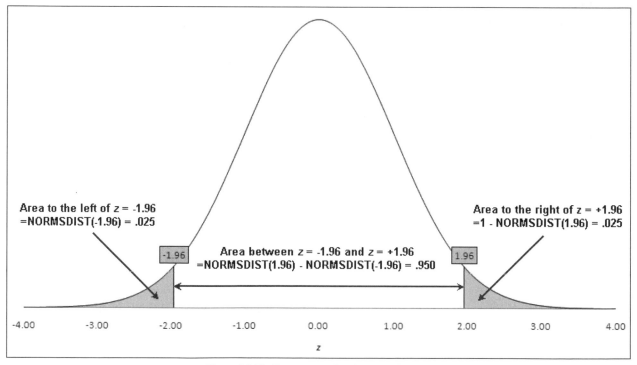

Figure 5.2 Finding areas under the normal curve

For practice, repeat the use of the formulas above, substituting the following values of *z*:

- $z = \pm 1.282$
- $z = \pm 1.645$
- $z = \pm 2.576$
- $z = \pm 3.291$

Your calculations will reveal that these are the critical two-tailed values of z for p values of .20, .10, .01, and .001, respectively, placing 80%, 90%, 99%, and 99.9% of the area between the two values, and p divided equally in the two tails of the distribution.

In addition to NORMSDIST, Excel also provides a function labeled NORMDIST (without the first "S") for normal distributions with any mean and standard deviation, and the inverse of this function, NORMINV, for finding the area associated with a given raw score in a normal distribution. Although it is usually simpler to convert raw data to standard scores and use the standard normal distribution, the NORMINV function is quite useful for finding cutoff scores, as you will see at the end of this chapter.

Calculating z Scores with the STANDARDIZE Function

Let us return to the CEO data from Chapter 3 (Table 3.5) and find the z scores for the ages of the CEOs. To simplify matters, we can name the range of 50 ages, and then use this name in functions and formulas. See the new column labeled *zAge* for the z scores (Figure 5.3). Observe in cell E2 the z score for the first age in cell C2, and notice the use of the STANDARDIZE function in the Formula Bar. This illustrates a powerful and flexible feature of Excel. You can use functions as arguments in other functions, and thus avoid having to calculate intermediate values.

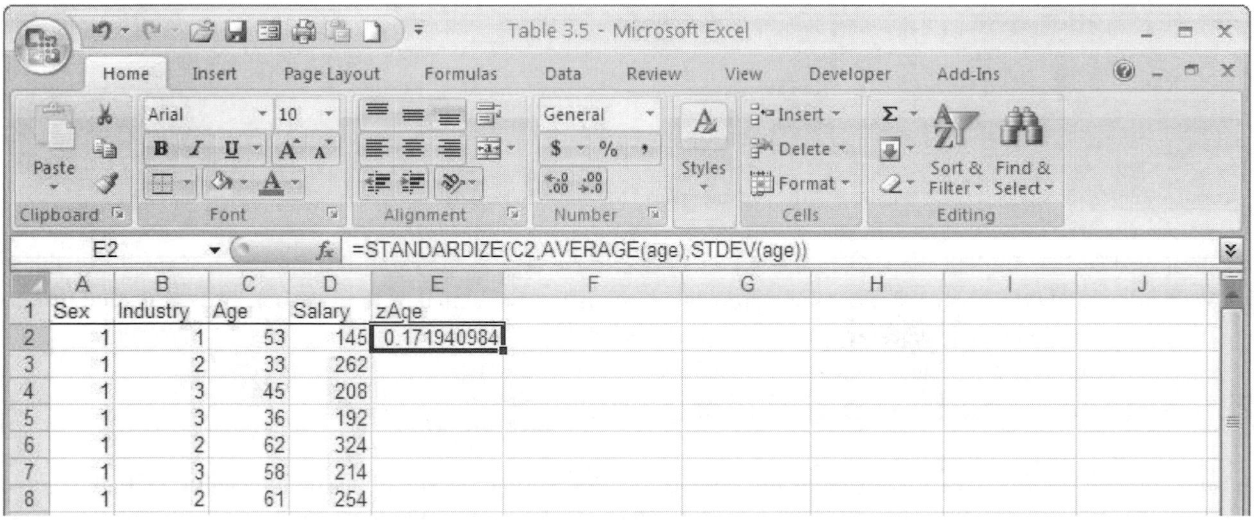

Figure 5.3 Using the STANDARDIZE function to find a z score

By using a relative reference to cell C2 (examine the Formula Bar in Figure 5.3 to see the formula), you can now copy the formula from cell E2 and paste it to the other cells in column E. The named range uses absolute cell references, so the formula will increment appropriately, and all the z scores will be computed correctly when you paste the formula to the remainder of the range in column E (see Figure 5.4).

The average z score is zero, and the standard deviation of the z scores is 1 by definition (Figure 5.4). Excel accumulates and reports rounding error, so the original average reported in cell E52 (see Figure 5.4) appeared in scientific notation as $-2.5313E-16$. This general number formatting confuses many students, but you should realize this number is essentially zero. In standard notation, it is a negative sign, followed by a zero, then a decimal, then fifteen zeros, and finally by 25313, or approximately –0.00000000000000025313. To see the result in a more expected and reassuring format, select the cell, then click on the Launch Number Format dialog icon in the **Number** group of the **Home** ribbon (or simply right-click to get the **Format Cells** option) and change the cell's number format to, say, four decimal places.

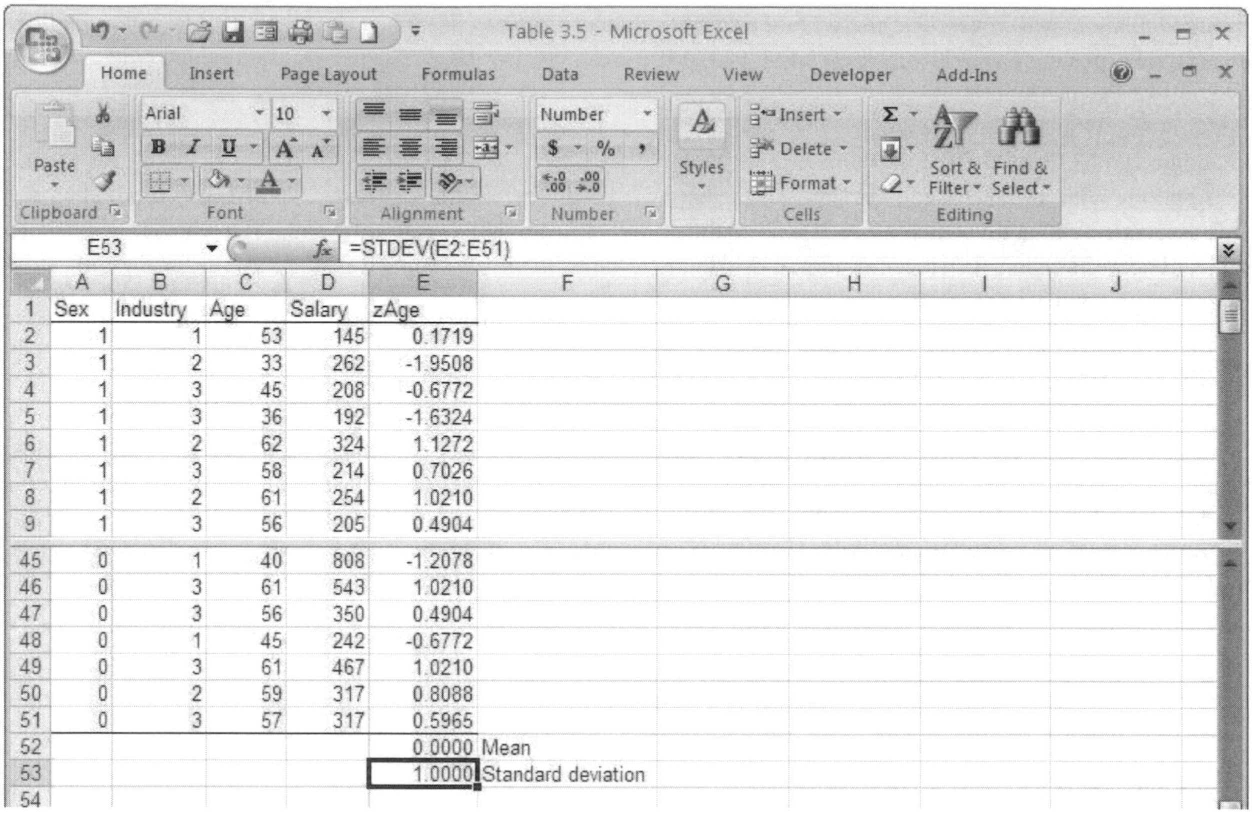

Figure 5.4 Mean of the *z* scores is 0 and standard deviation is 1

As discussed earlier, finding the area to the left of a *z* score, the area to the right of a *z* score, and the areas either between or beyond two *z* scores are common problems in statistics. Excel makes finding such areas easy, and makes the use of statistical tables unnecessary, as demonstrated below.

Finding the Area to the Left of a *z* Score

Assume the prices of homes in a given area of your city have a normal distribution with a mean of $220,000 and a standard deviation of $50,000. What is the probability that a randomly selected house in this area will have a price less than $150,000? First, calculate a *z* score, and then find the area to the *left* of the *z* score, because we are interested in a left-tailed ("less than") probability. For simplicity, let us express the prices in thousands of dollars:

$$z = \frac{150 - 220}{50} = -1.40$$

You can find this value in Excel by typing

$$= STANDARDIZE(150, 220, 50)$$

into a blank cell of the worksheet and then pressing <**Enter**>. As you have seen, the three arguments for the STANDARDIZE function are, in order, the value of X being evaluated, the value of the population or sample mean, and the value of the population or sample standard deviation.

Examine the table of the standard normal distribution in the back of virtually any statistics text and you will find that the area to the left of a z score of the value -1.4 is approximately .0808. As illustrated earlier, you can use the NORMSDIST(z) function in Excel to find that the probability is, more precisely, 0.080756659. The argument for the NORMSDIST function is the value of z or a pointer to the cell containing the value. In this case, we simply type

$$= \text{NORMSDIST}(-1.40)$$

into a blank cell and press <**Enter**>. As mentioned previously, this function works for any value of z, positive, zero, or negative.[3] Because of the symmetry of the normal distribution, we know the area to the right of a z score of $+1.40$ is also .0808, and the area to the left of $+1.40$ must therefore be $1 - .0808 = .9192$. Verify this by typing

$$= \text{NORMSDIST}(1.40)$$

and pressing <**Enter**>. Remember in this problem you are finding the cumulative probability *up to* a z score of -1.40 by using the NORMSDIST function. Figure 5.5 shows this area, which we call a "left-tailed" probability.

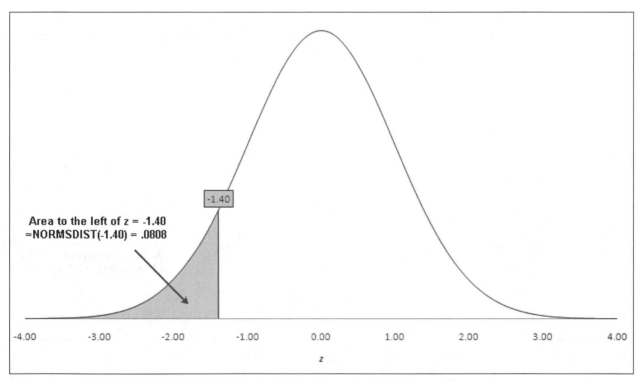

Figure 5.5 The shaded area is the area to the left of $z = -1.40$

---

[3] Recall, as we discussed earlier, extreme values of z will have probabilities reported as 0 or 1 by Excel. For APA-reporting purposes, any value reported as less than .001 should be reported as $p < .001$, and any value reported as greater than .999 should be reported as $p > .999$. Because the normal distribution ranges from $-\infty$ to $+\infty$, every possible z score has a nonzero cumulative probability.

Finding the Area to the Right of a z Score

For a standardized test with a mean of 500 and a standard deviation of 100, what is the probability that an individual will score above 750, if the test scores are normally distributed? First, calculate a z score by typing

$$= \text{STANDARDIZE}(750, 500, 100)$$

in a blank cell of the worksheet and pressing <**Enter**>. The value of z is 2.50. In this case, you are looking for a "right-tailed" (above 750) probability. Remembering probabilities sum to 1, and the area to the left of z is found by the function NORMSDIST(z), you can use subtraction to find the area to the right of z. To determine the area to the right (beyond) a z score of 2.5 (or, equivalently, a raw score of 750), you can use the following formula in a blank cell of the workbook:

$$= 1 - \text{NORMSDIST}(2.50)$$

This formula instantly returns the value 0.006209665. The probability an individual will score above 750 is approximately .006. Remember when you subtract the cumulative probability for a z score from 1, you are finding the area to the right of z in the standard normal distribution (see Figure 5.6). This approach to finding a "right-tailed" probability" works with any value of z: Positive, zero, or negative, with the exceptions previously noted for extreme z scores.

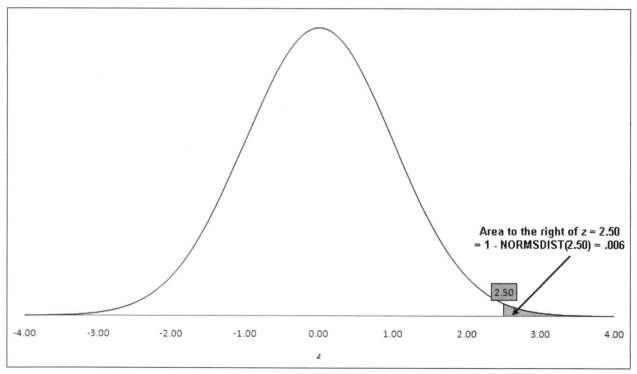

Figure 5.6 The shaded area is the area to the right of z = 2.50

Determining the Area Between two z Scores

We can also use a subtraction strategy to find the area between two z scores. For example, just to prove the obvious point one more time, confirm that 95% of the standard normal distribution lies between $z = \pm 1.960$ approximately. Enter the following simple formula into any blank worksheet cell:

$$= \text{NORMSDIST}(1.96) - \text{NORMSDIST}(-1.96)$$

When you press <**Enter**>, <**Tab**>, or click on a different cell, the result 0.95000421 appears in the cell. Of course, the formula will display in the Formula Bar. This helpful subtraction strategy can be used to find the area in any normal distribution between two raw score values. Simply convert each score to a z score, and then subtract the cumulative probability for the lower z score from the cumulative probability for the higher z score. Remember always to subtract the cumulative probability for the z score for the lower raw score from the cumulative probability for the z score for the higher raw score. Otherwise, you will calculate a negative probability, which is theoretically impossible.

To illustrate, assume you have data from a normally distributed standardized test with a mean of 100 and a standard deviation of 15. What percentage of scores will lie between the raw scores of 80 and 120? First, convert these scores to standard scores. Let us use the notation z_1 and z_2, with z_2 representing the z score for the higher raw score.

$$z_2 = \text{STANDARDIZE}(120,100,15) = 1.33$$

$$z_1 = \text{STANDARDIZE}(80,100,15) = -1.33$$

To find the area between these scores, use the subtraction strategy, remembering to subtract the cumulative probability for the lower z score from that of the higher z score:

$$= \text{NORMSDIST}(1.33) - \text{NORMSDIST}(-1.33)$$

When you press <**Enter**>, the result, .816, appears in the cell. About 82% of the scores on this test are between 80 and 120 (see Figure 5.7). This means, of course, that $1 - .816 = .184$ or 18% of the scores will be in the tails of the distribution, with half (9%) higher than 120, and the other half (9%) lower than 80.

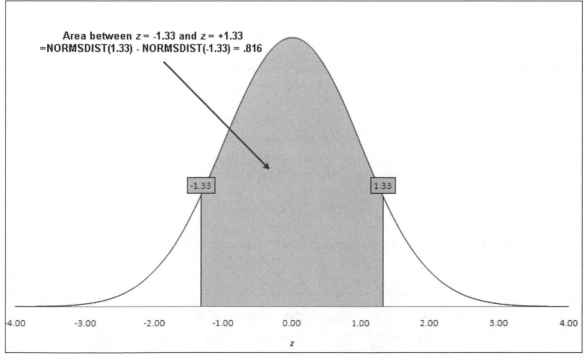

Figure 5.7 The shaded area is the area between $z = -1.33$ and $z = +1.33$

Finding the *z* Score for a Given Probability

You have already seen the NORMSINV function. It is the "inverse" of the standard cumulative normal distribution. You supply a probability, and the function returns the *z* score for that particular probability. This will be the *z* score dividing the standard normal distribution into two areas, p (the supplied probability) and $1 - p$ the remainder of the area under the standard normal curve. The two probabilities must total to 1 by definition. For example, you may want to know the *z* score that divides the upper 7.76 percent of the standard normal distribution from the lower 92.24 percent. Because the NORMSINV function is the inverse of the standard cumulative normal distribution, you would supply the value .9224 as the argument by typing

$$= NORMSINV(.9224)$$

into a blank cell of your worksheet, and you would instantly find the answer to be $z = 1.421401743$. If you wanted the lower critical value for separating the bottom 7.76 percent of the standard normal distribution from the upper 92.24 percent, you would type

$$= NORMSINV(.0776)$$

and find the answer to be $z = -1.421401743$.

As a reminder, you can use this function to find one- and two-tailed critical values of *z*. For example, the critical values for a two-tailed test with alpha = .01 will be found by dividing alpha in half. So you can find the upper limit by using the NORMSINV function

$$= NORMSINV(.995)$$

and the lower limit by typing

$$= NORMSINV(.005)$$

With .005 of the total area in each tail of the distribution, we are left with .99 in the center between the critical values, which are $z = \pm 2.576$. To find the critical value for a one-tailed test in the left tail of the distribution, just type in

$$= NORMSINV(alpha)$$

and to find the critical value for a one-tailed test in the right tail of the distribution, type in

$$= NORMSINV(1-alpha)$$

Supply the desired values for alpha and $1 - alpha$. We will examine one- and two-tailed tests more closely in Chapter 6.

THE BOTTOM LINE

- To find the *z* score for any value of *X*, use STANDARDIZE(*X*, Mean, Std_Dev).
- To find the area to the left of a *z* score in the standard normal distribution, use NORMSDIST(*z*).
- To find the area to the right of a *z* score, use 1 − NORMSDIST(*z*).
- To find the area between two *z* scores where *z*1 < *z*2, use NORMSDIST(*z*2) − NORMSDIST(*z*1).

Comparing Empirical and Theoretical Probabilities

We can use the standard normal curve to obtain theoretical probabilities, that is, the areas or frequencies we would expect to see if the data were normally distributed. We can then compare these expected values to the areas or frequencies we actually observe in the data to determine whether the normal distribution is an appropriate model for the data.

When you use the NORMSDIST and NORMSINV functions, you are assuming the data are approximately normally distributed. When the data are not normally distributed, the normal probabilities may not be very close to the observed probabilities. But even when the data are decidedly non-normal, the more generous limits of the Chebyshev Inequality will always apply. Return to the CEO ages discussed earlier in the chapter and use the table feature you learned in Chapter 3 to determine some observed probabilities and compare them to the ones you would expect if the ages were normally distributed. The age distribution appears to be roughly normal (see Figure 5.8), so the two probabilities should be close to each other.

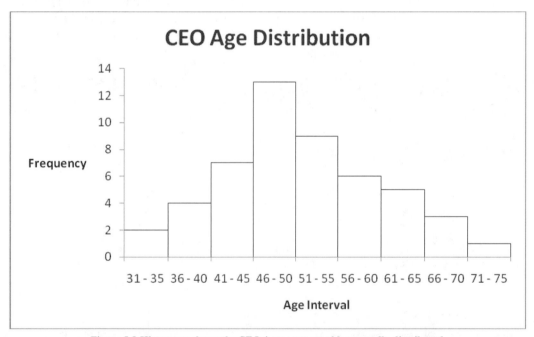

Figure 5.8 Histogram shows the CEOs' ages are roughly normally distributed

By the limits of the Empirical Rule, if the ages are normally distributed, approximately 68% of observations will be between ±1 standard deviation units of the mean (or will have z scores between -1 and $+1$). You could manually count the number of observations with z scores between -1 and $+1$. Counting these scores would be a laborious and error-prone task if you did it by hand. The Total Row and number filtering features of the table make the task faster, easier, and more accurate.

To examine the empirical probability and compare it with the expected probability, open the CEO data again, convert the data to a table, and then add a Total Row (see Figure 5.9). For column E, set the Total Row to display the count of the selected z scores by clicking on the dropdown arrow at the right of the field in the Total Row. You can also sort or filter one or more columns without using a table by selecting **Home** > **Editing** > **Sort & Filter** or **Data** > **Sort & Filter** > **Filter**. Filtering data this way, however, will not allow you to use a Total Row.

⁪	A	B	C	D	E
46	0	3	61	543	1.0210
47	0	3	56	350	0.4904
48	0	1	45	242	-0.6772
49	0	3	61	467	1.0210
50	0	2	59	317	0.8088
51	0	3	57	317	0.5965
52	**Total**				50

Figure 5.9 CEO Table with Total Row (partial data)

You can use the advanced filtering abilities of the Excel table to examine the empirical probabilities by working with the column of *z* scores. Set the upper and lower limits as –1 and +1, and filter the data to count how many of the 50 CEOs have ages between these two limits. In the row of column headings, click on the dropdown arrow at the right of the *zAge* column (see Figure 5.10). Select **Number Filters** and **Between**. When you click on **Between**, you will open a Custom AutoFilter dialog box. Type the desired limits as shown in Figure 5.11, and then click **OK.** In the **Total Row,** notice there are 34 CEOs whose ages are between ±1 standard deviations of the mean. Because the ages are roughly normal, the empirical probability 34/50 = .68 (or 68%) agrees with the theoretical one in this instance.

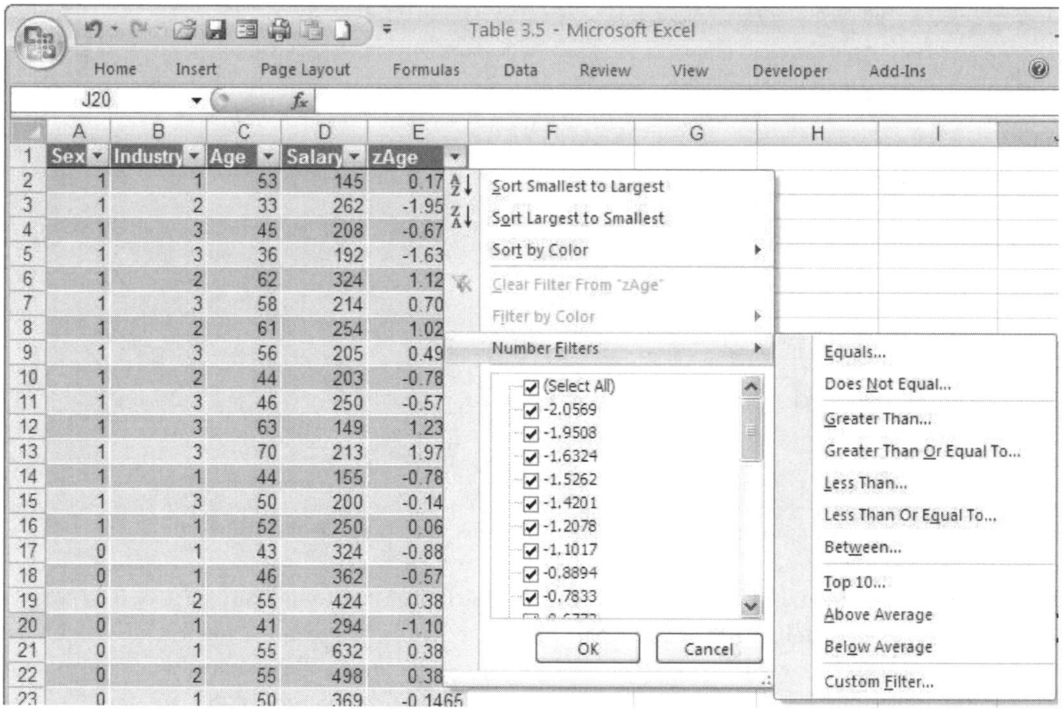

Figure 5.10 Using a number filter

Note in Figure 5.12 that although the records for the remaining CEOs are filtered from view, they are still present in the dataset, and will reappear when the filter is removed. As a visible indicator the filter is "on," notice the little funnel icon at the right side of the column header row (row 1) for *zAge* in column E. To remove the filter, click on the funnel icon and then click on **Clear Filter from "zAge."** You just found the observed frequency between two *z* scores. You could obviously use this same approach to find observed frequencies to the right of a *z* score or to the left of a *z* score as well. Look again at Figure 5.10 for the wide variety of filtering options.

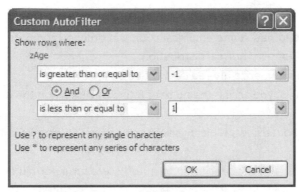

Figure 5.11 Custom AutoFilter dialog

	A	B	C	D	E
1	Sex ▾	Industry ▾	Age ▾	Salary ▾	zAge ▾
34	0	1	53	298	0.1719
36	0	1	53	406	0.1719
37	0	2	47	862	-0.4649
38	0	1	48	298	-0.3587
41	0	1	60	726	0.9149
43	0	1	51	536	-0.0403
44	0	3	50	291	-0.1465
47	0	3	56	350	0.4904
48	0	1	45	242	-0.6772
50	0	2	59	317	0.8088
51	0	3	57	317	0.5965
52	Total				34

Figure 5.12 Counting the result of applying the custom filter (partial data)

Finding a Cutoff Score Using Excel

We can use Excel's NORMINV (without the "S") function to find the raw score that cuts off any desired proportion of scores in a normal distribution with any mean and standard deviation. This function makes it very easy to find cutoff scores, and greatly reduces the number of steps involved. To illustrate, what is the cutoff score for selecting the top 10% of applicants from a normally distributed standardized test with a mean of 500 and a standard deviation of 100? Using what you have already learned in this chapter, you could solve this problem by first finding the z score separating the lower 90% of the standard normal distribution from the upper 10%:

$$= \text{NORMSINV}(.90) = 1.28$$

Then you could use the inverse transformation of z to X introduced earlier:

$$X = z(s) + \overline{X} = 1.28(100) + 500 = 628$$

The cutoff score is 628. It is even easier to solve this problem in one step using the NORMINV function. For this function, supply the desired cumulative probability, the mean, and the standard deviation as arguments:

$$= \text{NORMINV}(.90, 500, 100) = 628$$

To find a different cutoff, simply change the probability. For example, to select the top 5%, use the following syntax:

$$= \text{NORMINV}(.95, 500, 100) = 664 \text{ (rounded)}$$

THE BOTTOM LINE

- You can use number filters to determine empirical counts in order to compare these counts with theoretical probabilities based on the standard normal distribution.
- Using a table allows you to summarize filtered data with a Total Row.
- When your data are in a table, you access the number filters by clicking on the dropdown arrow at the right of the column label.
- You can also filter data without using a table by selecting **Home** > **Editing** > **Sort & Filter** or **Data** > **Sort & Filter** > **Filter**.
- Excel's NORMINV function allows the user to find a cutoff score for a normal distribution with any mean and standard deviation.

Chapter 5 Exercises

1. A normal distribution has a mean of 75 with a standard deviation of 10.
   a. Compute the *z* score for a raw score of 62.
   b. About what percent of observations are greater than 95?
   c. About what percent of observations are lower than 65?
   d. About what percent of observations are between 60 and 90?

2. A normal distribution has a mean of 20 and a standard deviation of 4.
   a. Compute the *z* score associated with a score of 25.
   b. About what percent of observations are lower than 16?
   c. About what percent of observations are higher than 30?
   d. About what percent of observations are between 20 and 25?

3. Assume the commute time from downtown Chicago to O'Hare Airport using the Chicago Transit Authority train system has a normal distribution with a mean of 65 minutes and a standard deviation of 5 minutes.
   a. What is the *z* score associated with a commute time of 53 minutes?
   b. About what percent of commutes will be faster than 60 minutes?
   c. About what percent of commutes will be longer than 70 minutes?
   d. About what percent of commutes will be between 60 and 70 minutes?

4. Return to the data reported in the worksheet from Table 2.1 on the average wages of covered workers in the 50 states and the District of Columbia. These data are positively skewed (as are most income data). Chebyshev's Inequality states that at least 75% of the data must be between ±2 standard deviations of the mean, while the Empirical Rule states for a normal distribution approximately 95% of the data will be between ±2 standard deviations. Use the Table's **Total Row** and filtering capabilities to determine which rule better describes the actual percentages for 2001 and 2002 wages.

5. What *z* score separates the upper 15% of the standard normal distribution from the lower 85%?

6. What *z* score separates the lower 20% of the standard normal distribution from the upper 80%?

7. A standardized test follows a normal distribution with a mean of 1000 and a standard deviation of 150. Your score on the test is 1200. What is your percentile?

8. Bob takes an online IQ test and finds his score is 120. If the test score distribution is normal with a mean of 100 and a standard deviation of 15, what percentage of respondents will score higher than Bob? Lower than Bob?

9. A standardized test has a mean of 100 and a standard deviation of 15. Assuming the test follows a normal distribution, what is the cutoff score for selecting the top 15% of applicants? The top 10% of applicants? The top 5% of applicants?

10. A standardized test has a mean of 500 and a standard deviation of 50. Assuming the test follows a normal distribution, what is the cutoff score for selecting the top 5% of applicants? The top 1% of applicants?

6   Confidence Intervals and Introduction to Hypothesis Testing

Because they have repeatedly heard the phrase "margin of error" related to opinion polls, most people have an intuitive grasp of confidence intervals. In fact, the margin of error is a confidence interval for a proportion, which is a kind of mean. Stating confidence intervals for estimates of parameters such as the population mean, and for functions of parameters, such as the differences in means, is an effective way of reporting results, according to the *Publication Manual of the American Psychological Association* (APA, 2010). For additional information on reporting statistical results in APA format, refer to Appendix B. At the end of this chapter, you will learn some important concepts that provide a context and terminology for the hypothesis tests presented in the remaining chapters of this book. In the process, you will also learn a simple statistical test known as the one-sample z test.

A single value, such as the sample mean, is a ***point estimate*** of the population mean. A confidence interval is a range of possible values for the parameter or function we are estimating, and constitutes an ***interval estimate***. We are not very confident in a point estimate because of sampling error. We expect the means of different samples from the same population to have different values. However, if we calculate a range of possible values, we can be more confident the parameter we are estimating is located within the interval. The wider the interval, the greater our confidence. As the interval increases in size, so does our confidence that we have "captured" the value of the population mean within the interval. At the same time, however, as the interval increases in size, the precision of our estimate decreases. We are trading confidence for precision.

In behavioral research, the most commonly reported confidence intervals are 95% intervals. As the above discussion indicates, a confidence interval is not a single value, but a range of values. The confidence interval has a lower limit and an upper limit, and values between those limits are "in" the confidence interval. The correct interpretation of the interval is a statement of confidence. We can be 95% confident the interval contains the value of the parameter or function we are estimating.

In this chapter, you will learn how to construct confidence intervals for the population mean using the normal distribution and t distribution, as well as how to build correct confidence intervals for proportions using the normal distribution. You will also learn the basics of hypothesis testing, including the definitions of important terms. In the process, you will learn a simple hypothesis test known as the one-sample z test.

Defining a Confidence Interval for the Population Mean

We can use the normal distribution to construct confidence intervals in situations where we know the population standard deviation or when the sample size is very large. Because the concepts build on those from the previous chapter, we will use the normal distribution to explain the definition and calculation of confidence intervals and a simple one-sample test of hypothesis. In real life situations, we hardly ever know the population parameters, and our practice thus far has been to use sample statistics as estimates. In keeping with this, from this chapter forward we will use the t distribution rather than the normal distribution for confidence intervals for reasons that will become apparent in this chapter.

The standard deviation of the sampling distribution of means for samples of size n is

$$\sigma_{\bar{X}} = \sqrt{\frac{\sigma_X^2}{n}} = \frac{\sigma_X}{\sqrt{n}}$$

As discussed previously, this is the standard error of the mean, and represents the standard deviation of the sampling distribution of means for samples of size n. Examine the formula above to see that as n increases, the variability of the distribution of sample means decreases. If the population standard deviation were 15, the standard deviation of the sampling distribution of means for samples of size 10 would be $15/\sqrt{10} = 4.74$, while the standard deviation of the sampling distribution of means for samples of size 100 would be $15/\sqrt{100} = 1.50$. With very large samples, the sample means will differ very little from each other, and the sample mean and standard deviation will become better and better estimates of the population parameters.

We can use the standard normal distribution to find a confidence interval for the population mean. Let us define the interval as follows:

$$\text{CI} = \bar{X} \pm z_{\alpha/2}(\sigma_{\bar{X}})$$

The value $z_{\alpha/2}(\sigma_{\bar{X}})$ is one-half the width of the confidence interval. Estimates of the population mean for samples of size n will differ from the sample mean by an amount no larger than $\left| z_{\alpha/2}(\sigma_{\bar{X}}) \right|$. Let us call this quantity E, the "maximum error of estimate."

$$E = z_{\alpha/2}(\sigma_{\bar{X}})$$

We can now more easily represent our confidence interval for the population mean as

$$\text{CI} = \bar{X} \pm E$$

We add E to the sample mean to find the upper limit of the confidence interval, and subtract the same value from the sample mean to find the lower limit. We center the confidence interval on the sample mean because the sample mean is an unbiased estimate of the population mean. Many statistics authors report such confidence intervals as follows:

$$\bar{X} - z_{\alpha/2}(\sigma_{\bar{X}}) \leq \mu \leq \bar{X} + z_{\alpha/2}(\sigma_{\bar{X}})$$

or

$$\bar{X} - E \leq \mu \leq \bar{X} + E$$

The APA publication manual (APA, 2010) requires a slightly different format for reporting confidence intervals, as you will learn shortly.

A Graphical Representation of a Confidence Interval

Consider a graphical representation of a confidence interval based on the standard normal distribution. Assume we want to construct a 95% confidence interval. As you learned in the previous chapter, 95% percent of the area under the standard normal curve is between the z scores of -1.960 and $+1.960$. Let us call this area our level of "confidence" and calculate it as $1 - \alpha = .95$ (or 95%). The value of α is thus .05 (or 5%). As a reminder from our previous discussion, the area to the right of 1.96 is $\alpha/2 = .025$, and the area to the left of -1.960 is also $\alpha/2 = .025$, so these two areas add up to .05 or 5%, meaning that we have covered "all the area" under the standard normal curve.

Assume for purposes of illustration a rather strange situation in which we know the population standard deviation, but we do not know the mean of the population. We might have a standardized test with a sample mean of 100, a population standard deviation of 15, and a sample size of $n = 100$. Note the values of the mean and sample size are only coincidentally the same, and are chosen simply to make the calculations easier. For a 95% confidence interval, the maximum error of estimate, E, is found by applying our formulas above as

$$E = z_{\alpha/2}(\sigma_{\bar{X}}) = 1.960\left(\frac{15}{\sqrt{100}}\right) = 1.960(1.50) = 2.94$$

The lowest possible estimate of the population mean in this case is therefore $100 - 2.94 = 97.06$, and the highest possible estimate is $100 + 2.94 = 102.94$. These are the lower and upper limits of the 95% confidence interval. Figure 6.1 shows how the lower and upper limits, the maximum error of estimate, and the confidence interval are interrelated. For convenience, the scaling includes both the standard normal distribution and the raw score measurement units from the sample. Ninety-five percent of the probability (our confidence level of $1 - \alpha$) is between the two limits, and 5% (α) is divided equally in the two tails of the normal distribution. We are 95% confident the true population mean for the standardized test is somewhere between 97.06 and 102.94.

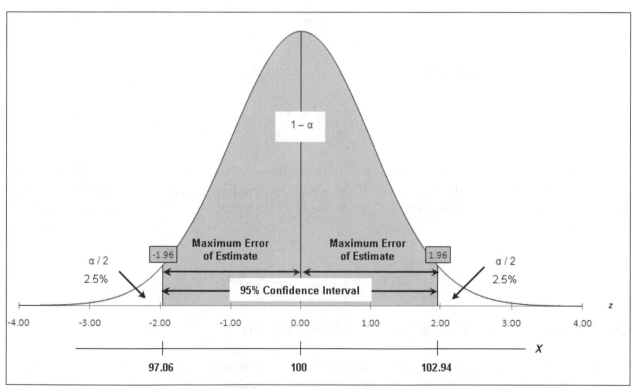

Figure 6.1 Confidence interval using the normal distribution

Using Excel's CONFIDENCE Function

Excel's built-in CONFIDENCE function allows us easily to find the value of E, the maximum error of estimate. The function takes three arguments, which are the alpha level, the population standard deviation, and the sample size. Instead of doing the calculations ourselves, let us use the CONFIDENCE function for the current problem, with $\alpha =$

.05 as discussed above, the population standard deviation, σ, of 15, and the sample size of $n = 100$. Type the following into a blank worksheet cell:

$$= \text{CONFIDENCE}(0.05, 15, 100)$$

When you press <**Enter**>, the result, $E = 2.94$, appears in the cell, and agrees with our calculations above. With large samples of $n = 200$ or more, you can use the CONFIDENCE function to calculate confidence intervals. For a 99% confidence interval, enter 0.01 for α. For a 90% confidence interval, use .10 for α.

Determining Required Sample Size

Another very useful application of confidence intervals is the determination of the required sample size to achieve a certain level of precision in our estimates of the population mean. In the example above, our estimate of the population mean with a sample of $n = 100$ was within ± 2.94 of the sample mean. Assume we are interested in determining how large a sample we would need to ensure that our estimate of the population mean would differ from the sample mean by no more than 2 points. Recall the formula for the maximum error of estimate, E:

$$E = z_{\alpha/2}(\sigma_{\bar{X}})$$

Further, recall that we defined the standard error of the mean as

$$\sigma_{\bar{X}} = \frac{\sigma_X}{\sqrt{n}}$$

We can now solve for n, using algebraic manipulation of the formula for E:

$$n = \left(\frac{z_{\alpha/2}(\sigma_X)}{E}\right)^2$$

Thus, to ensure our estimate of the population mean differs by no more than ± 2 points from the sample mean, we must have a minimum of $n = 217$ observations. We should always round our sample size estimates up to the next integer. We can now use this formula with different values of E to determine the required values of n for different error estimates.

$$n = \left(\frac{z_{\alpha/2}(\sigma_X)}{E}\right)^2 = \left(\frac{1.960(15)}{2}\right)^2 = 216.09$$

Confidence Intervals Using the t Distribution

We have thus far imposed an artificial and unrealistic condition on our confidence intervals by assuming that we know the population standard deviation. When we do not know the population standard deviation, and we usually do not, we should use the t distribution rather than the normal distribution for confidence intervals. The work of statistician William S. Gosset (who wrote under the pseudonym "Student") led to the development of the t distribution as a way to estimate the "probable error" of the sample mean for small samples. This distribution is simply an estimate of z for different sample sizes. Like the normal distribution, the t distribution is a theoretical abstraction, and we can use a mathematical formula to generate the theoretical curve. As the sample size increases, the t distribution gets closer and closer to the normal distribution, and with very large samples of $n = 200$ or more, confidence intervals developed from the normal and the t distributions will be virtually identical. Consider the following table (Table 6.1) showing the critical values of t for a 95% confidence interval for different sample sizes. The degrees of freedom are $n - 1$ in this, the simplest of cases. Notice as the sample size increases, the value of t gets closer to our standard critical z value of ± 1.96. As the sample size becomes large, there are no material differences between t-based and z-based confidence intervals. Because of the wide discrepancies between z and t with small samples, it is obviously important to use the t distribution with smaller samples.

Table 6.1 Critical values of t for 95% confidence intervals with different sample sizes

n	df	t_{crit}
2	1	12.71
5	4	2.78
10	9	2.26
15	14	2.14
20	19	2.09
30	29	2.05
50	49	2.01
100	99	1.98
200	199	1.97
500	499	1.96
1000	999	1.96

As another way to understand the relationship between the standard normal and t distributions, consider Figure 6.2. The t distribution is flatter and has wider tails (extending farther into the upper and lower regions) than the normal distribution. These differences, however, quickly diminish as the degrees of freedom increase.

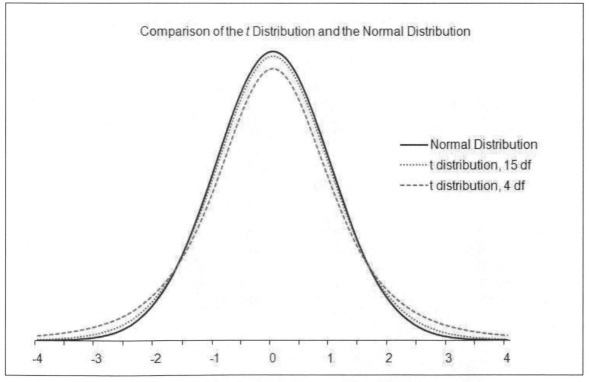

Figure 6.2 Comparing the standard normal and t distributions

To develop confidence intervals using the t distribution, we substitute the appropriate value of t for z and use the sample standard deviation in our calculation of the standard error of the mean:

$$E = t_{\alpha/2}(s_{\bar{X}})$$

where $t_{\alpha/2}$ is the critical value of t separating the upper and lower $\alpha/2$ % of the t distribution from the middle $(1 - \alpha)(100\%)$. The value of t has $n - 1$ degrees of freedom. We can find critical values of t in a table, or even more easily with the TINV function, as you will see shortly. The formula for a 95% confidence interval using the t distribution is

$$95\% \text{ CI} = \bar{X} \pm E$$

As before, we center the confidence interval on the sample mean. The quantity $s_{\bar{X}}$ is the standard error of the mean estimated from sample data, and defined previously as

$$s_{\bar{X}} = \sqrt{\frac{s_X^2}{n}} = \frac{s_X}{\sqrt{n}}$$

Remember this value is routinely calculated and reported by the Descriptive Statistics tool in the Analysis ToolPak. Consider the results from a sample of 38 college students to pairings of faces and adjectives in an implicit association test. The data are the reaction or judgment times required for the participant to evaluate stereotype-congruent pairings (associating one's own race with favorable attributes and another race with unfavorable attributes) and stereotype-incongruent pairings (associating one's own race with unfavorable attributes and another race with favorable attributes). Table 6.2 shows the data for the congruent pairings only.

Table 6.2 Reaction times for stereotype-congruent pairings of faces and adjectives

0.90	1.14
0.66	0.91
0.74	0.92
0.93	0.92
0.91	0.38
1.17	0.90
0.92	0.79
0.81	0.85
1.03	1.08
0.74	0.77
0.68	1.03
1.11	0.68
0.93	0.75
0.71	0.75
0.80	0.75
0.70	0.78
0.61	0.83
1.11	0.82
0.80	0.68

The mean reaction time is 0.842 seconds, and the standard deviation is 0.164 seconds. We can use the TINV function to find the critical values of t for 37 degrees of freedom that separate the middle 95% of the distribution from the upper and lower 2.5%. These values are $t = \pm 2.026$:

$$= \text{TINV}(.05, 37) = 2.026$$

The TINV function automatically reports the two-tailed value for the requested degrees of freedom, so the user supplies the value of α rather than $\alpha/2$. As our previous discussion indicated, because the t distribution is an estimate of the normal distribution, its standard deviation is greater than 1, and we will find the value of $t = 2.026$ to be slightly larger than the value of $z = 1.960$ for a 95% confidence interval. Most statistical packages use the t distribution to calculate confidence intervals regardless of the sample size. Let us calculate our 95% confidence interval using the t distribution. First we calculate E, the maximum error of estimate:

$$E = t(s_{\bar{X}}) = 2.026\left(\frac{0.164}{\sqrt{38}}\right) = 0.054$$

Now we can calculate the confidence interval

$$\text{CI} = \bar{X} \pm E$$

$$\text{LL} = \bar{X} - 0.054 = 0.788$$
$$\text{UL} = \bar{X} + 0.054 = 0.896$$

Placing the data from Table 6.2 in an Excel worksheet, we will use the Descriptive Statistics tool (**Data > Data Analysis > Descriptive Statistics)** and check both "Summary Statistics" and "Confidence Level for Mean," which defaults to 95% (see Figure 6.3). If you want a 99% confidence interval, just click in the "%" field and change the value to 99. Similarly, you could change the confidence level to find a 90% CI, an 80% CI, or even a 99.9% CI. In any of these cases, Excel will determine the critical value of t for the degrees of freedom, and calculate the appropriate value of E.

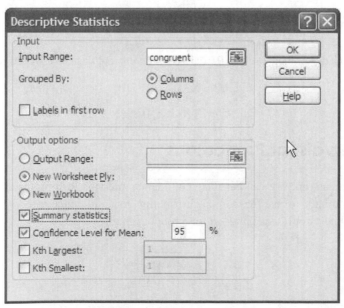

Figure 6.3 Descriptive Statistics dialog

If you simply want to find the *t*-based confidence interval, you can check that box only (see Figure 6.3). Check "Labels in first row" to give the output the correct label if you have included a label in the data range. Click **OK**. The value of *E* (labeled as "Confidence Level") reported by Excel corresponds to our calculations above (see Table 6.3).

Table 6.3 Descriptive statistics for stereotype-congruent reaction times

Congruent	
Mean	0.842
Standard Error	0.027
Median	0.815
Mode	0.920
Standard Deviation	0.164
Sample Variance	0.027
Kurtosis	0.619
Skewness	-0.059
Range	0.790
Minimum	0.380
Maximum	1.170
Sum	31.990
Count	38
Confidence Level(95.0%)	0.054

Reporting a Confidence Interval

A graphic representation of the confidence interval we just developed would be similar to the one shown earlier in Figure 6.1, but would obviously use the *t* distribution instead of the normal distribution. The APA publication manual (APA, 2010, p. 117) requires the following format for reporting a confidence interval, with the lower and upper limits in square brackets and separated by a comma.

$$X\% \text{ CI [LL, UL]}$$

Replace *X* with the appropriate number, such as 95 or 99. In the current case, we would report the 95% confidence interval as

$$95\% \text{ CI } [0.788, 0.896]$$

Confidence Intervals for Proportions

A proportion is a kind of mean, and we can calculate confidence intervals for proportions. Although we could use the *t* distribution, it is customary to use the normal distribution for confidence intervals for proportions. Use the following formula to calculate a confidence interval for a proportion, *p*:

$$\text{CI} = p \pm z_{\alpha/2}\left(\sqrt{\frac{pq}{n}}\right)$$

where $z_{\alpha/2}$ is the value of z that places half the alpha in each tail of the distribution, leaving $1 - \alpha$ in the middle. The quantity $\sqrt{pq/n}$ is the "standard error of the proportion," and used in exactly the same sense as the standard error of the mean. To illustrate, let us recall the Rasmussen poll discussed in Chapter 4, in which 37% of respondents reported support for the economic recovery plan. Assume 200 people participated in the poll. Calculate a 95% confidence interval as follows:

$$CI = p \pm z_{\alpha/2}\left(\sqrt{\frac{pq}{n}}\right) = .37 \pm 1.96\left(\sqrt{\frac{.37 \times .63}{200}}\right)$$
$$= .37 \pm .0669$$

In APA format, we report this as:

$$95\% \text{ CI } [.3031, .4369]$$

Because our sample contained only 200 people, we are not very confident the true population proportion is .37, but we can be 95% confident the population proportion is between .3031 and .4369. Pollsters and journalists usually report such confidence intervals in percentage terms, as in "this poll had a margin of error of plus or minus 6.69%."

Confidence intervals for proportions developed using the formula shown above are easy to calculate and to interpret. However, such intervals are really only appropriate (and only accurate) when the sample size is very large (Moore, 2004). We can achieve a more accurate confidence interval by using the "plus four" method. Essentially, we add four imaginary observations, two of which are successes, and two of which are failures, and approximate the confidence interval as follows. Let the new estimate of p be

$$\tilde{p} = \frac{\text{count of successes in the sample} + 2}{n + 4}$$

We can now calculate a corrected confidence interval as:

$$CI = \tilde{p} \pm z_{\alpha/2}\left(\sqrt{\frac{\tilde{p}(1 - \tilde{p})}{n + 4}}\right)$$

We should use this method whenever the confidence interval is at least 90% and the sample size is 10 or more. Let us use our corrected formula to calculate a confidence interval in the current example. With 200 respondents, the 37% "successes" represent 74 individuals. So our revised estimate of p is $76/204 = .3725$. The new confidence interval is

$$CI = \tilde{p} \pm z_{\alpha/2}\left(\sqrt{\frac{\tilde{p}(1 - \tilde{p})}{n + 4}}\right) = .3725 \pm 1.96\left(\sqrt{\frac{.3725 \times .6275}{204}}\right)$$
$$= .3725 \pm .0666$$
$$= [.3059, .4391]$$

Computational studies have shown that this corrected confidence interval is more accurate than the uncorrected one.

> **THE BOTTOM LINE**
> - Confidence intervals provide a range of possible values within which we can be reasonably confident the true population mean or proportion is located.
> - The most commonly reported confidence intervals are 95% confidence intervals, the default in Excel and in most statistics packages.
> - Excel's CONFIDENCE function uses the normal distribution to return a margin of error, which is one-half the width of the confidence interval. We call this value *E*, the maximum error of estimate. The syntax is = CONFIDENCE(alpha, standard_deviation, sample_size).
> - We can determine the required sample size for a given level of precision.
> - The "Confidence Level" provided by Excel's Descriptive Statistics tool is *E* based on the *t* distribution.
> - You can use the normal distribution to develop confidence intervals for proportions. A "plus four" correction improves the accuracy of confidence intervals for proportions.

An Introduction to Hypothesis Testing

Before discussing *t* tests and other hypothesis tests, we need to establish and clarify some important statistical terminology. These terms include hypothesis, Type I and Type II error, statistical significance, effect size, and statistical power. You have already learned in this chapter that we can use the mean of a sample as a point estimate of the population mean and a confidence interval centered on that sample mean as an interval estimate of the population mean. In this section, we will expand our discussion to examining the difference between a sample mean and the known or hypothesized population mean. In the process, we will define the terms we need to explore tests of hypothesis. This new terminology allows us to broach the subject of inferential statistics, which involves making decisions about the likelihood of sample results when a specific state of affairs is true in the population.

The One-Sample *z* Test

Let us provide a context for our discussion of hypothesis testing with a very simple example, building on the concepts from Chapters 5 and 6. The test we will use is a one-sample *z* test. We will again impose the artificial condition that we know the population standard deviation. As you will see in the following chapters, we hardly ever make that assumption in real life, so our purpose here as it was with confidence intervals is simply to introduce the concepts by showing how we can use the standard normal distribution in hypothesis testing. We would be more likely to perform a one-sample *t* test than a one-sample *z* test, as you will learn in Chapter 7.

Imagine researchers report that in the United States, the average happiness score on a 10-point scale is 7.4, with a population standard deviation of 1.3. You collect happiness scores from 100 randomly selected individuals in your community, and find that the average happiness score for your sample is 7.67. You want to compare the happiness of people in your community to the national average. Is the difference of 0.27 between your community's happiness score and the national average significant, or would you expect to see a difference that small based on sampling error alone? To answer this question, we must first determine the standard error of the mean:

$$\sigma_{\bar{X}} = \frac{\sigma_X}{\sqrt{n}} = \frac{1.3}{\sqrt{100}} = \frac{1.3}{10} = 0.13$$

Now, let us calculate a *z* score, but in this case, we will subtract the ***population mean*** from the sample mean. We are determining how far away from the population mean our community's mean happiness is, in standard deviation units, on a scale representing the sampling distribution of means for samples of size 100.

$$z = \frac{\overline{X} - \mu}{\sigma_{\overline{X}}} = \frac{7.67 - 7.4}{0.13} = \frac{0.27}{0.13} = 2.077$$

We can find the area beyond $z = 2.077$ by using the NORMSDIST function, as you have learned.

$$= 1 - NORMSDIST(2.077) = .019 \text{ (rounded to 3 decimals)}$$

Recall this is a "one-tailed" probability because we found only the probability in the upper tail of the standard normal distribution. We had no reason initially to expect that our community's happiness score would be higher or lower than the population's, so we need to use a "two-tailed" test. To find the two-tailed probability that our community's happiness score would differ from the population by ±2.077 standard deviation units, we can double the one-tailed probability, and we will report our "p value" as .038. This value is lower than the conventional .05 required for statistical significance, and we conclude that our community is indeed happier than the national average.

Excel provides a one-sample z test function, as discussed below (and again in Chapter 7). This function compares the sample mean to a known or hypothesized population mean. You can optionally supply the population standard deviation, if you know it or are willing to assume you do. The syntax is

$$= ZTEST(array, x, [sigma])$$

Replace "array" with the reference(s) to the sample data, "x" with the hypothesized population mean, and, optionally, "[sigma]" with the known population (or assumed) standard deviation. Assume we named the data range "happiness," based on the data in Table 6.4, which represent the 100 happiness scores in our hypothetical sample.

Table 6.4 Hypothetical happiness scores for 100 people

7	8	8	9	8	9	6	8	7	8
8	7	8	7	8	5	7	9	7	7
9	6	8	8	9	7	9	8	7	9
9	9	8	10	9	7	9	9	7	9
7	8	7	7	8	8	6	9	8	7
9	5	8	5	6	6	8	8	5	6
9	9	9	7	7	7	9	8	6	8
7	8	7	9	4	8	8	8	7	6
9	9	6	8	7	6	8	7	8	9
9	7	9	9	8	7	7	8	9	8

Enter the following in a blank worksheet cell:

$$= ZTEST(happiness, 7.4, 1.3)$$

When you press <**Enter**>, you achieve the same result, $p = .019$, that we obtained through the calculations above. Remember the ZTEST function performs a one-tailed test, so we must double the reported probability for a two-tailed test. The function returns the p value, but not the value of z. In order to find the value of z, we can use the NORMSINV function you learned in Chapter 5:

$$= NORMSINV(1 - ZTEST(happiness, 7.4, 1.3))$$

Because the sample mean is higher than the population mean, we evaluate the "right-tailed" probability to find the correct z score, 2.077, which, of course, corresponds to our calculations above. If you omit the population standard deviation, Excel will use the sample standard deviation, and you will actually be doing a t test instead of a z test. We discuss this issue further in Chapter 7. The reader should be aware that the ZTEST function uses Excel's NORMSDIST function, and the formula shown above will return a #NUM error for z scores larger than approximately 8 or lower than approximately –12.

A Confidence Interval for the One-Sample z Test

Recall that z scores of ±1.96 separate the middle 95% of the standard normal distribution from the upper 2.5% and the lower 2.5%. Let us develop a 95% confidence interval for the difference between our community's happiness score and the population mean. We center this confidence interval on the observed difference.

$$95\% \text{ CI} = \left(\overline{X} - \mu\right) \pm z_{\alpha/2}(\sigma_{\overline{X}}) = (7.67 - 7.4) \pm 1.960(0.13)$$
$$= 0.27 \pm 0.2548$$
$$= [0.0152, \ 0.5248]$$

We are 95% confident that our community's happiness score is between 0.0152 and 0.5248 points higher than the population mean on the 10-point scale. Zero or "no difference" is not in the interval. Our lower limit is still a positive nonzero difference. As you have already learned, we could also report a 95% confidence interval for our sample mean of 7.67 as 95% CI [7.4152, 7.9248]. Because the population mean of 7.4 is not "in" the interval we just calculated, both intervals are telling us the same thing in different ways. Both indicate that we can reject the null hypothesis of "no difference" between our community's happiness and the national average.

The Null Hypothesis and the Alternative Hypothesis

When we perform hypothesis tests, there are two competing hypotheses, the ***null hypothesis*** and the ***alternative hypothesis***. We state these hypotheses in such a fashion that one must be true, and the other must be false. If the null hypothesis is true, then the alternative hypothesis is false. If the alternative hypothesis is true, then the null hypothesis is false. We also state these hypotheses in such a way that there are no other possible explanations. Formally, the null hypothesis and the alternative hypothesis are mutually exclusive and collectively exhaustive: Only one of them can be true, and one of them must be true. Our hypotheses are statements about population parameters, in the case of z and t tests, population means (or differences between population means). The null hypothesis is a statement that there is no difference or effect in the population. The alternative hypothesis is a statement that there is a difference or effect in the population. We usually abbreviate the null hypothesis as H_0, with the zero subscript indicating no difference or no effect in the population. We will abbreviate the alternative hypothesis as H_1, though you will also see it abbreviated as H_a. The reason it is important to differentiate between these hypotheses is that we make our statistical inferences by assuming that the null hypothesis is true. We obviously would not need to do hypothesis tests if we actually knew the population state of affairs, but when we do not know the population, we still want to make informed decisions from sample results. In order to do this, we must assume some state of affairs in the population.

In the case of our one-sample z test, the null hypothesis of no difference states that the mean happiness score of our community does not differ from the population average, and therefore is equal to it. Symbolically:

$$H_0: \mu = 7.4$$

This is saying that our community comes from a population with a happiness average of 7.4. We can also state our null hypothesis as "no difference," by using the following symbols. The two statements are equivalent ways of saying the same thing.

$$H_0: \mu - 7.4 = 0$$

Our alternative hypothesis is that the sample does not come from a population with an average of 7.4:

$$H_1: \mu \neq 7.4$$

or equivalently,

$$H_1: \mu - 7.4 \neq 0$$

"Equality" or "no difference," is always in the null hypothesis, while "not equal to" or "inequality") is always in the alternative hypothesis. In inferential statistics, the null hypothesis is *presumptively correct*. We make this presumption, even when we believe the null hypothesis to be false, because we know the distribution of the test statistic under the null hypothesis. This allows us to compare our sample results to a presumed population "state of affairs."

We examine how likely it would be to observe the sample results we obtained if the null hypothesis is true. If this probability is very small (usually lower than .05), we *reject* the null hypothesis. If the probability of obtaining the sample results is large (usually greater than .05), we *retain* (or fail to reject) the null hypothesis. Because our two hypotheses are mutually exclusive and collectively exhaustive, when we make a decision about the null hypothesis, we have also made a decision about the alternative hypothesis. Because we do not know the population state of affairs, we could have made the correct decision concerning the null hypothesis, or we could have made an error.

Type I and Type II Errors

When the null hypothesis is true (there is no difference or effect in the population) and we retain it, we have made the correct decision. When the null hypothesis is false (there is a real difference or effect in the population) and we reject it, we have also made a correct decision. But when the null hypothesis is true, and we reject it, we have made an error. We will call this kind of error a Type I error. We use the symbol α to represent the probability of making a Type I error. Thus, when the null hypothesis is true, we will make the correct decision with probability $1 - \alpha$, which is our *confidence* in our results.

When the null hypothesis is false, and we retain it, we have made a different kind of error. We will call this kind of error a Type II error. The symbol β represents the probability of Type II error. When the null hypothesis is false and we reject it, we make the correct decision with probability $1 - \beta$, which is the *power* of our statistical test, as discussed later in this section. Table 6.5 shows the relationships between the decisions we make from our samples and the state of affairs in the population.

Table 6.5 Type I and Type II errors

		Population State of Affairs	
		H_0 is True	H_0 is False
Decision from Sample	Reject H_0	Type I Error (α)	Correct Decision ($1 - \beta$)
	Retain H_0	Correct Decision ($1 - \alpha$)	Type II Error (β)

Statisticians generally consider Type I errors to be very serious. When we reject a true null hypothesis, we are claiming, based on our sample results, an effect or a difference that is not true in the population. Consider the example of a food supplement developed as a preventive for colds. Either the food supplement works or it does not work (the population state of affairs). Assume our sample evidence indicates that the supplement works, so we market it as effective. Sales soar. But what if the product does not really work as advertised? We have committed a Type I error in that case. We have misrepresented the product through false advertising, and are now liable for that misrepresentation. We may have to face many dissatisfied customers, and even potential lawsuits. Now assume our sample evidence indicates that the supplement does not work, so we do not develop and market it. If the supplement really does not work, we have made the right decision to keep it off the market. But if it really works, we have not committed false advertising, have made no money through misrepresentation, and are not liable, though we have still made an error, in this case a Type II error. Though we have lost an opportunity, we have not committed any fraud.

Because of the serious nature of Type I errors, we want to make sure that we reject true null hypotheses very infrequently. We control the probability of Type I error by specifying a required significance level in advance of the statistical test. As you know, we usually set this level to .05, limiting our Type I errors to 5% of the cases when the null hypothesis is true. We call this significance level alpha (α). We could reduce alpha to a more conservative level of .01, and assure ourselves that we are making the correct decision 99% of the time when the null hypothesis is true. However, when we lower our alpha level, we reduce the likelihood of rejecting the null hypothesis both when it is true and when it is false. Similarly, we could increase the alpha level to .10, and still make the correct decision 90% of the time when the null hypothesis is true. In this case, we have increased the probability that we will reject the null hypothesis both when it is true and when it is false, making our test less conservative and more powerful by increasing the probability of Type I error.

Rejecting the null hypothesis when it is false is a correct decision, and the probability of this outcome is $1 - \beta$. As mentioned above, we call this probability the ***statistical power*** of our hypothesis test. Other things equal, lowering our alpha level to reduce the probability of Type I error also decreases the power of the test, while raising the alpha level increases the power of the test. By convention, researchers in many fields have accepted an alpha level of .05 as a good compromise between power (finding a result if one exists in the population) and conservatism (retaining the null hypothesis when it is false). We can also increase the power of a statistical test by increasing the sample size. We are more likely to find an effect of any given size as we increase the size of the sample. As you have seen, the standard error of the mean decreases when the sample size increases. This is also true of other standard error terms, such as the standard error of the difference between means. The practical result is that with larger samples, you are more likely to detect a difference or effect if there is a difference or effect in the population.

Statistical Significance and Effect Size

Assume we have adopted the conventional alpha level of .05. When we perform our statistical test, we will determine a *p* value, the probability of observing the effect or difference we obtained from our sample, or an effect larger than the one we observed, if the null hypothesis is true. This is our observed level of Type I error. This *p* value could be higher than alpha or lower than alpha. If the *p* value is lower than alpha, we reject the null hypothesis as untenable in light of the sample results. This decision is equivalent to the claim of ***statistical significance***. Saying that you reject the null hypothesis is the same thing as saying that your results are statistically significant. If the *p* value is higher than alpha, we retain (fail to reject) the null hypothesis. When we claim statistical significance, we indicate that we have found support for the alternative hypothesis, and state our results as though the alternative hypothesis is true. For instruction on reporting statistical results in the format required by the American Psychological Association (APA), refer to Appendix B.

When we claim statistical significance, we are not really proving anything, because we do not know the population, but we are saying that if the null hypothesis is true, it would be very unlikely to obtain the sample results we achieved, and in fact, this would happen so infrequently that we are willing to reject the null hypothesis. Statistical significance is not the same thing as practical significance or utility. With larger and larger samples, any effect or difference, practically important or not, will eventually become statistically significant. Similarly, even if the effect is a large one, we will be less likely to obtain statistical significance when the sample size becomes smaller and smaller. We need another way to describe the importance of our results irrespective of sample size. The concept of *effect size* addresses this problem. Effect size indexes tell us "how big" a difference or effect we have detected, regardless of the level of statistical significance.

The concepts of sample size, effect size, and statistical power are interrelated, and by making assumptions about any two of these, we can determine the other one mathematically. For example, in this chapter, we were able to determine the required sample size to obtain a required (assumed) level of precision in our estimates of a population mean. In similar fashion, we can determine required sample size to detect a difference between two means, the effect size needed to achieve a certain level of statistical power, and the observed power of a statistical test given the sample size and the effect size.

One- and Two-Tailed Tests

You learned to construct two-sided confidence intervals in this chapter by placing half of the alpha level in each tail of the test distribution (t or z). Two-sided confidence intervals correspond to two-tailed significance tests. In two-tailed tests, we are interested in extreme findings on either side of the test distribution. By contrast, in one-tailed tests, we are only interested in one tail of the test distribution.

Let us return to the example of our happiness scale. What if we were willing to assume, at the outset, that our community's happiness score was indeed higher than the national average? In this case, we would have to rephrase our null and alternative hypotheses slightly. We are no longer interested in the possibility that our community's happiness is only "different" from the national average, so we will not test the lower tail of the normal distribution. The two-tailed test has two regions of rejection or "critical regions," while the one-tailed test has only one critical region. We are only interested in finding significance if our community's happiness is higher than the national average. Our null hypothesis is now:

$$H_0: \mu \le 7.4$$

and the alternative hypothesis is

$$H_1: \mu > 7.4$$

Examine the restated null and alternative hypotheses. "Equality" is still in the null hypothesis, but the null hypothesis now says we are only interested in a directional, one-sided outcome. We are risking everything on that outcome. As long as the sample results are in the hypothesized direction, we have just made our test more powerful. To see why, understand that the probability of Type I error (α) is now concentrated in the upper tail of the standard normal distribution. Our "critical value" of z is now +1.65, not ±1.96, and a smaller difference would be detectable as statistically significant, again as long as the results are in the hypothesized direction. Figure 6.3 shows the difference between a one-tailed test and a two-tailed test. Depending on the null and alternative hypotheses, you could just as easily have a one-tailed test with the critical region in the left tail of the test distribution. Figure 6.4 shows critical values of the standard normal distribution for one- and two-tailed hypothesis tests with alpha = .05. When we find the p value for our z score of 2.077 for the one-tailed test, we report only the right-tailed probability, p = .019. recall we find this value from the Excel formula:

$$= 1 - \text{NORMSDIST}(z) = 1 - \text{NORMSDIST}(2.077) = .019$$

Remember that if our sample mean is lower than 7.4, even if it is much lower, we are not entitled to a claim of statistical significance if the results are in the "wrong" direction when we do a one-tailed test. The same approach applies with one- and two-tailed t tests, but the critical values will vary according to sample size, as you have already learned.

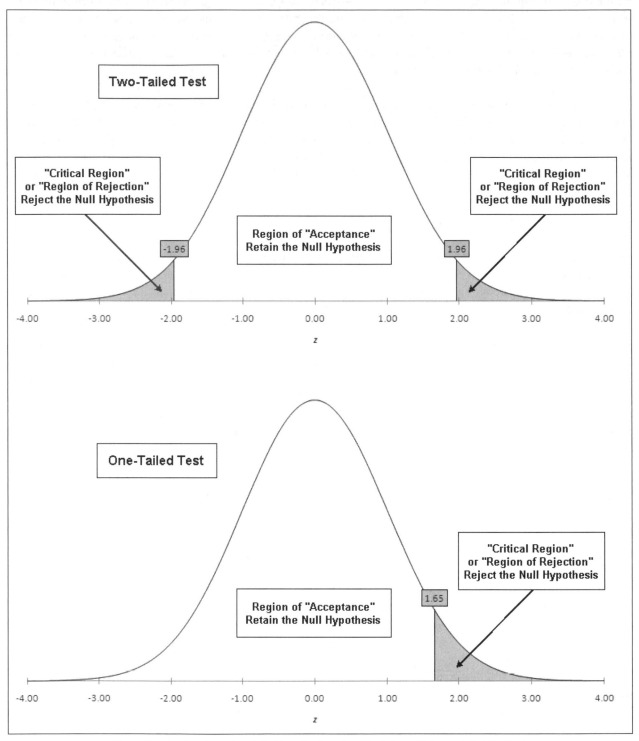

Figure 6.4 One-tailed and two-tailed hypothesis tests with alpha = .05 (normal distribution)

We have now developed the terminology and the logic we need to proceed with hypothesis testing in Chapter 7. The reader should understand that we rarely know the population standard deviation, and that the use of the z test in this chapter was simply for introducing the logic and steps of hypothesis testing. You should also know that not all modern statisticians are enthralled with the classic null hypothesis significance testing (NHST) approach presented in this book. There are different ways to make inferences besides estimating population parameters from sample statistics, and indeed, there are other ways to report probabilities besides the traditional ones shown here. Appendix B introduces the concept of the "probability of replication" as a way to report results. The interested reader can find many references in the current statistical literature to techniques known as resampling and bootstrapping. These sample-based techniques have only recently come into wide use because they rely on extensive computing capabilities, and though interesting, are beyond our current scope.

THE BOTTOM LINE

- Important terms in hypothesis testing include null and alternative hypothesis, Type I and Type II errors, statistical significance, power, and effect size.

- We perform hypothesis tests by presuming that the null hypothesis is true. This allows us to determine how likely our sample results are under this assumption. If the probability of the result we obtained, or an even more extreme result, is less than alpha, we reject the null hypothesis.

- The one-sample z test compares a sample mean to a known or hypothesized population mean when the population standard deviation is known.

- Excel provides the ZTEST function for a one-tailed one-sample z test.

- All things equal, statistical power increases when we increase sample size, increase the alpha level, and use one-tailed hypothesis tests (as long as the results are in the hypothesized direction).

Chapter 6 Exercises

1. The following data are the stereotype-incongruent reaction times for 38 college students on an implicit association test (see the text for an explanation). Develop a 95% confidence interval for the population mean using the t distribution. Report the confidence interval in APA format.

1.80	1.16
0.74	1.69
0.96	0.98
1.65	0.98
1.04	1.43
1.65	1.40
1.26	1.23
1.08	1.16
0.69	1.48
0.96	1.04
1.39	1.06
1.25	1.08
1.21	1.22
0.92	1.22
1.32	1.22
1.14	0.86
1.13	1.03
1.05	0.93
0.88	0.77

2. Using the same data as in Exercise #1, develop a 99% confidence interval for the population mean using the t distribution. Report the confidence interval in APA format. Why is the 99% confidence interval wider than the 95% confidence interval?

3. The following data represent the total number of text messages sent and received in a month[4] by a sample of 16 teenagers. Construct a 95% confidence interval for the population mean using the t distribution. Report the confidence interval in APA format.

1470	1384	2345	1942
1896	2055	2055	1990
2159	2245	1751	1552
2004	1362	1745	1720

4. For the same data as in Exercise #3, develop a 99% confidence interval for the population mean using the t distribution. Report the confidence interval in APA format.

5. For the data from Table 3.5, use the t distribution to develop 95% and 99% confidence intervals for the population mean of the ages of the 50 CEOs. Report the confidence intervals in APA format.

6. A political candidate has his staff poll randomly-selected voters. Of those voters contacted, 361 responded. Of the respondents, 173 said they would vote for the candidate in the next election. Develop a 95% confidence interval for the proportion of voters who will vote for the candidate. Use the correction shown in the text. Report the confidence interval in APA format.

7. For the data from exercise #6 above, develop a 99% confidence interval for the proportion. Use the correction shown in the text. Report the confidence interval in APA format.

8. You conducted a survey of 300 college students and found that 30 of the students reported being vegetarians. Develop 95% and 99% confidence intervals for this proportion. Use the correction shown in the text. Report each interval in APA format.

9. The Nielsen Television Audience Report (July 2009) indicates the number of televisions in the average American home is now 2.86, with a population standard deviation of 0.75. You select a random sample of 64 households in your community and find that the average number of TVs is 2.68. Conduct a one-sample z test (two-tailed) with alpha = .05. Is the number of TVs per household in your community significantly different from the population average?

10. For the information in Exercise #9 above, assume you had prior reason to assume that your community would have a lower number of TVs on average than the population. Conduct and interpret a one-tailed one-sample z test with alpha = .05. Why are the results of the one- and two-tailed tests different?

---

[4] This example is based on information provided by the Nielsen Mobile Survey on September 22, 2008.

7   *t* Tests for Means

In this chapter, you will learn to use Excel for *t* tests for a single mean, for the means from two independent samples, and for the means from paired samples. Excel does not have a built-in one-sample *t* test, but the computations are not difficult, and you can use other tools for this test. Excel's Analysis ToolPak provides independent-samples *t* tests and paired samples *t* tests.

As with the normal distribution, Excel provides a function for determining the probability of an obtained value of *t* for a given degrees of freedom and number of tails in the hypothesis test. This function is TDIST. The TDIST function only works for positive values of *t*, unlike the NORMSDIST function, which works for both positive and negative values of *z*. Like the *z* distribution, the *t* distribution is symmetrical, so this limitation is not material. In most statistics texts, only the upper halves of both the *z* and the *t* distributions are tabled to conserve space. To get around this limitation, we can simply ignore the sign of the value of *t* by using the ABS function with the TDIST function, as in

$$= \text{TDIST}(\text{ABS}(t), \textit{df}, \text{tails})$$

when finding *p* values. In addition to the value of *t*, you must supply the degrees of freedom and the number of tails for the hypothesis test, 1 or 2. This function does not work in the same way as the NORMSDIST function. It provides the probability in the tail (or tails) of the *t* distribution, rather than the cumulative probability up to the value of *t*.

As you may recall from the previous chapter, Excel also provides the "inverse" of the *t* distribution. By supplying a given probability, the degrees of freedom, and the number of tails in the hypothesis test, the user can find critical value(s) of *t*. This function is called TINV, and like TDIST, only works with positive values of *t*. The *t* distribution exhibits many similarities to the normal distribution. It is also symmetrical and "bell-shaped," with a mean of zero. However, as you saw previously, the standard deviation of the *t* distribution is larger than 1. Unlike the standard normal distribution, the *t* distribution is really a family of distributions, one for each value of the parameter known as the degrees of freedom, based on the sample size.

The One-Sample *t* Test

The one-sample *t* test is a simple parametric statistical test with a purpose identical to the one-sample *z* test you learned in the previous chapter. The *z* test is technically only appropriate when we know the population standard deviation or when we have very large samples. The one-sample *t* test, however, works well with both large and small samples and when we do not know the population standard deviation. The one-sample *t* test compares a given sample mean, $\overline{X}$, to a known or hypothesized value of the population mean, μ_0. We use the sample standard deviation to estimate the population standard deviation. As you learned in the previous chapter, it is especially important to use the *t* test when sample sizes are small.

The null hypothesis is that any observed difference between the sample mean and the population mean (known or hypothesized) is due to sampling error, or in other words, that the difference between the sample mean and the population mean is zero. Our hypotheses are about population means, even though we are using sample data. More formally, we can state the null hypothesis as:

$$H_0: \mu = \mu_0$$

or equivalently,

$$H_0: \mu - \mu_0 = 0$$

One statement stresses the equality of the two means, saying that the sample comes from a population with mean μ_0, while the other statement stresses "no difference," that is, no difference between the sample mean and the hypothesized population mean.

The alternative hypothesis for a two-tailed test is that the observed difference between the sample mean and the population mean is greater than zero, or said differently, that the difference is so large we are unwilling to assume that the observed difference is due to sampling error. We can also state this alternative hypothesis in two ways, one stressing "no difference," and the other stressing inequality:

$$H_1: \mu \neq \mu_0$$

or

$$H_1: \mu - \mu_0 \neq 0$$

When the null hypothesis that the sample mean equals the hypothesized value is true, the value derived from the equation

$$t = \frac{\bar{X} - \mu_0}{s_{\bar{X}}}$$

is distributed as *t* with *n* − 1 degrees of freedom. The denominator

$$s_{\bar{X}} = \sqrt{\frac{s_X^2}{n}} = \frac{s_X}{\sqrt{n}}$$

is the standard error of the mean introduced in the previous chapters, and as you recall, is the standard deviation of the sampling distribution of means for samples of size *n*. Recall Excel reports this value for sample data via the Descriptive Statistics tool. Though there is not a tool labeled "one-sample *t* test" in Excel, the calculations are routine. Those who want a built-in procedure can use the ZTEST function you learned in Chapter 6, and even the paired-samples *t* test procedure, for a one-sample *t* test, as demonstrated in this chapter.

As explained earlier with the one-sample *z* test, we can also have a one-tailed alternative hypothesis. In order to cover all the outcomes, we will need to modify our null hypothesis. Assume we are willing to hypothesize that our sample mean comes from a population with a mean higher than the original hypothesized population mean. This might be the case, for example, if we take a random sample from a population with a certain hypothesized mean, and we then apply some treatment to our sample. We can use our "happiness" data from Chapter 6 to illustrate. Assume that we have had a campaign in our community to improve peoples' attitudes. We did not have a "before," measure, but we still know the national average. We want to compare our community's average happiness to the national average. We are not interested in testing the possibility that happiness decreased after the campaign, only that it improved. Our null hypothesis is now:

$$H_0: \mu \leq \mu_0$$

or

$$H_0: \mu - \mu_0 \leq 0$$

Now, we can state the alternative hypothesis:

$$H_1: \mu > \mu_0$$

or

$$H_1: \mu - \mu_0 > 0$$

Let us work out the calculations for the one-sample t test using "happiness data" from Table 6.4. In the current case, we are not willing to assume that we know the population standard deviation, and we use the t distribution as our sampling distribution for the difference between our sample mean and the population mean. Let us assume that we will do a two-tailed test with $\alpha = .05$. Knowing that there are $100 - 1 = 99$ degrees of freedom, we can find the two-tailed critical values of t using the TINV function:

$$= TINV(.05, 99) = \pm1.984$$

The value of t is not much larger than the standard normal distribution's critical value of ±1.96 for $\alpha = .05$ because the sample size is large. Using the Descriptive Statistics tool, we find the sample standard deviation to be 1.181 and the standard error of the mean to be 0.1181. Remembering the hypothesized population mean is 7.4, we now can find our value of t and test its significance.

$$t = \frac{\bar{X} - \mu_0}{s_{\bar{X}}} = \frac{7.67 - 7.4}{\left(1.181/\sqrt{100}\right)} = \frac{0.27}{0.1181} = 2.286$$

This value is larger than the critical value of 1.984, so we reject the null hypothesis. To determine the actual p value (the observed probability of a Type I error if the null hypothesis is true), we can use the TDIST function:

$$= TDIST(2.286, 99, 2) = .024$$

Comparing this value to our alpha level of .05, we also reach the conclusion that we should reject the null hypothesis. In fact, using the p value approach avoids the necessity of finding a critical value and provides a more precise statement of the probability of Type I error than does the critical value approach. As with the one-sample z test, if we can justify a one-tailed t test and if the results are in the hypothesized direction, we can report the p value as $p = .012$.

Example Data

Let us use another example for the one-sample t test, and in the process introduce a reusable worksheet template. A statistics professor decided to change her approach from handheld calculators to the use of Microsoft Excel as a teaching tool and for student homework assignments. The professor knows the average score on the first quiz in her statistics course for the past courses is 74, but she does not have the standard deviation from those previous administrations. This term's class of 25 students had an average score of 77.72 on the first quiz, with a standard deviation of 3.542. Table 7.1 shows the data. We will conduct a one-sample t test to compare this term's scores with the average from previous courses. The null hypothesis is that the observed difference between 77.72 and the previous mean of 74 is due to sampling error. The alternative hypothesis is that the current class's mean of 77.72 is significantly different from the previous mean of 74.

Table 7.1 Hypothetical statistics quiz scores

74	81	77	77	76
79	83	77	80	75
82	73	80	76	76
80	84	80	82	78
74	81	75	72	71

The Descriptive Statistics tool provides the mean and the standard error of the mean (see Table 7.2). Remember to select **Data** > **Analysis** > **Data Analysis** > **Descriptive Statistics**.

Table 7.2 Descriptive statistics for the quiz scores

QuizScores	
Mean	77.72
Standard Error	0.708
Median	77
Mode	80
Standard Deviation	3.542
Sample Variance	12.543
Kurtosis	-0.873
Skewness	-0.085
Range	13
Minimum	71
Maximum	84
Sum	1943
Count	25
Confidence Level(95.0%)	1.462

We apply the formula for *t*

$$t = \frac{\bar{X} - \mu_0}{s_{\bar{X}}} = \frac{77.72 - 74}{0.708} = 5.25$$

Now we can use the TDIST function to determine the two-tailed probability of this value of *t* with 24 degrees of freedom:

$$= \text{TDIST}(5.25, 24, 2)$$

The result, rounded to three decimals, is 0.000, and we report it as $p < .001$. Our summary statement might be as follows: A one-sample *t* test revealed this term's statistics class ($M = 77.72$, $SD = 3.54$) had a significantly higher average score on the first quiz than the previous classes, $t(24) = 5.25$, $p < .001$. The completed one-sample *t*-test results from the generic worksheet template are in Figure 7.1. The template reports both one-tailed and two-tailed probabilities. The user must first determine whether the results are in the hypothesized direction before deciding the appropriateness of a one-tailed test. In our case, the alternative hypothesis was nondirectional, so we should report the two-tailed *p* value.

Sample Size	25
Population Mean	74
Sample Mean	77.72
Mean Difference	3.72
Standard Deviation	3.541656863
Standard Error	0.708331373
t	5.25
df	24
Two-tailed Probability	0.000
One-tailed Probability	0.000
Cohen's *d*	1.05
95% Confidence Interval	
Max. Error of Estimate	1.462
Lower Limit	2.258
Upper Limit	5.182

Figure 7.1 One-sample *t* test results

When you omit the value of the population standard deviation, the one-sample ZTEST function discussed in Chapter 6 uses the sample standard deviation calculated from the raw data. Therefore, Excel performs a one-sample *t* test in that case. By naming the range of data, entering the hypothesized mean, and omitting the population standard deviation, we are actually finding *t* rather than *z*. With the data range named "data," the following formula will produce the same result as the multiple formulas and functions shown above and by the worksheet template:

$$= NORMSINV(1-ZTEST(data, 74))$$

Because it uses the sample standard deviation, this formula will find the value of *t* rather than *z*. The value of *t* is 5.25 (see Figure 7.2), in agreement with our calculations and the template. Then it is easy to use the TDIST function to find the probability for a given number of tails and degrees of freedom, as illustrated above. Recall the previous discussion of the limitations of the NORMSDIST function. The value returned by the formula in Figure 7.2 will be reported as #NUM (a number error) if the value returned by the ZTEST function is 0 or 1 (indicating an extreme value of *t* or *z*).

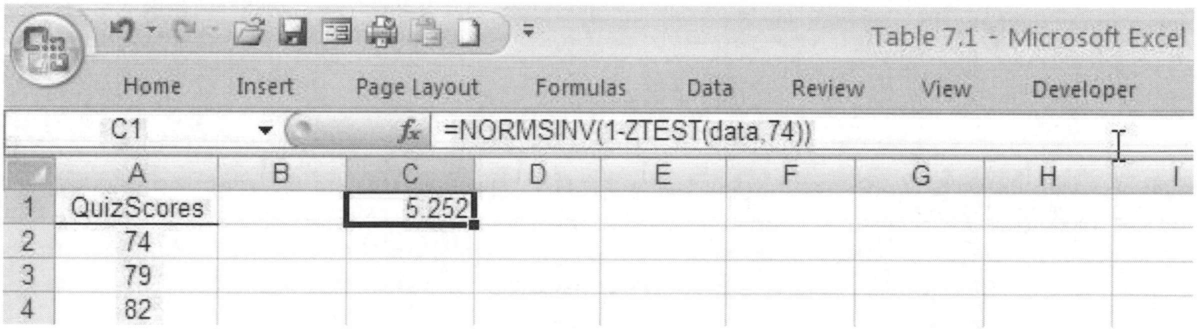

Figure 7.2 Using the ZTEST function and the NORMSINV function to find a one-sample *t* (partial data)

Though it seems strange at first, we can even use the paired-samples *t* test in Excel to conduct a one-sample *t* test (Patterson & Basham, 2006). Insert a vector of the constant value of the hypothesized population mean as the second item in the pair (see Figure 7.3). Because the paired-samples *t* test is the subject of a later section in this chapter, only the results appear here. The results from the paired-samples *t* test are the same as those from the template and the ZTEST function. Because the vector of constants has no variance, the correlation between the two values is undefined, but the value of *t* and the degrees of freedom are correct, as is the reported *p* value.

	A	B	C	D	E	F	G
1	QuizScores	μ_0		t-Test: Paired Two Sample for Means			
2	74	74					
3	79	74			QuizScores	µ0	
4	82	74		Mean	77.72	74	
5	80	74		Variance	12.543	0	
6	74	74		Observations	25	25	
7	81	74		Pearson Correlation	#DIV/0!		
8	83	74		Hypothesized Mean Difference	0		
9	73	74		df	24		
10	84	74		t Stat	5.252		
11	81	74		P(T<=t) one-tail	0.000		
12	77	74		t Critical one-tail	1.711		
13	77	74		P(T<=t) two-tail	0.000		
14	80	74		t Critical two-tail	2.064		
15	80	74					
16	75	74					
17	77	74					
18	80	74					
19	76	74					
20	82	74					
21	72	74					
22	76	74					
23	75	74					
24	76	74					
25	78	74					
26	71	74					

Figure 7.3 Using the paired-samples *t* test tool for a one-sample *t* test

Confidence Interval for a One-Sample *t* Test

We can develop a confidence interval for the one-sample *t* test as follows. First, we locate the critical values of the *t* distribution for the relevant degrees of freedom that will place α/2 in each tail, leaving us with 1 – α in the middle of the distribution. Then we multiply this value of *t* by the standard error of the sample mean. Subtract this margin of error from the mean difference for the lower limit of the confidence interval, and add it to the mean difference for the upper limit. Symbolically,

$$CI = \left(\bar{X} - \mu_0 \right) \pm t_{\text{crit}} \left(s_{\bar{X}} \right)$$

Assume we want the 95% confidence interval. Using the TINV function, we find the critical values of *t* for 24 degrees of freedom are *t* = ±2.064:

=TINV(.05,24)

Taking the appropriate values from our worksheet template, or from the Descriptive Statistics tool, we calculate the confidence interval. The generic template automates these calculations (see Figure 7.1).

$$95\% \text{ CI} = \left(\overline{X} - \mu_0\right) \pm t_{\text{crit}}(s_{\overline{X}})$$
$$= \left(77.72 - 74\right) \pm 2.064 \left(0.70833\right)$$
$$= 3.72 \pm 1.462$$
$$= \left[2.258, 5.182\right]$$

Note the difference between this confidence interval and the ones we constructed earlier in Chapter 6. In this case, we center the interval on the difference between the sample mean and the hypothesized population mean, as we did with the one-sample z test. The confidence interval shows that we are 95% confident that the true mean difference is between 2.258 and 5.182. Because "no difference," that is, a mean difference of 0, is not contained in the interval, we can reject the null hypothesis. We can interpret the additional confidence intervals shown in this chapter in a similar fashion.

THE BOTTOM LINE

- The one-sample t test compares a sample mean to a known or hypothesized population mean when sample sizes are small and when the population standard deviation is not known.

- Excel does not provide a one-sample t test tool.

- The TDIST and TINV functions only work for positive values of t.

- The ZTEST function performs a one-sample t test when you omit the population standard deviation.

- You can also use the paired-samples t test tool for a one-sample t test.

Independent-Samples *t* Test

The independent-samples t test compares the means from two separate samples. The key to this procedure is that there is no overlap in group membership. Each observation belongs to only one sample. The two samples may represent experimental conditions, such as a control group and an experimental group, or they may represent naturally-occurring groups such as males and females. You are interested in determining whether the observed difference between the sample means is statistically significant, or whether you can only conclude the observed differences are attributable to sampling error. As in the case of the one-sample z test and the one-sample t test, the null hypothesis of no difference in the population is presumptively true. As with the one-sample t test, we can have a one-tailed or a two-tailed alternative hypothesis. In this case, the sampling distribution of the difference between two means is distributed as t when the null hypothesis is true. The mechanics of specifying one- and two-tailed tests for the independent-samples t test are similar to those for the one-sample t test. We will examine the two-tailed version. The reader is left to develop the one-tailed hypotheses, using the examples for the one-sample t test as a guide.

The null hypothesis is that the population means for the independent samples are equal (or that the difference between the two means is zero):

$$H_0: \mu_1 = \mu_2$$

or

$$H_0: \mu_1 - \mu_2 = 0$$

The alternative hypothesis is that the population means are unequal (or that the difference between the two means is not zero):

$$H_0: \mu_1 \neq \mu_2$$

or

$$H_0: \mu_1 - \mu_2 \neq 0$$

Because they are independent, the two samples are not required to have the same number of observations. The Analysis ToolPak performs both one- and two-tailed independent-samples *t* tests. The independent-samples *t* test assumes the data are ratio or interval, the observations in each group are independent, the samples are drawn from normally distributed populations. Excel provides *t* tests for both equal variances and unequal variances in the population. When we are not willing to assume the population variances are equal, an adjustment to the degrees of freedom for the *t* test can accommodate this inequality. For the unequal variances *t* test, the value of *t* is calculated as

$$t = \frac{\left(\bar{X}_1 - \bar{X}_2\right) - \left(\mu_1 - \mu_2\right)}{\sqrt{\dfrac{s_1^2}{n_1} + \dfrac{s_2^2}{n_2}}}$$

where the hypothesized mean difference, μ_1-μ_2, is often assumed to be zero. The unequal variances *t* test uses the Welch-Satterthwaite equation to approximate the degrees of freedom:

$$df = \frac{\left(\dfrac{s_1^2}{n_1} + \dfrac{s_2^2}{n_2}\right)^2}{\dfrac{\left(\dfrac{s_1^2}{n_1}\right)^2}{n_1 - 1} + \dfrac{\left(\dfrac{s_2^2}{n_2}\right)^2}{n_2 - 1}}$$

Note the result may be a fractional number. Excel uses the above formula for degrees of freedom for the unequal variances *t* test, but rounds the degrees of freedom to the nearest integer. The Welch test is more conservative than the *t* test assuming equal variances.

The equal variances test is the more commonly taught and performed in behavioral research. In the case of two independent groups, we can use a simple *F* test to examine the equality of the variances in order to determine which *t* test is appropriate. The ratio of the larger of the two sample variances to the smaller variance is distributed as *F* with $n_1 - 1$ and $n_2 - 1$ degrees of freedom. If the *F* ratio is significant at $p < .05$, one should use the unequal variances test. Instead of the Welch-Satterthwaite approximation for the degrees of freedom, one may use the even more conservative approach of $df =$ smaller of $n_1 - 1$ or $n_2 - 1$.

The formula for the independent-samples *t* test for equal variances used by Excel is based on a pooled variance estimate. This value weights the estimate by the relative sizes of the two samples. The value of *t* is calculated as

$$t = \frac{\bar{X}_1 - \bar{X}_2 - \left(\mu_1 - \mu_2\right)}{\sqrt{\left(\dfrac{\left(n_1 - 1\right)s_1^2 + \left(n_2 - 1\right)s_2^2}{n_1 + n_2 - 2}\right)\left(\dfrac{1}{n_1} + \dfrac{1}{n_2}\right)}}$$

This formula is appropriate when we can assume the population variances are equal. Although the formula looks imposing, it may help to see that the denominator term is the estimated standard error of the difference between means of two samples. The first part of the term under the radical in the above formula

$$s_p^2 = \frac{(n_1 - 1)s_1^2 + (n_2 - 1)s_2^2}{n_1 + n_2 - 2}$$

is the pooled variance estimate, s_p^2, and understanding that the hypothesized mean difference $\mu_1 - \mu_2$ is usually zero, we can use a simpler form for t

$$t = \frac{\overline{X}_1 - \overline{X}_2}{\sqrt{\dfrac{s_p^2}{n_1} + \dfrac{s_p^2}{n_2}}}$$

The degrees of freedom for the independent-samples t test assuming equal variance are $n_1 - 1 + n_2 - 1 = n_1 + n_2 - 2$, as each sample loses one degree of freedom. By this point in their statistics course, even with a simpler presentation of the formula, most students are relieved to let a software program find the value of t for them.

Example Data

The data in Table 7.3[5] represent psychological need for competence scores on a 100-point scale for selected student leaders and a nonequivalent control group consisting of a randomly selected class of college students at the same university. We will use an independent-samples t test to determine whether the two groups have equal need for competence. Because we expect student leaders to express a higher need for competence, let us perform a one-tailed test.

Excel allows one to use side-by-side data like those in Table 7.3 for an independent-samples t test. However, some statistics packages such as SPSS require the dependent variable scores to be placed in a single column with an additional column for the grouping variable, which can be an indicator (1, 2) or a dummy-coded (0, 1) column to identify the group to which the observation belongs. This format is called "stacked" data. Figure 7.4 shows the use of dummy-coding with a 1 to represent the leader group and 0 to represent the randomly-selected class. Clearly, you could still use named ranges with such a coding scheme in Excel. Many instructors prefer the stacked coding with indicator variables because they use a statistical package in combination with Excel. In addition to compatibility with other programs, another advantage of the column of group membership codes is that it makes sorting and filtering the data easier. For now, we will just leave the columns side-by-side with appropriate labels (see Figure 7.5). We will return to the issue of stacked data in Chapter 10.

---

[5] These are a sample of data collected by the author.

Table 7.3 Need for competence scores

Leaders	Control
78.6	66.7
76.2	71.4
85.7	57.1
81.0	52.4
97.6	57.1
61.9	85.7
88.1	76.2
59.5	64.3
73.8	54.8
57.1	92.9
81.0	73.8
92.9	97.6
83.3	64.3
78.6	69.1
100.0	85.7
88.1	50.0
76.2	69.1
76.2	92.9
78.6	61.9
	61.9
	66.7
	73.8
	85.7

	A	B
1	Value	Group
2	78.6	1
3	76.2	1
4	85.7	1
5	81.0	1
6	97.6	1
7	61.9	1
8	88.1	1
9	59.5	1
10	73.8	1
34	69.1	0
35	85.7	0
36	50.0	0
37	69.1	0
38	92.9	0
39	61.9	0
40	61.9	0
41	66.7	0
42	73.8	0
43	85.7	0

Figure 7.4. Use of dummy-coding for groups (partial data)

	A	B
1	Leaders	Control
2	78.6	66.7
3	76.2	71.4
4	85.7	57.1
5	81.0	52.4
6	97.6	57.1
7	61.9	85.7
8	88.1	76.2
9	59.5	64.3
10	73.8	54.8
11	57.1	92.9
12	81.0	73.8
13	92.9	97.6
14	83.3	64.3
15	78.6	69.1
16	100.0	85.7
17	88.1	50.0
18	76.2	69.1
19	76.2	92.9
20	78.6	61.9
21		61.9
22		66.7
23		73.8
24		85.7

Figure 7.5 Side-by-side data in Excel

The Independent-Samples t Test in the Analysis ToolPak

First, we will check the homogeneity of variance assumption by using the F-Test tool in the Analysis ToolPak (**Data > Analysis > Data Analysis > F-Test Two-Sample for Variances**). Though it is technically not necessary, when using this tool, it helps to divide the larger sample variance by the smaller one in order to make the F ratio greater than one. To ensure this, assign the scores for the control class to Variable 1 and the scores for the leaders to Variable 2. The FTEST dialog appears in Figure 7.6, and the test results in Figure 7.7. The lack of significance for the obtained F ratio indicates the equal variances test is appropriate. This tool performs a one-tailed test. If you divide the smaller variance by the larger variance, the F ratio will be less than 1, and the critical value will be in the left tail of the F distribution. If you reverse the variable ranges, the value of F and the critical value will both change, but the reported p value will be the same. In contrast to the homogeneity of variance test, the F tests performed in the analysis of variance discussed in Chapters 8 and 9 are two-tailed tests, even though they are performed only in the upper tail of the F distribution.

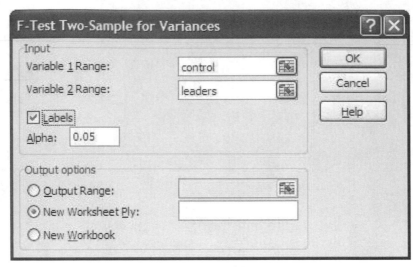

Figure 7.6 F-Test dialog box

	A	B	C	D
1	F-Test Two-Sample for Variances			
2				
3		*Control*	*Leaders*	
4	Mean	70.9173913	79.70526316	
5	Variance	186.0542292	133.9460819	
6	Observations	23	19	
7	df	22	18	
8	F	1.389023304		
9	P(F<=f) one-tail	0.241517509		
10	F Critical one-tail	2.168473511		
11				

Figure 7.7 Nonsignificant *F* ratio indicates variances are approximately equal

To perform the independent-samples *t* test, select **Data > Analysis > Data Analysis > t-test: Two-Sample Assuming Equal Variances**. Click **OK**, and the *t* test Dialog Box appears (Figure 7.8). Supply the ranges for the two variables, including labels if desired. Click **OK** to run the *t* test. The resulting *t*-test output appears in a new worksheet (see Table 7.4).

The significant *t* test indicates we can reject the null hypothesis that student leaders and the nonequivalent control group have the same psychological need for competence. Because the hypothesis was directional, a one-tailed test is appropriate. Student leaders expressed significantly higher levels of need for competence than did randomly selected students, $t(40) = 2.22$, $p = .016$ (one-tailed).

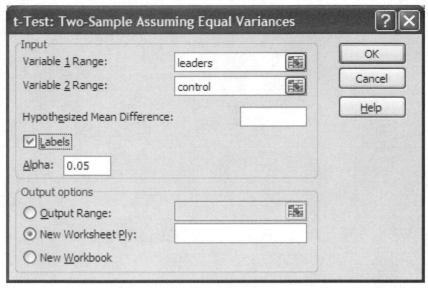

Figure 7.8 Independent-samples *t* test dialog box

Table 7.4 Output from *t* test

t-Test: Two-Sample Assuming Equal Variances

	Leaders	Control
Mean	79.705	70.917
Variance	133.946	186.054
Observations	19	23
Pooled Variance	162.606	
Hypothesized Mean Difference	0	
df	40	
t Stat	2.223	
P(T<=t) one-tail	0.016	
t Critical one-tail	1.684	
P(T<=t) two-tail	0.032	
t Critical two-tail	2.021	

An Independent-Samples *t* Test Template

Figure 7.9 shows a generic independent-samples *t* test template for the *t* test assuming equal variances. A template (not shown) for the *t* test assuming unequal variances is also available from the author. The independent-samples *t*-test template automates the calculations and includes measures of effect size (Cohen's *d* and eta-squared) in addition to a 95% confidence interval for the difference between the sample means. We will discuss effect-size estimates in more detail later in this chapter. Let us first turn our attention to a confidence interval for the mean difference.

	A	B	C	D	E	F	G	H	I
1	Group1	Group2		Statistic	Group1	Group2			
2	78.6	66.7		Sum	1514.4	1631.1			
3	76.2	71.4		Count	19	23			
4	85.7	57.1		Mean	79.70526316	70.9173913			
5	81	52.4		Variance	133.9460819	186.0542292			
6	97.6	57.1		Standard Deviation	11.57350776	13.64016969			
7	61.9	85.7		Pooled Variance	162.6055629				
8	88.1	76.2		Pooled Standard Deviation	12.75168863				
9	59.5	64.3		Mean Difference	8.787871854				
10	73.8	54.8		Standard Error of Mean Difference	3.953225848				
11	57.1	92.9		df	40				
12	81	73.8		t obtained	2.22				
13	92.9	97.6		one-tailed probability	0.016				
14	83.3	64.3		two-tailed probability	0.032				
15	78.6	69.1		Cohen's d	0.69				
16	100	85.7		Eta squared	0.11				
17	88.1	50.0							
18	76.2	69.1			Lower Limit	Upper Limit			
19	76.2	92.9		95% Confidence Interval for Mean Diff.	0.798	16.778			
20	78.6	61.9							
21		61.9							
22		66.7		Enter two groups of observations in the green-shaded data entry areas in columns A and B,					
23		73.8		starting with cells A2 and B2. The worksheet conducts an independent-samples *t* test assuming					
24		85.7		equal variances. The worksheet is protected to keep you from changing the formulas.					
25									

Figure 7.9 Independent-samples *t* test template

Confidence Interval for the Difference between Means

We can construct a confidence interval for the difference between means by making use of the *t* distribution. Let us locate the critical value of *t* separating the middle 95% of the distribution from the upper and lower 2.5% with 40 degrees of freedom. As a reminder, the Excel syntax is

$$= \text{TINV}(.05, 40)$$

Recall the standard error of the difference between means is

$$s_{\bar{X}_1 - \bar{X}_2} = s_{\text{pooled}} \sqrt{\left(\frac{1}{n_1} + \frac{1}{n_2}\right)}$$

and we can find the 95% confidence interval for the difference between means as

$$\left(\bar{X}_1 - \bar{X}_2\right) \pm t_{\text{crit}} \left(s_{\bar{X}_1 - \bar{X}_2}\right)$$

Using the TINV function, we find the critical value of *t* with 40 degrees of freedom to be approximately ±2.021. Multiply this value by the standard error of the difference between the means, and then subtract the value from the mean difference for the lower limit and add the value to the mean difference for the upper limit. To illustrate, the pooled variance estimate was 162.606, so the pooled standard deviation estimate is its square root, 12.752, $n_1 = 19$ and $n_2 = 23$, so the standard error of the mean difference is approximately

$$s_{\bar{X}_1 - \bar{X}_2} = s_{\text{pooled}} \sqrt{\left(\frac{1}{n_1} + \frac{1}{n_2}\right)} = 12.752 \sqrt{\frac{1}{19} + \frac{1}{23}} = 3.953$$

And our 95% confidence interval for the mean difference is

$$\left(\overline{X}_1 - \overline{X}_2\right) \pm t_{\text{crit}}\left(s_{\overline{X}_1 - \overline{X}_2}\right) = (79.71 - 70.92) \pm 2.021(3.953)$$

$$LL = 0.798$$

$$UL = 16.778$$

As shown above, the independent-samples t test template automates the calculation of the confidence interval. The APA format for reporting this interval is

$$95\% \text{ CI} = [0.798, 16.778]$$

THE BOTTOM LINE

- The independent-samples t test compares the means from two separate groups.
- The t test assumes interval or ratio data, normality of population distribution, and independence of the observations within the groups.
- Excel provides t tests that assume the population variances are equal and that assume the population variances are not equal.
- Place the data in side-by-side columns or use named ranges.
- You can test the homogeneity of variance by using the F-Test tool (**Data > Analysis > Data Analysis > F-Test Two-Sample for Variances**).
- To perform the independent-samples t test when the variances are equal, select **Data > Analysis > Data Analysis > t-Test: Two-Sample Assuming Equal Variances**.
- Enter the appropriate information and Click **OK** to run the t test.

Paired-Samples *t* Test

The paired-samples t test applies to data in which the observations from one sample are paired with or linked to the observations in the second sample. This test has different names in different fields. It is variously called the correlated t test, the non-independent t test, the dependent t test, or even the related t test. All these names indicate that we are considering pairs of observations, rather than independent observations. An obvious example is before and after measurements such as a pretest and a posttest for the same individuals. Each person provides two scores, and sorting one column of scores would destroy the relationship between the pairs of scores. Note that in the independent-samples t test, by contrast, sorting either column or both columns would have no effect on the value of t, because each participant provides only one score. The paired-samples t test assumes the data are interval or ratio, the separate observations within each group are independent, and the differences between the two scores for each pair are normally distributed.

Although formulas for the paired-samples t test using the correlation between the pairs of measures are possible, and instructive, they are also computationally complicated. Most modern texts use the simpler direct-difference method for the paired-samples t test, stressing that the only required values for the test are the differences between the pairs of observations. To calculate t, create a column for the differences between the paired measurements. Because the differences are based on the two measures, they are not constrained to have a mean of zero. They will have a mean of zero only when, on average, there are no differences between the two measurements. Take this column of difference scores, and calculate its mean, standard deviation, and standard error. Of course, the simplest way to do this is to use the Descriptive Statistics tool in the Analysis ToolPak. Then we can calculate the value of t as

$$t = \frac{\overline{X}_D}{s_{\overline{X}_D}}$$

where $\overline{X}_D$ is the average difference, and $s_{\overline{X}}$ is the standard error of the mean difference, found by dividing the standard deviation of the difference scores by the square root of *n*, the number of pairs of observations. The similarity of this formula to that for the one-sample *t* should be obvious. When the null hypothesis that the average difference is zero is true, the value obtained above is distributed as *t* with $n - 1$ degrees of freedom, where *n* is the number of pairs of observations. It is very easy to conceive the paired-samples *t* test as a special case of the one-sample *t* test, and the one-sample *t* test worksheet template shown earlier can be used for this test by entering the column of difference scores as the data values and 0 representing "no difference on average" as the test value or "population mean." Let us specify the two-tailed hypotheses for the paired-samples *t* test. The null hypothesis is that the mean difference in the population is zero. The alternative hypothesis is that the population mean difference is not zero. The reader may want to develop the one-tailed versions using the previous examples as guides.

$$H_0: \mu_D = 0$$

$$H_1: \mu_D \neq 0$$

Example Data

Fifteen students completed an Attitudes Toward Statistics (ATS) scale at the beginning and at the end of a basic statistics course.[6] The data are as shown in Table 7.5. Higher scores indicate more favorable attitudes toward statistics. We want to test the hypothesis that the ATS score after the statistics course is significantly higher (one-tailed) than the score at the beginning. Let us adopt an alpha level of .05. The data entered in Excel appear in Figure 7.10.

Table 7.5 Attitudes Toward Statistics

Student	Time1	Time2
1	84	88
2	45	54
3	32	43
4	48	42
5	53	51
6	64	73
7	45	58
8	74	79
9	68	72
10	54	52
11	90	92
12	84	89
13	72	82
14	69	82
15	72	73

---

[6] Data collected by the author.

	A	B	C
1	Student	Time1	Time2
2	1	84	88
3	2	45	54
4	3	32	43
5	4	48	42
6	5	53	51
7	6	64	73
8	7	45	58
9	8	74	79
10	9	68	72
11	10	54	52
12	11	90	92
13	12	84	89
14	13	72	82
15	14	69	82
16	15	72	73

Figure 7.10 Data for paired-samples *t* test

A Paired-Samples *t* test Template

A generic paired-samples *t* test template (see Figure 7.11) makes use of the direct difference method described above. The template also calculates and reports descriptive statistics, a 95% confidence interval, and effect size estimates.

	A	B	C	D	E	F	G	H
1	Pair	Measure1	Measure2	Difference		Statistic	Measure1	Measure2
2	1	84	88	-4		Count	15	15
3	2	45	54	-9		Mean	63.6	68.66666667
4	3	32	43	-11		Standard Deviation	16.830245	17.178336
5	4	48	42	6				
6	5	53	51	2		Mean Difference	-5.066666667	
7	6	64	73	-9		Std. Error	1.491	
8	7	45	58	-13		*t*	-3.40	
9	8	74	79	-5		*df*	14	
10	9	68	72	-4		*p* (*t*) one-tailed	0.002	
11	10	54	52	2		*p* (*t*) two-tailed	0.004	
12	11	90	92	-2				
13	12	84	89	-5		95% Confidence Interval		
14	13	72	82	-10		Lower Limit	-8.265	
15	14	69	82	-13		Upper Limit	-1.868	
16	15	72	73	-1				
17						Effect Size		
18						Cohen's *d*	-0.88	
19						Eta squared	0.45	

Figure 7.11 Paired-samples *t* test template

The calculated *t* statistic of –3.40 indicates that the average Time2 ATS score is significantly higher than the ATS score for Time1. We can conclude that taking a statistics course is associated with significantly more positive attitudes toward statistics after the class is finished, $t(14) = -3.40$, $p = .002$ (one-tailed).

Paired-Samples *t* Test in the Analysis ToolPak

To perform the analysis using the Analysis ToolPak, select **Data** > **Analysis** > **Data Analysis** > **t-Test: Paired Two Sample for Means**. The dialog box appears in Figure 7.12. Enter the Variable1 and Variable2 ranges as shown. If you did not name your ranges, you can just enter the cell references or drag through the data. You may place the output in a new worksheet or in the same worksheet as the data. In this case, keep the default and select a new worksheet (see Figure 7.12). The output table for the paired-samples *t* test appears in Figure 7.13. The results are consistent with those from the worksheet template.

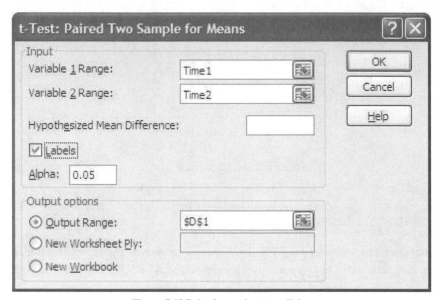

Figure 7.12 Paired-samples *t* test dialog

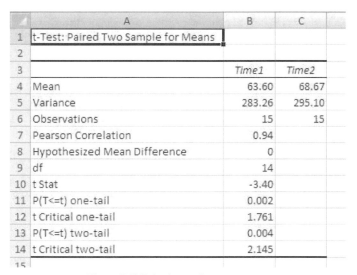

	A	B	C
1	t-Test: Paired Two Sample for Means		
2			
3		Time1	Time2
4	Mean	63.60	68.67
5	Variance	283.26	295.10
6	Observations	15	15
7	Pearson Correlation	0.94	
8	Hypothesized Mean Difference	0	
9	df	14	
10	t Stat	-3.40	
11	P(T<=t) one-tail	0.002	
12	t Critical one-tail	1.761	
13	P(T<=t) two-tail	0.004	
14	t Critical two-tail	2.145	
15			

Figure 7.13 Paired-samples *t* test output

Confidence Interval for the Paired-Samples *t* Test

As with the one-sample and independent-samples *t* tests, we can construct a confidence interval for the paired-samples *t* test. The TINV function determines the critical values of *t* for the relevant alpha level and degrees of freedom. We then construct the confidence interval as follows:

$$CI = \bar{X}_D \pm t_{\alpha/2}\left(s_{\bar{X}_D}\right)$$

For a 95% confidence interval, we use TINV function to find that the critical values of t for 14 degrees of freedom are ± 2.145, and the confidence interval is

$$95\%\ CI = \bar{X}_D \pm t_{crit}\left(s_{\bar{X}_D}\right) = -5.067 \pm 2.145(1.491)$$
$$= [-8.265, -1.868]$$

The generic worksheet template (Figure 7.11) automates the calculation of the confidence interval.

THE BOTTOM LINE

- The paired-samples t test compares the means for pairs of observations.
- The paired-samples t test assumes interval or ratio data, independence of observations within each group, and that the differences between pairs are normally distributed.
- The paired-samples t test can easily be seen as a one-sample (the differences) t test.
- Enter data in two columns with appropriate labels.
- Select **Data > Analysis > Data Analysis > t-Test: Paired Two Sample for Means**.
- Enter data ranges or names for the two variables.
- Check Labels if the data have labels.
- Accept or change the default .05 alpha level.
- Click **OK** to run the paired-samples t test.

Effect Size for t Tests

There are several possible effect size indexes for the t test. One of the most popular and easiest to compute and interpret is Cohen's d (Cohen, 1988), which is a standardized effect size index calculated in standard deviation units. For the independent-samples t test, d can be calculated as

$$d = \frac{\bar{X}_1 - \bar{X}_2}{s_{pooled}}$$

Although Excel does not compute effect size indexes automatically, the calculations are simple. Remember Excel's Analysis ToolPak reports the pooled variance estimate (see Table 7.4), so the square root of that value is the pooled standard deviation. For the paired-samples t test, one could calculate a value of d as follows:

$$d = \frac{\bar{X}_D}{s_D}$$

Finally, for the one-sample t test, we can use the following formula to find the value of d:

$$d = \frac{\bar{X} - \mu_0}{s}$$

Cohen suggests these guidelines for interpreting the magnitude of the effect (see Table 7.6). Note that *d* can be positive or negative, and in the interpretation, you can simply use the absolute value of *d*.

Table 7.6 Guidelines for interpreting Cohen's *d*

Value of *d*	Size of Effect
0.20	Small
0.50	Medium
0.80	Large

Another useful effect-size index for the *t* test is eta squared, which is also used with analysis of variance. For *t* tests, we can calculate eta squared as:

$$\eta^2 = \frac{t^2}{\left(t^2 + df\right)}$$

The interested reader should consult a theoretical statistics text for an explanation of the relationship between t^2 and the *F* distribution discussed in the next chapter. Eta squared is directly interpretable as the proportion of variation in the dependent variable explained by the independent variable(s). For the example used in this chapter to illustrate the independent samples *t* test, recall *t* = 2.223 with 40 degrees of freedom. We can calculate eta squared as

$$\eta^2 = \frac{t^2}{\left(t^2 + df\right)} = \frac{2.223^2}{\left(2.223^2 + 40\right)} = \frac{4.942}{44.942} = .11$$

This value indicates knowledge of whether the student was a leader or not explains approximately 11% of the variation in psychological need for competence.

THE BOTTOM LINE

- Cohen's *d* is a popular effect-size index for *t* tests.
- Cohen's *d* is a standardized effect size index expressing the magnitude of a difference or effect in standard deviation units.
- The mean difference divided by the standard deviation (or pooled standard deviation) is Cohen's *d*.
- Eta squared is proportion of variation in the dependent variable that can be explained by the independent variable(s).

Chapter 7 Exercises

1. Using the dataset from Table 2.1, conduct a one-sample *t* test of the two-tailed hypothesis that the average percent change in wages from 2001 to 2002 was different from zero. Use an alpha level of .05. Calculate and interpret Cohen's *d* as a measure of effect size.

2. According to the Nielson Mobile Survey, the average teenager in the United States sends and receives an average of 1742 text messages each month. For the data from Exercise 6.3 (repeated below), conduct a one-sample *t* test to determine if this sample of 16 teenagers is significantly different from the population average of 1742. Use a two-tailed test and an alpha level of .05. Calculate and interpret Cohen's *d* as a measure of effect size.

1470	1384	2345	1942
1896	2055	2055	1990
2159	2245	1751	1552
2004	1362	1745	1720

3. Using the data from Table 2.1, conduct a paired-samples t test to compare the average wages in 2001 and 2002. Test the two-tailed hypothesis that the average wages for 2002 are different from the average wages for 2001. Use an alpha level of .05. Calculate and interpret Cohen's d as a measure of effect size.

4. Twenty college students participated in a word recognition experiment in which words were flashed on a computer screen for increasingly longer time intervals until the student recognized the word. Half the words were flashed to the right of a fixation point and thus stimulated the left side of the brain, while the other words were flashed to the left of the fixation point and thus stimulated the right side of the brain. The reaction times in seconds to recognize the stimulus word for the two hemispheres are shown below. Conduct and interpret a paired-samples t test to determine if the left hemisphere recognizes words more quickly than the right hemisphere. Use a one-tailed test and an alpha level of .05.

Participant	Left	Right	Participant	Left	Right
1	0.094	0.100	11	0.094	0.143
2	0.098	0.096	12	0.113	0.116
3	0.109	0.135	13	0.105	0.121
4	0.103	0.090	14	0.126	0.179
5	0.090	0.143	15	0.090	0.090
6	0.098	0.128	16	0.105	0.121
7	0.120	0.105	17	0.126	0.179
8	0.124	0.134	18	0.098	0.096
9	0.113	0.116	19	0.119	0.120
10	0.099	0.123	20	0.095	0.108

5. The following data are the stereotype-congruent and stereotype-incongruent reaction times for 38 college students on an implicit association test. Conduct and interpret a paired-samples t test to determine if there is a difference in reaction times for the two conditions. Calculate and interpret Cohen's d as a measure of effect size.

UserID	Congruent	Incongruent	UserID	Congruent	Incongruent
1	0.90	1.80	20	1.14	1.16
2	0.66	0.74	21	0.91	1.69
3	0.74	0.96	22	0.92	0.98
4	0.93	1.65	23	0.92	0.98
5	0.91	1.04	24	0.38	1.43
6	1.17	1.65	25	0.90	1.40
7	0.92	1.26	26	0.79	1.23
8	0.81	1.08	27	0.85	1.16
9	1.03	0.69	28	1.08	1.48
10	0.74	0.96	29	0.77	1.04
11	0.68	1.39	30	1.03	1.06
12	1.11	1.25	31	0.68	1.08
13	0.93	1.21	32	0.75	1.22
14	0.71	0.92	33	0.75	1.22
15	0.80	1.32	34	0.75	1.22
16	0.70	1.14	35	0.78	0.86
17	0.61	1.13	36	0.83	1.03
18	1.11	1.05	37	0.82	0.93
19	0.80	0.88	38	0.68	0.77

6. Using the data from Table 3.5, conduct and interpret an independent-samples *t* test to determine whether the salaries of male and female CEOs are different. Use an alpha level of .05. Calculate and interpret Cohen's *d* as a measure of effect size.

7. Using the data from Table 3.5, conduct and interpret an independent-samples *t* test to determine whether the ages of male and female CEOs are different. Use an alpha level of .05. Calculate and interpret Cohen's *d* as a measure of effect size.

8. Independent samples of undergraduate and graduate statistics students completed an Attitudes Toward Statistics scale. Higher scores indicate more favorable attitudes toward statistics. The results appear below. Perform an independent-samples *t* test to determine whether the attitudes of the two groups are different. Use an alpha level of .05. Calculate and interpret Cohen's *d* as a measure of effect size.

Undergrad	Grad
63	67
47	78
65	54
79	76
65	61
63	78
41	51
41	67
75	69
49	71
41	59
60	75
42	88
75	44
52	

9. Researchers compared two weight loss supplements. Two independent groups of 15 randomly selected participants took each supplement, and researchers recorded the amount of weight lost in a month. A negative number indicates weight gain. Conduct and interpret an independent-samples *t* test to determine if the two brands are equally effective. Use an alpha level of .05. Calculate and interpret Cohen's *d* as a measure of effect size.

BrandA	BrandB
6.8	4.7
13.2	11.4
8.8	6.7
7.2	5.0
10.5	8.6
2.1	0.0
7.4	-1.5
13.6	11.8
7.3	5.1
9.8	7.8
6.6	4.4
7.1	4.9
13.7	11.9
14.2	12.4
6.8	4.8

8   Analysis of Variance

The one-way analysis of variance (ANOVA) is an extension of the independent-samples t test to three or more groups. ANOVA partitions or "analyzes" the variation in the dependent variable into two sources. Some of the variation is due to differences between the means of the groups. This variation is ***between-groups*** variation or treatment effect. Some of the variation is due to differences among the scores within the separate groups. This is ***within-groups*** variation or error variance. We calculate a mean square (MS) for each source of variation by dividing the sum of squares for the particular source by the appropriate degrees of freedom. In ANOVA, the MSs are the actual "variances being analyzed." The F ratio used to test the hypothesis of equality among the group means is a ratio of two variance estimates, in this case, the MS between groups or MS_b divided by the MS within or MS_w. Like the t distribution, the F distribution is a family of distributions, each defined by the degrees of freedom for the numerator and the degrees of freedom for the denominator. Unlike the t distribution, the F distribution is not symmetrical. It ranges between 0 and $+\infty$. If the two variance estimates are equal, we would expect the value of F to be 1, so the F distribution tends to peak at the value 1. As the between-groups variance increases and the within-groups variance decreases, the F ratio becomes larger, but also less probable under the null hypothesis that the variances are equal. We perform most of our F tests in the right tail of the distribution, and these are nearly always two-tailed tests because the F distribution is based on squared values. The one-way ANOVA assumes the populations being sampled are normally distributed, the variances in the populations are equal (homoscedasticity), and the observations in each sample are independent.

Partitioning the variance in the one-way ANOVA is straightforward, and Excel allows the learner to use definitional formulas to calculate the terms. Assume we have k independent groups with $n_1 + n_2 + \ldots + n_k = N$ total observations. The total sum of squares is simply the sum of the squares of the deviations of each individual score from the overall mean of the dataset, which we will symbolize with a double bar:

$$SS_{\text{tot}} = \sum_{i=1}^{N} \left(X_i - \overline{\overline{X}} \right)^2$$

The total degrees of freedom are $N - 1$, and the astute reader will note the total sum of squares is found by the DEVSQ function in Excel, and when divided by the total degrees of freedom, is the estimate of the population variance treating all scores as a single dataset.

The within-groups sum of squares is the sum of the squared deviations from the group mean for all scores within that group. We sum these values across the k groups. The only source of variation in this term is deviations from its own group mean for each score. The degrees of freedom for the within-groups sum of squares are $N - k$.

$$SS_{\text{w}} = \sum_{j=1}^{k} \sum_{i=1}^{n_j} (X_i - \overline{X}_j)^2$$

The between-groups sum of squares is based on the deviations between the group means and the overall mean, weighted by the number of observations in each group:

$$SS_{\text{b}} = \sum_{j=1}^{k} n_j (\overline{X}_j - \overline{\overline{X}})^2$$

The degrees of freedom for the between-groups sum of squares are $k - 1$.

Excel's Analysis ToolPak provides one-way between-groups analysis ANOVA, one-way within-subjects (repeated-measures) ANOVA, and two-way ANOVA for a balanced factorial design. There is a brief treatment of two-way ANOVA at the end of this chapter, but you will find Excel's two-way ANOVA tool is limited, and therefore for practical purposes you will want to use a dedicated statistics package, an Excel statistics add-in, or regression models with coding variables for more complex ANOVA designs. In Chapter 10, you will get an introduction to the manner in which you can repurpose t tests and ANOVA as regression problems. Excel provides no facility for follow-up comparisons after a significant F test, but it is possible to write formulas to perform these tests, and several Excel add-ins provide post hoc comparisons.

The null hypothesis for the ANOVA is that the k population means are equivalent:

$$H_0: \mu_1 = \mu_2 = \ldots = \mu_k$$

The alternative hypothesis is not as easy to put into symbols. It specifies that the difference between at least one pair of means is not zero.

Example Data

We will use the following hypothetical data to illustrate the one-way between-groups ANOVA. A statistics professor taught three sections of the same statistics class one semester. One section was in a traditional classroom, the second section was an online class that did not meet physically, and the third section was a hybrid class with classroom lecture and an online homework component. There were 10 students in each section. The classes used the same text. All students took the same final examination, and their scores appear in Table 8.1.

Table 8.1 Scores on a statistics final examination

Online	Classroom	Hybrid
65	72	87
75	82	94
83	87	75
80	82	95
64	69	70
81	85	80
85	90	86
62	70	91
84	92	87
80	86	93

The properly formatted data in Excel might appear as in Figure 8.1. For application of the Analysis ToolPak's analysis of variance tool and of the worksheet template shown in this book, side-by-side groups of observations are possible, and aid in visualization. For the one-way ANOVA, some statistical packages like SPSS require the data to be in a "stacked format" with a group identification number coded as a separate variable in a different column, as discussed briefly in the previous chapter, and illustrated in more detail in Chapter 10. Because of its flexibility, Excel can handle either format.

	A	B	C
1	Online	Classroom	Hybrid
2	65	72	87
3	75	82	94
4	83	87	75
5	80	82	95
6	64	69	70
7	81	85	80
8	85	90	86
9	62	70	91
10	84	92	87
11	80	86	93
12			

Figure 8.1 Data for one-way ANOVA in Excel

Find the total sum of squares by use of the DEVSQ function, treating all the observations as a single dataset. The value is 2463.87, and the total degrees of freedom are $N - 1 = 29$. We can also calculate the within-groups sum of squares by using the DEVSQ function for each group and adding the three.

= DEVSQ(A2:A11) + DEVSQ(B2:B11) + DEVSQ(C2:C11) = 1971.00

The mean square within has $N - k = 27$ degrees of freedom, so the mean square within is 1971.00 / 27 = 73.00. We can calculate the between-groups sum of squares by finding the mean for each condition and then multiplying the squared deviation scores for those means from the overall mean by the number of observations in the groups and adding across the groups. The means for online, classroom, and hybrid are 75.9, 81.5, and 85.8, respectively. The overall mean is 81.07. There are 10 observations in each group. The sum of squares between groups is:

$$SS_b = 10(75.9 - 81.07)^2 + 10(81.5 - 81.07)^2 + 10(85.8 - 81.07)^2 = 492.87$$

The degrees of freedom for the between groups sum of squares are $k - 1 = 2$, so the mean square between is 492.85 / 2 = 246.43. The F ratio is the MS_b divided by the MS_w, or 246.43 / 73.00 = 3.38. With 2 and 27 degrees of freedom, this F ratio is significant, $F(2, 27) = 3.38$, $p = .049$, $\eta^2 = .20$, and we conclude the means for the three teaching methods are significantly different. After seeing how Excel's Analysis ToolPak can be used to perform a one-way ANOVA, we will discuss eta squared, our measure of effect size.

One-Way ANOVA in the Analysis ToolPak

To conduct the one-way ANOVA using the Analysis ToolPak, select **Data** > **Analysis** > **Data Analysis**. In the dialog box, select **Anova: Single Factor** and then click **OK**. The ANOVA tool Dialog box appears (see Figure 8.2). Provide the input range including the column labels, and click **OK**. If the group sizes are not equal, drag through the entire range to include the group with the largest number of observations, including any blank cells. The resulting descriptive statistics and ANOVA summary table are shown in Figure 8.3. The value "*F crit*" = 3.35 reported by Excel is the minimum value of F required for statistical significance at the .05 alpha level with 2 and 27 degrees of freedom.

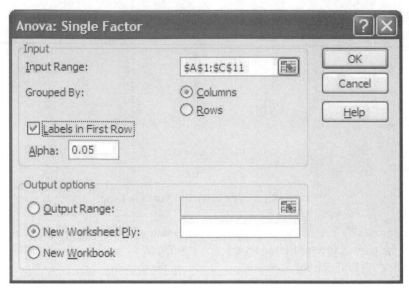

Figure 8.2 One-way ANOVA tool dialog box

	A	B	C	D	E	F	G
1	Anova: Single Factor						
2							
3	SUMMARY						
4	Groups	Count	Sum	Average	Variance		
5	Online	10	759	75.90	79.21		
6	Classroom	10	815	81.50	69.39		
7	Hybrid	10	858	85.80	70.40		
8							
9							
10	ANOVA						
11	Source of Variation	SS	df	MS	F	P-value	F crit
12	Between Groups	492.87	2	246.43	3.38	0.05	3.35
13	Within Groups	1971.00	27	73.00			
14							
15	Total	2463.87	29				
16							

Figure 8.3 Excel's ANOVA summary table

THE BOTTOM LINE

- The one-way ANOVA compares three or more means simultaneously.
- The one-way ANOVA assumes interval or ratio data, independence, normality of distribution, and equality of variance.
- Excel does not provide post hoc comparisons.
- Place data in side-by-side columns with appropriate headings or use named ranges.
- Select **Data > Analysis > Data Analysis > Anova: Single Factor**.
- Drag through the entire range of data, including the empty cells if the group sizes are not equal.
- Click **OK** to run the one-way ANOVA.

Effect Size for the One-Way ANOVA

As an effect-size index for the one-way ANOVA, the value η^2 (eta squared) is the between-groups sum of squares divided by the total sum of squares:

$$\eta^2 = \frac{SS_{between}}{SS_{total}}$$

This value shows how much of the total variation in the dependent variable we can explain or "account for" by "treatment" effects or differences among the means. In the current case, the value of η^2 is .20, indicating approximately 20% of the variation in the dependent variable is accounted for by knowledge of the treatment condition. The type of class explains a statistically significant but not practically very large proportion of the variation in the statistics exam scores, leaving 80% of the variation unexplained.

An ANOVA Worksheet Template

Figure 8.4 shows a generic ANOVA worksheet template (available from the publisher). The user simply supplies the raw data for up to 10 groups. The results are consistent with those from the Analysis ToolPak's ANOVA tool. This template also calculates η^2 as a measure of effect size.

	A	B	C	D	E	F	G	H	I	J
1	Groups	3						Group1	Group2	Group3
2	*Nmax*	10						65	72	87
3								75	82	94
4								83	87	75
5		Mean	*n*	Std. Deviation	Between			80	82	95
6	Group1	75.9	10	8.900062422	266.944444			64	69	70
7	Group2	81.5	10	8.329999333	1.87777778			81	85	80
8	Group3	85.8	10	8.390470785	224.044444			85	90	86
9	Group4							62	70	91
10	Group5							84	92	87
11	Group6							80	86	93
12	Group7									
13	Group8									
14	Group9									
15	Group10									
16	Overall	81.06666667	30	9.217424778						
17										
18										
19	Source	*Sum of Squares*	*df*	*MS*	*F*	*p*				
20	Between	492.867	2	246.433	3.38	0.049				
21	Within	1971.000	27	73.000						
22	Total	2463.867	29							
23										
24	η^2	0.20								

Figure 8.4 One-way ANOVA worksheet template

Multiple Comparisons in Excel

When you have found a significant F ratio, it is usually of interest to know which means differ from each other. As mentioned earlier, Excel does not provide multiple comparisons, but it is possible to write formulas to perform these comparisons. It often occurs to the beginning statistics student that he or she could just do an independent-samples t test between each pair of means in the dataset. However, doing pairwise t tests increases the likelihood of Type I error (rejecting a true null hypothesis). To see how substantial the compounding of Type I error is, you must first understand the term "experimentwise error rate." Assume you are using the conventional standard of .05 as the required level for overall significance for the ANOVA. As you perform multiple t tests, the probability of rejecting a true null hypothesis quickly surpasses the nominal alpha level. The experimentwise error rate can be found from the following formula:

$$\alpha_{tot} = 1 - (1 - \alpha_{crit})^c$$

Where α_{tot} is the experimentwise error rate, α_{crit} is the nominal alpha level for each test, and c is the number of tests performed. To illustrate, we just compared three groups. If the alpha level for each of the three pairwise comparisons is set at .05, then the actual experimentwise error rate would be

$$\alpha_{tot} = 1 - (1 - .05)^3 = 1 - .95^3 = .142625$$

We have slightly more than a .14 probability of rejecting a true null hypothesis when performing only three pairwise tests. As the number of tests increases, this probability compounds quickly. For example, with only four groups, there are six possible comparisons, and the experimentwise error rate with a nominal alpha of .05 for each comparison is .265. With 10 groups, there are 45 pairwise comparisons, and the experimentwise error rate when each of these tests is performed at an alpha level of .05 is a staggering .901.

The Fisher LSD Test

Controlling for the experimentwise error rate is obviously very important. There are several approaches. R. A. Fisher, the creator of ANOVA, suggested one perform a "protected t test," in which the overall alpha level for all comparisons is held at α_{crit}. The protection of the alpha level is accomplished by using the within-groups MS and the degrees of freedom from all groups rather than the pooled standard deviation from the two groups being compared. Fisher's test is called LSD for "least significant difference." We can find a critical value of LSD for comparing two group means from the following formula:

$$LSD_\alpha = t_{\alpha/2} \sqrt{MS_w \left(\frac{1}{n_1} + \frac{1}{n_2} \right)}$$

When the group sizes are equal, a simpler formula to find the value of LSD is:

$$LSD_\alpha = t_{\alpha/2} \sqrt{\frac{2MS_w}{n}}$$

where $n_1 = n_2 = \ldots = n_k = n$. Because all three groups had 10 observations in the current case, we will need to find only one LSD value. If the group sizes are different, we must compute different values of LSD for each comparison. In this equation, α is the chosen alpha level, conventionally the same as that for the overall F test, $t_{\alpha/2}$ is the two-tailed critical value of t for df_w (the within-groups degrees of freedom). MS_w is, of course, the within-groups mean square, and n is the number of observations in a single group. Using these values from the ANOVA and the critical value of t found from the TINV function, we can calculate an LSD for alpha = .05.

$$LSD_{.05} = 2.0518 \sqrt{\frac{2(73)}{10}} = 7.84$$

We then compare this "least significant difference" to the actual differences among the means. Any difference larger in absolute value than LSD is statistically significant. Building a simple table to display the absolute values of the mean differences (see Table 8.2) makes them easier to compare. This is a two-tailed test, as we could change the sign of the mean difference simply by reversing the order of subtraction.

Table 8.2 Fisher LSD test of mean differences (differences are in absolute value)

	Online	Classroom	Hybrid
Online	-	5.60	9.90*
Classroom	-	-	4.30
Hybrid	-	-	-

*$p < .05$

By the standard of the LSD, only the difference between the online and hybrid sections is significant. It is possible to calculate a value of t rather than an LSD using the "protected t test," and this, of course, will allow the user to determine a more exact probability of a mean difference using the TDIST function. The value of t is

$$t = \frac{\overline{X}_i - \overline{X}_j}{\sqrt{\dfrac{MS_w}{n_i} + \dfrac{MS_w}{n_j}}}$$

The p value for this t statistic is evaluated at df_w instead of $n_1 + n_2 - 2$ as in the case of the independent-samples t test. Although many modern statisticians object to the Fisher LSD test because of its liberality, it has two significant advantages. It makes use of the familiar t distribution, and it easily accommodates groups of different sizes (Howell, 2008; Thorne & Giesen, 2003).

The Tukey HSD Test

The Fisher LSD is less popular today than the Tukey HSD ("honestly significant difference") test and Bonferroni-corrected comparisons. The Tukey HSD test uses the "studentized range statistic," a distribution not currently available in Excel. A table of critical values of the studentized range distribution is in Appendix D of this book. The HSD test (Tukey, 1949) is somewhat more conservative than the LSD test. This dictates that a difference between two means will have to be larger to be significant with the HSD test than with the LSD test. We calculate a critical difference as:

$$HSD = q_k \sqrt{\frac{MS_w}{n}}$$

where q is the tabled value of the studentized range statistic with the desired alpha level, k is the total number of treatments or conditions being compared, and n is the number of observations per group. Although many authors assert that the Tukey HSD test cannot be used with unequal sample sizes (see, for example, Gravetter & Wallnau, 2009), that is not precisely true. We can calculate the harmonic mean of the sample sizes and use that value, $\tilde{n}$, in place of n in calculating HSD. The harmonic mean of k different sample sizes is

$$\tilde{n} = \frac{k}{1/n_1 + 1/n_2 + ... + 1/n_k}$$

Excel has a built-in function for calculating the harmonic mean, HARMEAN. In this case, the samples are of equal size so we simply use the group size, n. The HSD criterion for an alpha level of .05 is

$$\text{HSD}_{.05} = q\sqrt{\frac{MS_w}{n}} = 3.51\sqrt{\frac{73}{10}} = 9.483$$

where q is found by interpolation for three means, $\alpha = .05$, and $df_w = 27$ in Appendix C. HSD is larger than LSD, making this a more conservative test, as the discussion indicated it would be. By this criterion as well, only the difference between the online and hybrid sections is significant.

Bonferroni Corrections

The Bonferroni correction is a simple adjustment to the alpha level to control for the experimentwise error rate. In general, if you perform k tests and want overall protection at the level of α, then you should use α/k as the criterion for significance for each comparison (Moore, McCabe, Duckworth, & Sclove, 2003). Assuming the overall alpha level is .05, and three comparisons are being made, then pairwise t tests can be performed, but the required significance level for each test is $\alpha/3$ or .01667.

Other Post Hoc Tests

As mentioned earlier, statistics packages and some statistics add-ins for Excel include mechanisms for performing post hoc comparisons. For example, the current version of SPSS offers 14 choices for post hoc tests for the ANOVA. Pace (2006) provides Excel formulas and functions for various post hoc tests including the Tukey HSD, the Fisher LSD, the Scheffé test, and the Dunnett test for multiple comparisons to a control group.

THE BOTTOM LINE

- Excel does not provide multiple comparisons or effect size indices for the one-way ANOVA.
- Eta squared (η^2) is the between-groups sum of squares divided by the total sum of squares, and shows the proportion of the total variation that can be attributed to group differences or treatment effects.
- The Fisher LSD, Tukey HSD, and Bonferroni-corrected comparisons are popular post hoc tests.
- These post hoc comparisons can be achieved through functions or formulas in Excel.
- Some Excel add-ins provide post hoc comparisons.
- Dedicated statistics packages like SPSS provide many post hoc procedures.

A Brief Introduction to Two-Way ANOVA

Thus far, we have examined the one-way ANOVA. Let us now take a brief look at two-way ANOVA by considering the simplest case, a balanced factorial design. In the two-way ANOVA, we have two independent variables rather than one. In ANOVA terminology, these independent variables are *factors*. Each independent variable must have at least two levels. We are interested in examining the effects of these factors on the dependent variable separately and in combination. We call the separate effects ***main effects*** and the combined effect an ***interaction***. Because each cell involves a combination of factors, the two-way ANOVA is an economical design. Let us call the column factor A and the row factor B. Table 8.3 shows how these factors are combined in a two-way balanced factorial ANOVA with two levels of each independent variable:

Table 8.3 Combination of factors A and B with two levels each

Level of B	Level of A	
	A_1	A_2
B_1	A_1B_1—Group 1	A_2B_1—Group 2
B_2	A_1B_2—Group 3	A_2B_2—Group 4

Let the number of columns (levels of factor A) be C and the number of rows (levels of factor B) be R. For convenience and mnemonic value, we use G to refer to the number of observations in each group, where in a balanced factorial design $R \times C \times G = N$, the total number of observations. Partitioning the variance in the two-way ANOVA is a little more complicated than in the one-way ANOVA. We have three sources of "between-groups" variation, which include the main effects of factor A, the main effects of factor B, and the interaction of A and B. We can define the total sum of squares as before:

$$SS_{\text{tot}} = \sum_{i=1}^{N}(X_i - \overline{\overline{X}})^2$$

As in the one-way ANOVA, with $N - 1$ degrees of freedom, the total mean square is the estimate of the population variance treating the entire set of observations as one sample. The partition of the total sum of squares includes the sums of squares for A, B, the $A \times B$ interaction, and an error term:

$$SS_{\text{tot}} = SS_A + SS_B + SS_{AB} + SS_{\text{err}}$$

We calculate the sum of squares for *cells* as the sum of the squared deviations of the individual cell means from the overall mean multiplied by the number of observations per group. This is the overall "between groups" variation, which we partition further into SS_A, SS_B and SS_{AB}.

$$SS_{\text{cells}} = G\sum_{i=1}^{R}\sum_{j=1}^{C}(\overline{X}_{ij} - \overline{\overline{X}})^2$$

Use the marginal means for the column factor A, ignoring the row factor B, to calculate the sum of squares for A:

$$SS_A = RG\sum_{i=1}^{C}(\overline{X}_i - \overline{\overline{X}})^2$$

with $C - 1$ degrees of freedom. In a similar fashion, the sum of squares for factor B, ignoring the column factor A, is

$$SS_B = CG\sum_{j=1}^{R}(\overline{X}_j - \overline{\overline{X}})^2$$

with $R - 1$ degrees of freedom. Subtracting the sum of squares for A and B from the sum of squares for cells gives the sum of squares for the interaction of A and B,

$$SS_{AB} = SS_{\text{cells}} - SS_A - SS_B$$

with $(R-1) \times (C-1)$ degrees of freedom. Finally, we can also find the error sum of squares by subtraction:

$$SS_{err} = SS_{tot} - SS_{cells}$$

with $RC \times (G-1)$ degrees of freedom. We calculate the mean square for each term by dividing the sum of squares by the respective degrees of freedom and then calculate the F ratio for each effect by dividing the mean square for that effect by the error mean square.

A Worked-Out Example of Two-Way ANOVA

To revive an earlier example, suppose you are interested in the attitudes of middle-school students toward the use of computers in the classroom. You randomly assign equal numbers of male and female students to either a "hands-on" section in which students use the computers or a "lecture" section where the teacher demonstrates the use of the computer in a traditional lecture format while the students sit at their desks. Students complete an attitude scale at the end of the class, with higher scores indicating more positive attitudes. There are four independent groups with four students in each cell, as follows (see Table 8.4).

Table 8.4 Hypothetical scores on a scale measuring attitudes toward computers

	Hands-on	Lecture
Male	15	15
	20	15
	19	14
	18	12
Female	16	20
	19	19
	17	18
	19	17

To demonstrate the use of the formulas shown above, let us calculate the cell means, the marginal means, and the overall mean from the data. Table 8.5 shows these values.

Table 8.5 Cell means, marginal means, and overall mean

	Hands-on	Lecture	Total		
Male	18.000	14.000	16.000	$R =$	2
Female	17.750	18.500	18.125	$C =$	2
Total	17.875	16.250	17.0625	$G =$	4
				$N =$	16

We can use Excel's DEVSQ function to find the total sum of squares by treating all 16 values as a single dataset. The value is 82.9375. The sum of squares for the column factor A is

$$SS_A = RG \sum_{i=1}^{C} (\overline{X}_i - \overline{\overline{X}})^2 = 2(4) \sum_{i=1}^{2} (\overline{X}_i - \overline{\overline{X}})^2$$
$$= 8((17.875 - 17.0625)^2 + (16.25 - 17.0625)^2) = 10.5625$$

The sum of squares for row factor B is

$$SS_{\text{B}} = CG\sum_{j=1}^{R}(\bar{X}_j - \bar{\bar{X}})^2 = 2(4)\sum_{j=1}^{2}(\bar{X}_j - \bar{\bar{X}})^2$$
$$= 8((16.00 - 17.0625)^2 + (18.125 - 17.0625)^2 = 18.0625$$

The sum of squares for cells is

$$SS_{\text{cells}} = G\sum_{i=1}^{R}\sum_{j=1}^{C}(\bar{X}_{ij} - \bar{\bar{X}})^2$$
$$= 4((18.00 - 17.0625)^2 + (17.75 - 17.0625)^2 + (14.00 - 17.0625)^2 + (18.5 - 17.0625)^2)$$
$$= 51.188$$

We can now calculate the sum of squares for interaction and error by subtraction:

$$SS_{\text{AB}} = SS_{\text{cells}} - SS_{\text{A}} - SS_{\text{B}} = 51.118 - 10.5625 - 18.0625 = 22.563$$

and

$$SS_{\text{err}} = SS_{\text{tot}} - SS_{\text{cells}} = 82.938 - 51.188 = 31.75$$

The SS_{err} term is equivalent to the within-groups sum of squares from our one-way ANOVA example, and you can calculate it directly rather than by subtraction. Simply treat each cell as an independent group, and calculate the sum of squared deviations for each cell.

$$SS_{\text{err}} = \sum_{j=1}^{k}\sum_{i=1}^{n_j}(X_i - \bar{X}_j)^2$$

Sum these values for an alternate way to compute SS_{err} (and to double-check your calculations).

$$SS_{\text{err}} = 14.00 + 6.00 + 6.75 + 5.00 = 31.75$$

Using the sums of squares along with their respective degrees of freedom, we obtain three F ratios, one for factor A, one for factor B, and one for the interaction of A and B. All three F ratios use the same error term. An ANOVA summary table helps organize the results of our calculations (see Table 8.6):

Table 8.6 ANOVA summary table for the example problem

ANOVA Summary Table				
Source	SS	df	MS	F	p(F)
A	18.0625	1	18.0625	6.83	0.023
B	10.5625	1	10.5625	3.99	0.069
A × B	22.5625	1	22.5625	8.53	0.013
Error	31.7500	12	2.6458		
Total	82.9375	15			

The main effect of factor A (*method*) is significant, $F(1,12) = 6.83$, $p = .023$, and the interaction of factors A and B (*method* by *sex*) is also significant, $F(1,12) = 8.53$, $p = .013$. There is no significant main effect of factor B (*sex*), $F(1,12) = 3.99$, $p = .069$. A plot of the cell means helps us to interpret these effects (Figure 8.5). The plot reveals female students enjoy both the lecture and the hands-on class, but male students enjoy the hands-on class more than the lecture. In this situation, the interpretation of the interaction and the main effect of the method (*lecture* or *hands-on*) is straightforward. In other situations where the lines of the plotted cell means cross one another, we have a "disordinal" interaction, and in these cases, the interpretation of main effects is problematic at best.

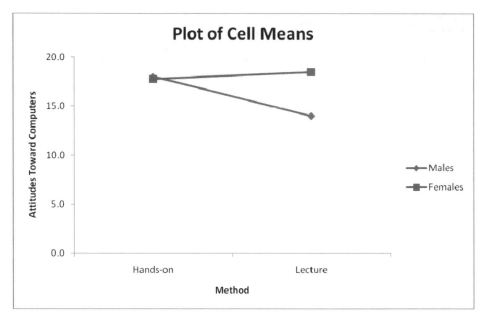

Figure 8.5 Plotting cell means reveals the pattern of interaction

Two-Way ANOVA in the Analysis ToolPak

For a balanced factorial design, Excel's "Anova: Two-Factor With Replication" tool automates all the above calculations and produces a summary table similar to the one shown in Table 8.6. Enter the data with appropriate labels (see Figure 8.6).

	A	B	C
1		Hands-on	Lecture
2	Male	15	15
3		20	15
4		19	14
5		18	12
6	Female	16	20
7		19	19
8		17	18
9		19	17
10			

Figure 8.6 Data arranged for a two-way ANOVA in Excel

To use the two-way ANOVA procedure, supply the input range from cell A1 to cell C9, including the text labels. The number of "Rows per sample" is G, the number of observations per group, in this case, 4. The **Anova: Two-Factor With Replication** dialog box appears in Figure 8.7. Let us accept the default to place the output in a new worksheet.

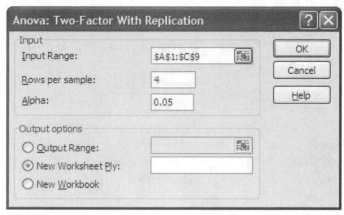

Figure 8.7 Two-way ANOVA dialog box

The summary statistics and the ANOVA summary table (after cell formatting) appear as follows (see Table 8.7). The results agree with those we achieved by applying the formulas shown previously. The value $F\ crit = 4.75$ shown in the Excel summary table is the minimum value of F required for statistical significance at the stated alpha level of .05 with 1 and 12 degrees of freedom. Verify this by using the FINV (inverse of the F distribution) function in Excel:

$$= \text{FINV}(0.05, 1, 12)$$

The result, 4.75 (rounded), appears when you press <**Enter**>.

Table 8.7 Output from the two-way ANOVA tool in Excel (after cell formatting)

Anova: Two-Factor With Replication

SUMMARY	Hands-on	Lecture	Total
Male			
Count	4	4	8
Sum	72	56	128
Average	18	14	16
Variance	4.67	2	7.43
Female			
Count	4	4	8
Sum	71	74	145
Average	17.75	18.5	18.125
Variance	2.25	1.67	1.84
Total			
Count	8	8	
Sum	143	130	
Average	17.875	16.25	
Variance	2.98	7.36	

ANOVA

Source of Variation	SS	df	MS	F	P-value	F crit
Sample	18.0625	1	18.0625	6.83	0.023	4.75
Columns	10.5625	1	10.5625	3.99	0.069	4.75
Interaction	22.5625	1	22.5625	8.53	0.013	4.75
Within	31.75	12	2.6458			
Total	82.9375	15				

Effect Size for the Two-Way ANOVA

We can determine the size of an effect in the two-way ANOVA by using a "partial" eta squared defined as follows:

$$\text{partial } \eta^2 = \frac{SS_{\text{effect}}}{SS_{\text{effect}} + SS_{\text{error}}}$$

Simply substitute the appropriate "effect" in the formula for main effects and interactions. For the current situation, partial η^2 for A (*method*) is $10.563/(10.563 + 31.750) = .25$, partial η^2 for B (*sex*) is $18.063/(18.063 + 31.750) = .36$, and partial η^2 for the A $\times$ B interaction is $22.563/(22.563 + 31.750) = .42$.

More Advanced ANOVA Designs

This very brief introduction illustrated the simplest case of two-way ANOVA—a balanced factorial design with only two levels each of two independent variables. In this case, with only two levels for each factor, post hoc comparisons are not possible or necessary. With more levels, post hoc comparisons are not only possible but also often necessary. There are many other ANOVA designs, including those with more than two levels and more than two factors, within-subjects or repeated-measures designs (the subject of Chapter 9), and mixed designs with one or more within-subjects and one or more between-groups factors. Another advanced topic is the analysis of covariance (ANCOVA). These more advanced designs are beyond the scope of this basic text. There is value in simplicity. The more complex the experimental design, the more difficult it becomes to interpret effects and interactions.

THE BOTTOM LINE

- Two-way ANOVA allows the examination of main effects for two independent variables (factors) plus their interaction.
- Excel's Analysis ToolPak provides the "Anova: Two-Factor With Replication" tool for conducting a two-way ANOVA for a balanced factorial design.
- Partial eta-squared is an appropriate effect-size index for the two-way ANOVA.
- More complex ANOVA designs are beyond the scope of this introductory text.

Chapter 8 Exercises

1. Using the dataset from Table 2.1, conduct a one-way ANOVA comparing the mean 2001 salaries for the separate regions. Use an alpha level of .05. Build an ANOVA summary table. What is the value of eta squared? If the overall F ratio is significant, conduct a Fisher LSD test or a Tukey HSD test to determine which pairs of means are significantly different at an experimentwise alpha level of .05. *Hint*: you will find it helpful to use the Table feature of Excel 2007 to sort and filter the data by region in order to perform the ANOVA. What are your conclusions?

2. Using the same dataset, conduct a one-way ANOVA comparing the mean 2002 salaries for the separate regions. Use an alpha level of .05. Build an ANOVA summary table. What is the value of eta squared? If the overall F ratio is significant, conduct a Fisher LSD test or a Tukey HSD test to determine which pairs of means are significantly different at an experimentwise alpha level of .05. What are your conclusions?

3. A training manager was interested in the effectiveness of three different methods of sharing job-related information. He randomly assigned employees to three groups of eight employees each. One employee did not complete the training, and was excluded from the analysis. The dependent variable is a mastery score of knowledge of the course material. The results are as follows. Conduct a one-way ANOVA to determine if the methods are equally effective. Use an alpha level of .05. Build an ANOVA summary table. What is the value of eta squared? If the overall F ratio is significant, conduct a Fisher LSD test or a Tukey HSD test to determine which pairs of means are significantly different at an experimentwise alpha level of .05. What are your conclusions?

Method1	Method2	Method3
49	69	60
62	80	62
55	76	72
61	81	65
56	73	65
62	77	75
64	86	68
53	76	

4. Three randomly selected groups of 15 clients each participated in a one-month exercise program. Two groups also received instruction in diet. Weight loss for the three groups is recorded below (negative numbers indicate weight gain). Conduct a one-way ANOVA to determine if the approaches are equally effective. Use an alpha level of .05. Build an ANOVA summary table. What is the value of eta squared? If the overall F ratio is significant, conduct a Fisher LSD test or a Tukey HSD test to determine which pairs of means are significantly different at an experimentwise alpha level of .05. What are your conclusions?

LowCarb	LowFat	Exercise
6.8	4.7	-1.6
13.2	11.4	4.9
8.8	6.7	6.2
7.2	5.0	4.3
10.5	8.6	7.2
2.1	0.0	4.7
7.4	-1.5	8.2
13.6	11.8	-1.8
7.3	5.1	4.1
9.8	7.8	7.9
6.6	4.4	-1.5
7.1	4.9	7.3
13.7	11.9	-2.8
14.2	12.4	11.7
6.8	4.8	6.3

5. Given the following raw data, test the hypothesis of equal means. Use an alpha level of .05. Build an ANOVA summary table. What is the value of eta squared? If the overall F ratio is significant, conduct a Fisher LSD test or a Tukey HSD test to determine which pairs of means are significantly different at an experimentwise alpha level of .05. What are your conclusions?

Group1	Group2	Group3	Group4
1	0	0	1
2	0	1	1
3	1	1	2
4	1	2	2
4	3	2	2
5	3	2	2
5	3	2	3
6	3	2	3
7	4	2	3
7	5	3	3
7	6	3	4
9	7	4	4

6. An Australian study compared the pain thresholds of blondes and brunettes. Hair color was identified as light blonde, dark blonde, light brunette, and dark brunette. Each participant was given a pain threshold test (higher scores indicate a higher tolerance for pain). The data are as follows:

LtBlonde	DkBlonde	LtBrunette	DkBrunette
62	63	42	32
60	57	50	39
71	52	41	51
55	41	37	30
48	43		35

Test the hypothesis that the means of the pain threshold scores are equal. Use an alpha level of .05. Build an ANOVA summary table. What is the value of eta squared? If the overall F ratio is significant, conduct a Fisher LSD test or a Tukey HSD test to determine which pairs of means are significantly different at an experimentwise alpha level of .05. What are your conclusions?

7. The following data from *Consumer Reports* (June, 1986) report the calorie content of different kinds of hot dogs. There were 54 total hot dog brands, labeled as all beef, meat (mostly pork), and poultry (turkey or chicken). Test the hypothesis that the calorie content of the different varieties of hot dogs is equal. Use an alpha level of .05. Build an ANOVA summary table. What is the value of eta squared? If the overall F ratio is significant, conduct a Fisher LSD test or a Tukey HSD test to determine which pairs of means are significantly different at an experimentwise alpha level of .05. What are your conclusions?

Beef	Meat	Poultry
186	173	129
181	191	132
176	182	102
149	190	106
184	172	94
190	147	102
158	146	87
139	139	99
175	175	107
148	136	113
152	179	135
111	153	142
141	107	86
153	195	143
190	135	152
157	140	146
131	138	144
149		
135		
132		

8. The following hypothetical data represent the pain ratings of headache sufferers after receiving either a placebo or a pain reliever. There were 20 patients randomly assigned to one of the treatments. The dependent variable is a rating of experienced pain from 1 (*No Pain*) to 7 (*Severe Pain*). Perform and interpret a one-way ANOVA to test the hypothesis that there is no treatment effect. Use an alpha level of .05. Build an ANOVA summary table. What is the value of eta squared? If the overall F ratio is significant, conduct a Fisher LSD test or a Tukey HSD test to determine which pairs of means are significantly different at an experimentwise alpha level of .05. What are your conclusions?

Placebo	Drug1	Drug2	Drug3
7	3	5	3
6	4	5	2
4	3	6	3
6	3	7	2
7	5	5	4

9. The fleet manager of a delivery service randomly assigned 15 identical Honda Civics to three groups of five each. Each vehicle was tested at 55 MPH for 400 highway miles. Gasoline mileage was recorded in miles per gallon. The results were as follows:

BrandA	BrandB	BrandC
34.0	35.3	33.3
35.0	36.5	34.0
34.3	36.4	34.7
35.5	37.0	33.0
35.8	37.6	34.9

Conduct a one-way ANOVA comparing the mean mileage for the three brands. Use an alpha level of .05. Build an ANOVA summary table. What is the value of eta squared? If the overall F ratio is significant, conduct a Fisher LSD test or a Tukey HSD test to determine which pairs of means are significantly different at an experimentwise alpha level of .05. Assuming the gasoline brands are all priced the same, what brand of gasoline should the fleet manager purchase?

10. The fleet manager wants to purchase new compact cars, and finds the following information concerning overall (combined highway and city) gasoline mileage for subcompact cars from different manufacturers (source: http://www.consumerreports.org). Conduct a one-way ANOVA comparing the gasoline mileage of the cars from the five different manufacturers. Use an alpha level of .05. Build an ANOVA summary table. What is the value of eta squared? If the overall F ratio is significant, conduct a Fisher LSD test or a Tukey HSD test to determine which pairs of means are significantly different at an experimentwise alpha level of .05. Based on your analysis, which manufacturer(s) would you recommend if the goal is to achieve the highest average gasoline mileage?

Honda	Kia	Chevy	Hyundai	Toyota
28	25	24	27	32
37	28	25	27	33
31	28	28	28	34
32	30	27	30	
34				

11. You are interested in the effects of observing violence on subsequent aggressive behavior. You randomly assign 32 children to 4 groups and expose each group to a video showing a combination of type of violence (real-action versus cartoon violence) and duration (10 minutes or 30 minutes). After watching the video, the children play a video game that allows them to cooperate or to aggress against the computerized opponent. The data represent the number of times the student chooses to agress when given the opportunity. The data are as follows. Conduct and interpret a two-way ANOVA.

		Type of Violence	
		Cartoon	Real-Action
Time of Exposure	10 Min.	47	52
		56	62
		48	57
		51	49
		46	64
		44	39
		50	50
		51	48
	30 Min.	67	81
		69	92
		65	82
		62	92
		67	82
		69	94
		59	86
		72	83

9   Repeated-Measures ANOVA

The repeated-measures (or within-subjects) ANOVA is an extension of the paired-samples t test to three or more repeated observations of the same participants or cases. The Analysis ToolPak tool that correctly performs one-way repeated-measures ANOVA is rather awkwardly labeled "Anova: Two-Factor Without Replication." This is because the repeated-measures ANOVA is a special case of two-way ANOVA with only one observation per cell. The two factors are "subjects" (rows of cases or participants) and "treatments" (columns containing the repeated measures). The ANOVA: Two-Factor Without Replication tool produces a summary table in which the subject (row) variable is the within-subjects source of variance, and the columns (conditions) factor is the between-groups source of variance. As with the one-way ANOVA, the null hypothesis for the repeated-measures ANOVA is that the means of the repeated measures are all equal in the population, and the alternative hypothesis is that the difference between at least one pair of means is significantly different from zero.

In general, the repeated-measures ANOVA is more powerful statistically than the between-groups ANOVA because individual differences are allocated to systematic variance. The error term is thus reduced, and the resulting test is more sensitive. This increased power, however, often comes with a price tag. Research designs making use of repeated measures are sensitive to such subject variables as learning, order effects, practice, and fatigue, whereas these variables are more readily controlled in the between-groups designs by random assignment to conditions. Researchers often address such factors in repeated-measures designs through counterbalancing.

The variance partition in the repeated-measures ANOVA is as follows. We have n subjects or cases and k repeated measures, so $nk = N$, the total number of observations. The total sum of squares and the between-groups sum of squares are the same as in the one-way between-groups ANOVA:

$$SS_{tot} = \sum_{i=1}^{N}(X_i - \overline{\overline{X}})^2$$

$$SS_b = \sum_{j=1}^{k} n_j (\overline{X}_j - \overline{\overline{X}})^2$$

As we have worked these computations out with examples in the previous chapter, they are not repeated here. The within-groups variation is now divided into two parts, subjects and residual (or error). The subjects sum of squares is based on the squared deviations between the mean across the k conditions for each subject and the overall mean. We can calculate the subjects sum of squares as follows:

$$SS_{subj} = \sum_{i=1}^{n}(\overline{X}_i - \overline{\overline{X}})^2$$

The degrees of freedom for the subjects sum of squares are $n - 1$. The residual term is most easily calculated by subtraction:

$$SS_{res} = SS_{tot} - SS_b - SS_{subj}$$

The repeated-measures ANOVA assumes the data are interval or ratio in nature, the sample is randomly selected from a population of normally-distributed observations, the observations within the sample are independent, the population variances of the treatments or conditions are equal, and finally, that the population covariances for all pairs of treatments are equal (the sphericity assumption).

Example Data

Twelve college students participated in a "mental rotation" task. A stimulus figure was presented and then either the same or a different (mirror-image) figure was presented rotated at 45, 90, 135, 180, 225, 270, or 315 degrees. Participants determined whether the rotated figure was the same as or different from the stimulus figure. To control for order effects, the computer randomized the presentation of the rotated figures. The dependent variable was the number of correct identifications a student made from the three matching figures for each angle. The data are in Table 9.1.

Table 9.1 Example data for repeated-measures ANOVA

Student	ANG45	ANG90	ANG135	ANG180	ANG225	ANG270	ANG315
1	3	2	2	2	1	2	3
2	3	1	0	3	2	3	3
3	2	3	3	2	3	3	3
4	2	3	3	3	2	3	3
5	3	3	2	0	3	3	2
6	3	3	2	2	2	2	3
7	3	3	2	2	3	3	3
8	2	1	2	1	2	1	3
9	3	3	1	3	2	0	2
10	3	3	3	3	3	3	3
11	3	3	3	3	3	3	3
12	3	2	0	0	1	1	2

The properly configured data in Excel appear as follows (see Figure 9.1). When you use Excel for repeated measures, it is helpful to include a column for the case or participant number.

	A	B	C	D	E	F	G	H
1	Student	ANG45	ANG90	ANG135	ANG180	ANG225	ANG270	ANG315
2	1	3	2	2	2	1	2	3
3	2	3	1	0	3	2	3	3
4	3	2	3	3	2	3	3	3
5	4	2	3	3	3	2	3	3
6	5	3	3	2	0	3	3	2
7	6	3	3	2	2	2	2	3
8	7	3	3	2	2	3	3	3
9	8	2	1	2	1	2	1	3
10	9	3	3	1	3	2	0	2
11	10	3	3	3	3	3	3	3
12	11	3	3	3	3	3	3	3
13	12	3	2	0	0	1	1	2

Figure 9.1. Excel data for repeated-measures ANOVA

Repeated-measures ANOVA in the Analysis ToolPak

To conduct the repeated-measures ANOVA, use the "Anova: Two-Factor Without Replication tool" in the Analysis ToolPak, as shown in Figure 9.2. Include the row of data labels, make sure you check the box in front of "Labels," and be sure to include the column of student numbers in the input range. It is the "rows" variable. If you are not using labels, then you should omit the student numbers along with the row of data labels.

The output is placed by default in a new worksheet, or optionally in the same worksheet with the data. The output includes descriptive statistics for each row and column (Figure 9.3) and an ANOVA summary table. The summary table formatted and then copied and pasted from Excel is in Table 9.2.

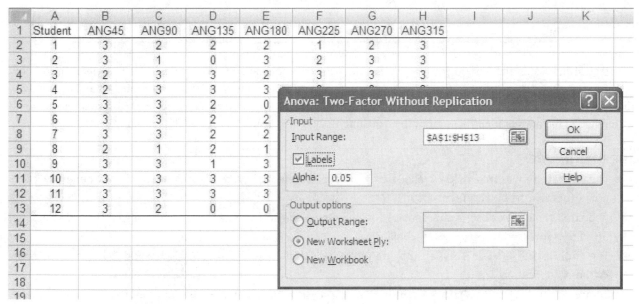

Figure 9.2. Using Excel for Repeated-measures ANOVA.

	A	B	C	D	E
1	Anova: Two-Factor Without Replication				
2					
3	SUMMARY	Count	Sum	Average	Variance
4	1	7	15	2.143	0.476
5	2	7	15	2.143	1.476
6	3	7	19	2.714	0.238
7	4	7	19	2.714	0.238
8	5	7	16	2.286	1.238
9	6	7	17	2.429	0.286
10	7	7	19	2.714	0.238
11	8	7	12	1.714	0.571
12	9	7	14	2.000	1.333
13	10	7	21	3.000	0.000
14	11	7	21	3.000	0.000
15	12	7	9	1.286	1.238
16					
17	ANG45	12	33	2.750	0.205
18	ANG90	12	30	2.500	0.636
19	ANG135	12	23	1.917	1.174
20	ANG180	12	24	2.000	1.273
21	ANG225	12	27	2.250	0.568
22	ANG270	12	27	2.250	1.114
23	ANG315	12	33	2.750	0.205

Figure 9.3 Descriptive statistics for columns and rows

Table 9.2 Summary output from repeated-measures ANOVA

ANOVA

Source of Variation	SS	df	MS	F	P-value	F crit
Rows	20.988	11	1.908	3.50	0.001	1.94
Columns	8.071	6	1.345	2.47	0.032	2.24
Error	35.929	66	0.544			
Total	64.988	83				

The test of interest is the F ratio for "Columns," the treatment comparison. It is typically of little interest to know whether the subjects or "Rows" F ratio is significant. This test is telling you what you probably already know— different individuals have differing levels of mental rotation skill. In summary, the angle of rotation makes a difference in the correct identification of the matching figures, $F(6,66) = 2.47$, $p = .032$, partial $\eta^2 = .18$.

THE BOTTOM LINE

- The repeated-measures ANOVA allocates individual differences to systematic error and is generally more powerful than the between-groups ANOVA.

- Repeated-measures designs are sensitive to learning, order effects, practice, and fatigue. These factors can often be addressed through counterbalancing.

- The tool in the Analysis ToolPak that performs repeated-measures ANOVA is labeled "Anova: Two-Factor Without Replication."

- To access this tool, select **Data > Analysis > Data Analysis > Anova: Two-Factor Without Replication**.

- The F ratio of interest is the "columns" or treatment comparison.

Multiple Comparisons in the Repeated-Measures ANOVA

As with the one-way ANOVA, Excel provides no follow-up or post hoc comparisons for the repeated-measures ANOVA. However, you can make a simple adjustment to the Fisher LSD or Tukey HSD tests introduced in the previous chapter and use the adjustment as the basis for multiple comparisons in the repeated-measures ANOVA.

The only minor adjustment for LSD or HSD with the repeated-measures ANOVA is that one uses MS_{error} and df_{error} rather than MS_w and df_w (Thorne & Giesen, 2003). Otherwise all calculations are identical to those shown earlier. Because there are repeated measures on the same individuals or cases, you will need only one value for LSD. We can easily find the two-tailed critical value of t for $\alpha = .05$ and 66 df by using the TINV function:

$$= \text{TINV}(.05, 66) = 1.9966$$

By use of the previous formula, we calculate $\text{LSD}_{.05}$ to be

$$\text{LSD} = t_\alpha \sqrt{\frac{2MS_{error}}{n}} = 1.9966\sqrt{\frac{2(0.5443)}{12}} = 0.601$$

Similarly, we can apply Tukey's HSD criterion:

$$\text{HSD} = q\sqrt{\frac{MS_{error}}{n}} = 4.15\sqrt{\frac{0.5443}{12}} = 0.88$$

The value of q was found by interpolation in Appendix C. As with the one-way ANOVA, you can report the post hoc comparisons with a table of mean differences using the LSD or the HSD test as follows (see Table 9.3). The LSD test produced significant comparisons for 45 degrees compared to 135 and 180 degrees, for 135 degrees compared to 315 degrees, and for 180 degrees compared to 315. None of the differences are significant by the HSD criterion, though the comparisons for 45 and 135 and 135 and 315 approach significance. Remember these tests are two-tailed, and the order of subtraction will change the sign of the mean difference, but the significance is the same.

Table 9.3 Post hoc comparisons for repeated-measures ANOVA (LSD test)

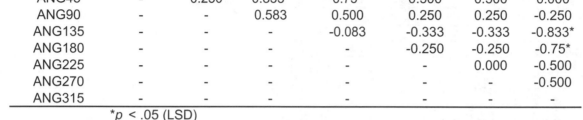

	ANG45	ANG90	ANG135	ANG180	ANG225	ANG270	ANG315
ANG45	-	0.250	0.833*	0.75*	0.500	0.500	0.000
ANG90	-	-	0.583	0.500	0.250	0.250	-0.250
ANG135	-	-	-	-0.083	-0.333	-0.333	-0.833*
ANG180	-	-	-	-	-0.250	-0.250	-0.75*
ANG225	-	-	-	-	-	0.000	-0.500
ANG270	-	-	-	-	-	-	-0.500
ANG315	-	-	-	-	-	-	-

*$p < .05$ (LSD)

A means plot assists in visual inspection of these differences (see Figure 9.4).

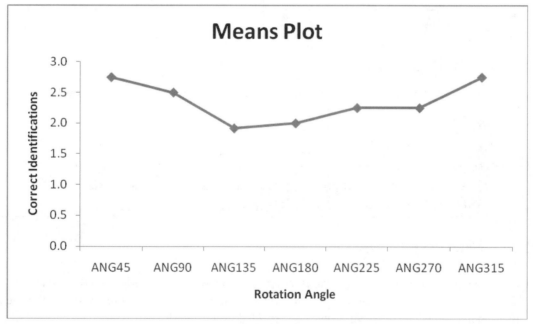

Figure 9.4 Means plot produced by Line Graph tool

The means plot makes it clear rotations closer to the original stimulus figure tended to produce a higher number of correct identifications, while more extreme rotations tended to produce a lower number of correct identifications.

A Worksheet Template for the Repeated-Measures ANOVA

For the repeated-measures ANOVA, a "partial eta squared" can be calculated by dividing $SS_{columns}$ by ($SS_{columns}$ + SS_{error}). In this case, partial $\eta^2 = 8.071/(8.071 + 35.929) = .18$. The generic worksheet template (Figure 9.5) conducts the ANOVA for up to ten repeated measures and calculates the value of partial eta squared as well as the LSD criterion for mean comparisons. Figure 9.5 shows the solution to the current problem in the worksheet template.

	A	B	C	D	E	F
1	Subjects	12				
2	Measures	7				
3						
4	ANOVA Summary Table					
5	Source	SS	df	MS	F	p(F)
6	Between groups	8.0714	6	1.3452	2.47	0.032
7	Subjects	20.9881	11	1.9080		
8	Error	35.9286	66	0.5444		
9	Total	64.9881	83	0.7830		
10	Partial η^2	0.1834				
11						
12	Statistics	Mean	Std. Dev.			
13	Measure1	2.7500	0.4523			
14	Measure2	2.5000	0.7977			
15	Measure3	1.9167	1.0836			
16	Measure4	2.0000	1.1282			
17	Measure5	2.2500	0.7538			
18	Measure6	2.2500	1.0553			
19	Measure7	2.7500	0.4523			
20	Measure8					
21	Measure9					
22	Measure10					
23						
24	LSD$_{.05}$	0.6014				

Figure 9.5 Solution to the current problem using the generic repeated-measures ANOVA template

THE BOTTOM LINE

- Excel provides no facility for post hoc comparisons in the repeated-measures ANOVA.
- LSD and HSD comparisons can be made by using MS_{error} and df_{error} rather than MS_w and df_w.
- Partial eta squared is an appropriate effect-size index for the repeated-measures ANOVA.
- Partial eta squared can be calculated as $SS_{columns} / (SS_{columns} + SS_{error})$.

Chapter 9 Exercises

1. The following scores represent job competency scores on a scale of 0 (*incompetent*) to 10 (*fully competent*) of 10 workers before a training program, immediately after the program, three months after the program, and six months after the program. Conduct a repeated-measures ANOVA with an alpha level of .05. If the overall F ratio for "columns" is significant, conduct a post hoc analysis using the modified Fisher LSD test or the modified Tukey HSD test. Did the training program appear to be effective?

Worker	Before	After	3Mo	6Mo
1	6	8	10	10
2	0	4	5	6
3	2	4	6	8
4	6	7	9	9
5	6	5	6	8
6	3	4	8	7
7	6	9	10	9
8	0	2	3	4
9	1	2	6	6
10	0	1	3	5

2. The following data represent the ratings of six different products by four different judges. Do the judges rate the products similarly? In this case, an insignificant "columns" F ratio would indicate agreement among the judges. Conduct a repeated-measures ANOVA using an alpha level of .05. If the overall F ratio for "columns" is significant, conduct a post hoc analysis using the modified Fisher LSD test or the modified Tukey HSD test. What do you conclude?

Product	Judge1	Judge2	Judge3	Judge4
1	2	4	3	3
2	5	7	5	6
3	1	3	1	2
4	7	9	9	8
5	2	4	6	1
6	6	8	8	4

3. Nine patients experiencing depression participated in a telephonic wellness coaching program. Each participant received a call from the same wellness coach every other week, thus participating in six sessions over a period of 12 weeks. At the end of each coaching session, the participant answered a series of 9 questions regarding the frequency over the past two weeks of various symptoms of depression. Scores for each question ranged from 0 (*not at all*) to 3 (*nearly every day*). Scores could range from 0 (*symptom free*) to 27 (*all symptoms present nearly every day*). The hypothetical results are as follows. Conduct a repeated-measures ANOVA using an alpha level of .05. If the overall F ratio for "columns" is significant, conduct a post hoc analysis using the modified Fisher LSD test or the modified Tukey HSD test. What do you conclude?

Participant	Session1	Session2	Session3	Session4	Session5	Session6
1	15	15	14	12	9	6
2	15	17	17	11	16	10
3	23	21	21	19	17	17
4	22	19	18	16	14	11
5	18	19	12	12	11	11
6	17	13	14	13	13	13
7	16	12	12	9	8	9
8	19	16	15	13	12	12
9	20	18	15	14	12	11

4. The following data represent seven customers' satisfaction levels from 1 (*very dissatisfied*) to 5 (*very satisfied*) for four consecutive visits to a restaurant. Conduct a repeated-measures ANOVA using an alpha level of .05. If the overall F ratio for "columns" is significant, conduct a post hoc analysis using the modified Fisher LSD test or the modified Tukey HSD test. What do you conclude?

Person	Time1	Time2	Time3	Time4
1	3	3	5	5
2	1	4	3	4
3	1	2	4	5
4	2	3	3	3
5	3	4	5	5
6	3	3	3	4
7	2	5	3	5

5. Nine clients participated in a group therapy session for three weeks, meeting once each week. With the client's permission, the therapist videotaped the session and then reviewed the tape to determine how many positive affirmations about him or herself the client made during the session. The results are as follows. Conduct a repeated-measures ANOVA using an alpha level of .05. If the overall F ratio for "columns" is significant, conduct a post hoc analysis using the modified Fisher LSD test or the modified Tukey HSD test. What do you conclude?

Client	Week1	Week2	Week3
1	6	7	8
2	2	6	6
3	13	15	15
4	12	16	17
5	4	8	12
6	10	12	15
7	10	15	13
8	2	6	7
9	14	12	14

6. Ten patients took four different treatments designed to lower cholesterol levels. The order of the four treatments was randomized for each patient, and each patient took the treatment daily for a month. At the end of each month, researchers recorded the patient's total serum cholesterol. The data are as follows. Conduct a repeated-measures ANOVA using an alpha level of .05. If the overall F ratio for "columns" is significant, conduct a post hoc analysis using the modified Fisher LSD test or the modified Tukey HSD test. What do you conclude?

ID	Treat1	Treat2	Treat3	Treat4
1	180	205	160	205
2	230	250	190	240
3	280	310	220	275
4	180	220	160	200
5	190	210	170	210
6	140	180	120	150
7	260	280	200	270
8	120	135	125	150
9	190	210	160	200
10	230	250	190	225

7. J.D. Power and Associates reported the following data concerning the North American Guest Satisfaction Index for eight midscale full-service hotel chains for the years 2004 – 2006. Is hotel quality improving? Conduct a repeated-measures ANOVA using an alpha level of .05. If the overall F ratio for "columns" is significant, conduct a post hoc analysis using the modified Fisher LSD test or the modified Tukey HSD test. What do you conclude?

Chain	2004	2005	2006
1	779	807	804
2	722	721	746
3	714	689	722
4	769	782	791
5	733	720	750
6	686	678	685
7	704	713	732
8	672	696	712

8. The following data represent customer quality ratings on a scale of 1 (*poor*) to 5 (*excellent*) for seven properties of a national hotel chain in a given city. The ratings are collected every month. Conduct a repeated-measures ANOVA with an alpha level of .05. If the overall F ratio for "columns" is significant, conduct a post hoc analysis using the modified Fisher LSD test or the modified Tukey HSD test. Is quality improving?

Location	Mo1	Mo2	Mo3	Mo4
1	3	3	5	5
2	1	4	3	4
3	1	2	4	5
4	2	3	3	3
5	3	4	5	5
6	3	3	3	4
7	2	5	3	5

9. The following data represent repeated measures on an Attitude Toward Statistics scale before, after, and six months after a statistics course. Higher numbers indicate more positive attitudes. Conduct a repeated-measures ANOVA using an alpha level of .05. If the overall F ratio for "columns" is significant, conduct a post hoc analysis using the modified Fisher LSD test or the modified Tukey HSD test. What do you conclude?

Student	Time1	Time2	Time3
1	84	88	90
2	45	54	60
3	32	43	44
4	48	42	50
5	53	51	50
6	64	73	80
7	45	58	65
8	74	79	83
9	68	72	73
10	54	52	60

10   Correlation and Regression

In this chapter, we will consider only the bivariate (two variables) case of correlation and regression. Let us return to our example from Chapter 3, where we looked at the relationship between study hours and grades. In correlation, we have a *predictor* or independent variable, X, and a *criterion* or dependent variable, Y. We are using study hours (X) to predict grade point average (Y), so the number of study hours for a given student is the predictor, and the student's GPA is the criterion. We are interested in determining whether these variables are related in a linear fashion. If these two variables have a positive relationship, students who study more will have higher grades, and those who study less will have lower grades. If the relationship is negative, students who study more will have lower grades (unlikely in this particular case). It is also possible that the variables have no relationship at all, so study hours and grades are independent of one another. We are not examining the cause and effect relationship between study hours and grades, but only their potential linear relationship. Before discussing how to do correlation and regression analyses in Excel, let us begin by defining covariance and correlation.

Covariance

You learned in Chapter 2 that the population variance is the average squared deviation for a single variable. The covariance in the population is the average cross-product of the paired deviation scores on X and Y for each observation. The population covariance is an index indicating the degree (if any) to which the two variables X and Y are related to each other in a linear fashion:

$$\sigma_{XY} = \frac{\sum_{i=1}^{N}(X_i - \mu_X)(Y_i - \mu_Y)}{N}$$

We calculate the covariance from the cross-products of deviation scores for the two variables, and every value for each variable contributes in a pairwise fashion to the covariance. When we do not know the population parameters, we use the corresponding sample statistics for an estimate of the population parameter:

$$\text{Cov}(X,Y) = \frac{\sum_{i=1}^{n}(X_i - \bar{X})(Y_i - \bar{Y})}{n-1}$$

For the sample covariance, we will use the term $\text{Cov}(X, Y)$ rather than s_{XY} to avoid any possible confusion with the standard deviation. We add the cross products of deviation scores, and then divide the total by N, the number of pairs in the population, or by $n - 1$ for an estimate of the population covariance using sample data. As you learned in Chapter 2, Excel's built-in statistical tools are usually based on the assumption we are using sample data to estimate population parameters. Excel's COVAR function is an exception. It uses the formula for the population covariance, and thus to calculate the sample covariance, you must multiply the result of the Excel function by $n / (n - 1)$ in order to arrive at the correct answer. See Appendix A for the Excel formulas.

The value of the covariance can be zero, positive, or negative. The sign of the covariance tells us whether the relationship is positive or negative. The magnitude of the covariance tells us how "big" the relationship is. However, the units of measurement of the two variables also affect the value of the covariance, making it difficult to determine the relative strength of the relationship. An additional example may help you understand both the concept of covariance and the inherent difficulty in interpreting its value. It is easy to observe that people's weights and heights tend to "go together." Though there are obvious exceptions, tall people are generally heavier than short people are. We would therefore expect the covariance of height and weight to be positive. Look at the following roster for the University of Georgia men's varsity basketball team from 2006 (Table 10.1). Height is measured in inches and weight is measured in pounds, and it appears at first glance that taller players are indeed heavier than shorter players are. To examine this relationship more closely, we can calculate the values of the deviation scores for both variables and cross-multiply them, as the formula for covariance requires. We then calculate the covariance from the formula shown above by dividing the sum of the cross products by $n - 1$. The descriptive statistics including the variances for both variables are also in Table 10.1. Note the covariance is positive, as we expected. But what does the value 103.59 mean? We can compare this value to the variances for height and weight to get some sense of "how big" the covariance is. Obviously, we need a better, more standardized, way to interpret the linear relationship between height and weight than the covariance, because we could just as easily measure weight in kilograms and height in meters, and if we did, we would get a completely different value for the covariance.

Table 10.1 Covariance of height and weight is positive

Player	Height	Weight	HeightDev	WeightDev	Cross-Product
1	71	182	-5.86	-27.36	160.23
2	80	240	3.14	30.64	96.31
3	73	179	-3.86	-30.36	117.09
4	73	184	-3.86	-25.36	97.81
5	72	170	-4.86	-39.36	191.16
6	77	178	0.14	-31.36	-4.48
7	76	202	-0.86	-7.36	6.31
8	75	195	-1.86	-14.36	26.66
9	76	194	-0.86	-15.36	13.16
10	79	221	2.14	11.64	24.95
11	81	247	4.14	37.64	155.95
12	83	265	6.14	55.64	341.81
13	81	210	4.14	0.64	2.66
14	79	264	2.14	54.64	117.09

	Height		Weight	
Mean	76.86	Mean		209.36
Standard Error	1.00	Standard Error		8.74
Median	76.5	Median		198.5
Mode	73	Mode		#N/A
Standard Deviation	3.76	Standard Deviation		32.72
Sample Variance	14.13	Sample Variance		1070.40
Kurtosis	-1.18	Kurtosis		-0.99
Skewness	-0.02	Skewness		0.65
Range	12	Range		95
Minimum	71	Minimum		170
Maximum	83	Maximum		265
Sum	1076	Sum		2931
Count	14	Count		14
Confidence Level(95.0%)	2.17	Confidence Level(95.0%)		18.89

Sum of Cross-Products	1346.71
Covariance	103.59

The Correlation Coefficient and the Coefficient of Determination

When we divide the covariance by the product of the two variables' standard deviations, we achieve a "scaleless" index ranging from −1 (perfect negative relationship) through 0 (no relationship) to +1 (perfect positive relationship). Unlike the covariance, this index is not affected by the units of measurement of X or Y, and any linear transformation of either variable will not affect its value. This index is the Pearson product-moment correlation, named after its creator, Karl Pearson. In the population:

$$\rho_{XY} = \frac{\sigma_{XY}}{\sigma_X \sigma_Y}$$

where ρ (lower case Greek rho) represents the population correlation. In a sample:

$$r_{XY} = \frac{\text{Cov}(X,Y)}{s_X s_Y}$$

From our previous example, we can find the value of the correlation between height and weight for the basketball players to be

$$r_{XY} = \frac{\text{Cov}(X,Y)}{s_X s_Y} = \frac{103.59}{(3.76)(32.72)} = .842$$

We are using the conceptual definition, but would rarely calculate a correlation coefficient this way. However, this approach helps us to understand what the term really means. Now, if we were to transform the weight measurements into kilograms or the heights into metric units, we would still have the same correlation because the units of measurement do not affect the value of the correlation as long as any transformations are linear. The correlation coefficient is standardized in the same way a z score is standardized. In fact, we can calculate a correlation coefficient by cross-multiplying and averaging the z scores for X and Y, and we will get the same value as we did from the previous equation. We divide by $n - 1$ because we are using the sample standard deviation with the $n - 1$ correction to calculate the z scores.

$$r_{XY} = \frac{\sum_{i=1}^{n} z_X z_Y}{n-1}$$

Once we have determined the value of the correlation coefficient, we can test its significance by a t test (or an equivalent analysis of variance). This test tells us how likely we would be to find a sample correlation as large as (in absolute value) or larger than the observed sample correlation if the correlation in the population is zero. We evaluate the following value of t at $n - 2$ degrees of freedom, where n is the number of pairs of observations.

$$t_{(n-2)} = r_{XY}\left(\sqrt{\frac{n-2}{1-r_{XY}^2}}\right)$$

The connection between the t distribution and the correlation coefficient is not accidental, and we will address this connection later in the chapter. In our current case, let us find the value of t and test its significance with the TDIST function.

$$t_{(n-2)} = r_{XY}\left(\sqrt{\frac{n-2}{1-r_{XY}^2}}\right) = .842\left(\sqrt{\frac{14-2}{1-.842^2}}\right) = 5.41$$

We determine the two-tailed significance of this value of t with 12 degrees of freedom:

$$= \text{TDIST}(5.41, 12, 2)$$

and the probability is $p < .001$ of observing a value of t this large or larger in absolute value if the population correlation coefficient is zero.

Although the correlation coefficient has the desirable property of ranging between -1 and $+1$ and is unaffected by linear transformations of either or both of the variables, it is still somewhat difficult to interpret. The sign of the correlation tells us whether the correlation is positive or negative, and the magnitude of the correlation indicates the strength of the linear relationship. However, the units are not on a ratio scale. We cannot say that a correlation of .50 represents twice as much relationship as a correlation of .25. A term much easier to interpret is the square of the correlation coefficient, r_{XY}^2. We can interpret this value directly as the proportion of the variation in the criterion variable, Y, that overlaps with the predictor variable, X. This value is called the "coefficient of determination," and corresponds to the value eta squared you learned earlier, as you will soon see. In our current example, almost 71% of the variation in weight can be explained by knowing the player's height.

As the above discussion implies, correlations can be positive or negative. You learned in Chapter 3 how to create a scatterplot to show the relationship between pairs of observations on two variables. If the relationship is a perfect positive correlation, all the points will fall on a straight line, and the line would tilt upward from left to right (positive slope). If the relationship is a perfect negative correlation, all the points will fall on a straight line, and the line would tilt downward from left to right (negative slope). If the relationship is not perfect, the points will not fall on a straight line, but we may still find that a line provides a good model to describe the general relationship even though it is imperfect. When there is close to a zero relationship, a line drawn through all the points would be flat, and would have close to zero slope.

We will now turn to the equation for the line of best fit that shows the linear relationship between X and Y.

The Regression Equation

In addition to calculating and testing the significance of a correlation, we are also often interested in examining the regression equation

$$\hat{Y} = b_0 + b_1 X$$

This equation shows us the formula for a line of "best fit" between the observed values of X and Y. For the regression equation, let us define the slope (regression coefficient), b_1, as

$$b_1 = r_{XY} \left(\frac{s_Y}{s_X} \right)$$

and the Y-intercept term, b_0, as

$$b_0 = \bar{Y} - b_1 \bar{X}$$

Excel has several useful built-in functions for correlation and regression. Simply to find the Pearson product-moment correlation between the two variables, we can use the built-in function CORREL(Array1,Array2) where Array1 and Array2 are the ranges for the X and Y variables. The regression coefficient (slope) for a bivariate correlation can be found by the function SLOPE(Array Y, Array X) where Array Y is the range of observed Y values and Array X is the range of observed X values. The intercept term can be found by use of the function INTERCEPT(Array Y, Array X) where the two arrays are defined as above. To determine a predicted value of Y for a given value of X, you can enter the function FORECAST(X, Array$Y$, Array$X$) and replace X with the value for which you want to predict the value of Y.

The Analysis ToolPak's Regression tool automates the calculation of the correlation, regression, and intercept coefficients. The tool also performs an analysis of variance of the significance of the regression and an equivalent t test of the slope coefficient. In addition to the simple correlation and regression analyses explored in this chapter, you can also use the Regression tool to conduct multiple regression analyses in which there are two or more predictor variables.

Example Data

Table 10.2 shows the data used in Chapter 3 to illustrate the scatterplot. You saw earlier (Figure 3.10) that the relationship was positive, indicating higher study hours were associated with higher grades. Using this example, you will learn the built-in functions for correlation, slope, intercept, and prediction. Then you will learn to perform a complete regression analysis of these example data using the Analysis ToolPak.

Table 10.2 Study hours and GPA for 20 students

Student	Hours	GPA	Student	Hours	GPA
1	10	3.33	11	13	3.26
2	12	2.92	12	12	3.00
3	10	2.56	13	11	2.74
4	15	3.08	14	10	2.85
5	14	3.57	15	13	3.33
6	12	3.31	16	13	3.29
7	13	3.45	17	14	3.58
8	15	3.93	18	18	3.85
9	16	3.82	19	17	4.00
10	14	3.70	20	14	3.50

When building your worksheet, place the data in an Excel workbook as shown in Figure 10.1. Although student numbers are not required, it is always good form to include a record number in case you want to sort or filter the data and then later return the data to their original sequence. Recall that we found a strong but not perfect relationship between the two variables, as the scatterplot shows (Figure 10.1). The figure also shows the equation for the line of best fit. Excel reports the "algebra" version of the equation, $\hat{Y} = mX + b$, but it is entirely equivalent to the statistical version, $\hat{Y} = b_0 + b_1 X$. Let us see how to use Excel functions to find the correlation, the slope, and the intercept, as well as to predict or forecast Y values.

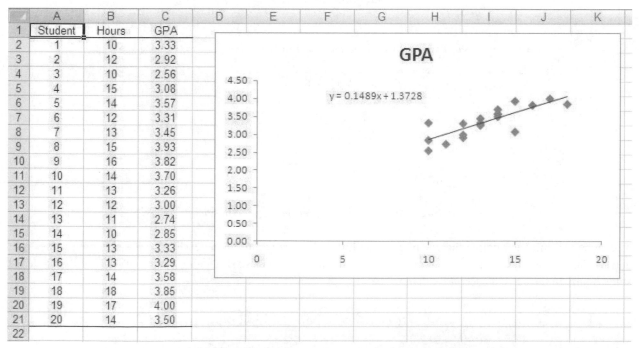

Figure 10.1 Excel data for regression analysis and resulting scatterplot

Correlation, Slope, Intercept, and Forecasting

For convenience, let us name the hours and GPA variable ranges. If you need a refresher, named ranges are discussed in Chapter 1. These named ranges make Excel formulas and functions easier to understand and easier to explain to others. Figure 10.2 displays the Formula View of the use of the functions for the correlation, intercept, and slope terms. Next, examine the Value View to show the results (Figure 10.3). The order of the variables does not affect the value of the correlation coefficient, but it does affect the values of the slope and intercept, as discussed below. You are "regressing" the criterion *Y* (GPA) onto the predictor *X* (study hours). Notice the CORREL, SLOPE, and INTERCEPT terms are reported by their respective functions, but there is no test for statistical significance.

Enter the CORREL function by going to the blank cell where you want the result to display, and then type

= CORREL(Array1, Array2)

If you have named the ranges, then just type the names of the ranges in your formula. For the CORREL function, it is immaterial whether you place the *X* array first or the *Y* array first, because $r_{XY} = r_{YX}$. Use the same approach for the slope and intercept. However, it is important you get the arrays in the right order for the SLOPE and INTERCEPT functions. For these functions, the *Y* array must come before the *X* array. If you accidentally enter the *X* array first, it will be treated as the criterion variable, and you will be regressing *X* onto *Y*, which although possible mathematically, is not what you want to do in this case.

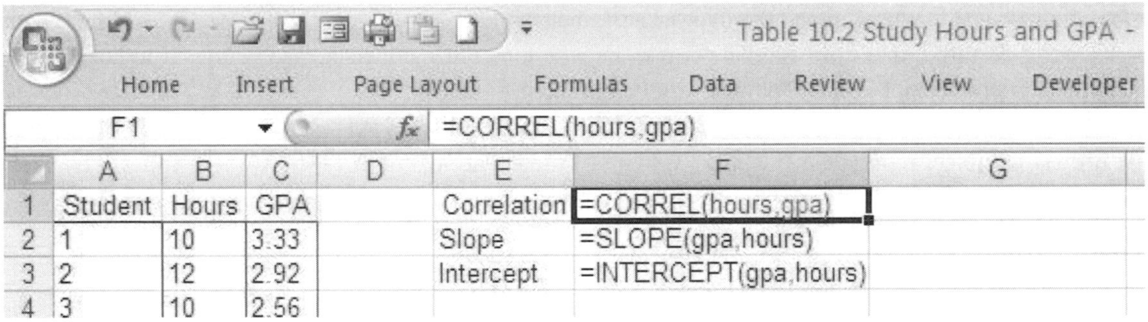

Figure 10.2 Using Excel functions for correlation, slope, and intercept terms (Formula View)

	A	B	C	D	E	F	G
1	Student	Hours	GPA		Correlation	0.817	
2	1	10	3.33		Slope	0.149	
3	2	12	2.92		Intercept	1.373	
4	3	10	2.56				
5	4	15	3.08				

Figure 10.3 Correlation, slope, and intercept (Value View)

The slope and intercept define the equation of the line of best fit we discussed earlier for the observed values of *Y* and *X*. This is the linear regression equation for predicting a student's GPA based on knowledge of the student's study hours. In the current case, the equation is:

$$\hat{Y} = b_0 + b_1X = 1.373 + 0.149 \times \text{hours}$$

Assuming the regression coefficient is statistically significant, we can use this equation to predict a GPA for any value of study hours, even values not observed in the sample. For example, to predict the GPA of a student who studies 8 hours per week, applying the regression equation would produce the following result:

$$\hat{Y} = 1.373 + 0.149 \times 8 = 2.56$$

Excel has a built-in function called FORECAST that can instantly produce this value, and the predicted value for any particular value of X. To use this function, supply the desired value of X, and the "known" or observed ranges of X and Y as shown in Figure 10.4. Examine in Figure 10.4 the FORECAST function displayed in the Formula Bar. We return briefly to forecasting at the end of this chapter. But first, you will learn more about using the Regression tool for regression analyses in Excel.

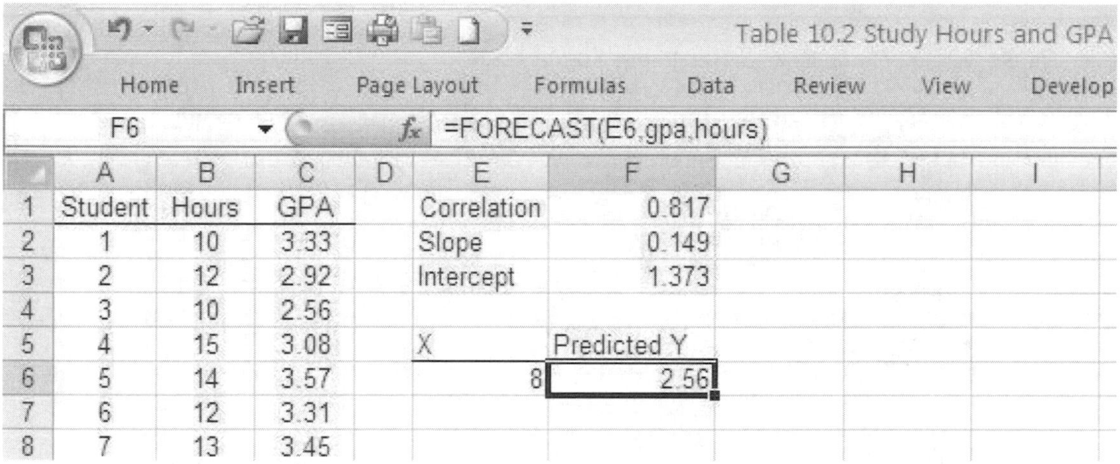

	A	B	C	D	E	F
1	Student	Hours	GPA		Correlation	0.817
2	1	10	3.33		Slope	0.149
3	2	12	2.92		Intercept	1.373
4	3	10	2.56			
5	4	15	3.08		X	Predicted Y
6	5	14	3.57		8	2.56
7	6	12	3.31			
8	7	13	3.45			

Figure 10.4 Using the FORECAST function

THE BOTTOM LINE

- The correlation between two variables can be found by use of the CORREL function, = CORREL(Array1, Array2) where Array1 and Array2 are the *X* and *Y* variables. The order of entry of *X* and *Y* is immaterial with correlation. The significance of the correlation coefficient is not tested.
- The slope of the line of best fit is found by use of the SLOPE function = SLOPE(ArrayY, ArrayX) where *Y* is the criterion variable and *X* is the predictor. The order of entry of the arrays is important for the correct slope to display.
- The *Y*-intercept is found by use of the INTERCEPT function, = INTERCEPT(ArrayY, ArrayX). The order of entry is important for the correct intercept to display.
- The FORECAST function can be used to predict a value of *Y* for any value of *X* by use of the linear regression equation.

Regression Analysis in the Analysis ToolPak

The Regression tool in the Analysis ToolPak reports the correlation coefficient, the slope, and the intercept, and performs a significance test on the overall regression, along with an equivalent test of the significance of the regression (slope) coefficient. The same tool is used for multiple regression with two or more predictors and a single criterion. Therefore, the absolute value of r_{XY} will be called "Multiple R." This value will always be zero or positive, but if the original correlation r_{XY} is negative, the slope term will be negative. To perform a regression analysis, select **Data** > **Analysis** > **Data Analysis** > **Regression** (see Figure 10.5).

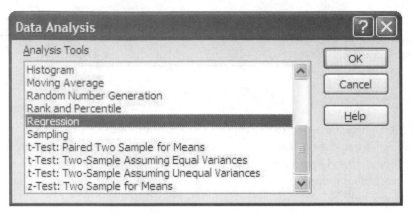

Figure 10.5 Selecting the Regression tool

Click **OK**. The Regression dialog appears (see Figure 10.6).

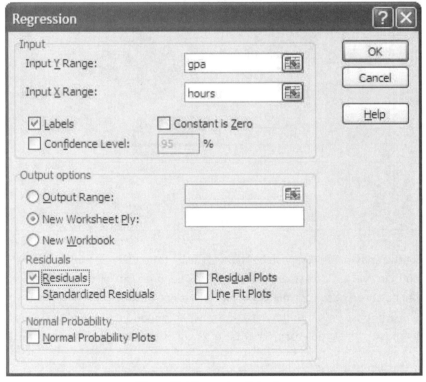

Figure 10.6 Regression dialog box

Enter the range of cell references or the named range for the *Y* variable (GPA) including the column heading. You can drag through the range, or type in the cell references. Enter the range for the *X* variable in the same way. Check the box to indicate the columns have labels in the first row. In this case, we have also asked for residuals and accepted the default to place the output in a new worksheet (see Figure 10.6). Click **OK** to run the analysis. The Regression tool output is in Table 10.3.

Table 10.3 Regression tool output

SUMMARY OUTPUT

Regression Statistics	
Multiple R	0.817
R Square	0.668
Adjusted R Square	0.650
Standard Error	0.240
Observations	20

ANOVA

	df	SS	MS	F	Significance F
Regression	1	2.089	2.089	36.261	0.000
Residual	18	1.037	0.058		
Total	19	3.126			

	Coefficients	Standard Error	t Stat	P-value	Lower 95%	Upper 95%
Intercept	1.373	0.333	4.119	0.001	0.673	2.073
Hours	0.149	0.025	6.022	0.000	0.097	0.201

The value "Multiple R" is the correlation between Y and $\hat{Y}$ (and the absolute value of the Pearson product-moment correlation between GPA and study hours we found earlier). In the two-variable case, the F test of the significance of the linear regression is mathematically and statistically identical to the t test of the significance of the regression coefficient for study hours. The square root of the F ratio, 36.26, equals the value of t, 6.02. The statistically significant regression indicates we can use study hours to predict GPA, and R^2 indicates that roughly 67 percent of the variation in grades can be explained by knowing a student's study hours. We can also calculate R^2 by dividing the $SS_{regression}$ by SS_{total}. As discussed earlier, this is equivalent to eta squared in ANOVA terms. The value labeled "standard error" is the standard error of estimate, a measure of the accuracy of predictions using the linear regression equation. For our example data, we calculate the standard error of estimate as:

$$S_{est} = \sqrt{\frac{\sum(Y-\hat{Y})^2}{n-2}} = \sqrt{\frac{SS_{residual}}{df_{residual}}} = \sqrt{MS_{residual}} = 0.240$$

Adjusted R-square is the estimate of the population R^2, taking into account both the sample size and the number of predictors. Though the calculated R^2 can never be negative, the adjusted value can be, when the sample value is very close to zero, or when the number of predictors is large relative to the number of observations.

We can determine the regression equation $\hat{Y} = b_0 + b_1 X$ from the output from the Regression tool output to be $\hat{Y} = 1.373 + 0.149 \times hours$, as discussed previously (see Table 10.3). A "residual" is the predicted value of Y subtracted from the observed value. Examination of residuals can be quite instructive, but is beyond our present scope. The optional residual output (see Table 10.4) appears below the summary output.

Table 10.4 Optional residual output from the Regression tool

RESIDUAL OUTPUT

Observation	Predicted GPA	Residuals
1	2.862	0.468
2	3.160	-0.240
3	2.862	-0.302
4	3.607	-0.527
5	3.458	0.112
6	3.160	0.150
7	3.309	0.141
8	3.607	0.323
9	3.756	0.064
10	3.458	0.242
11	3.309	-0.049
12	3.160	-0.160
13	3.011	-0.271
14	2.862	-0.012
15	3.309	0.021
16	3.309	-0.019
17	3.458	0.122
18	4.053	-0.203
19	3.905	0.095
20	3.458	0.042

THE BOTTOM LINE

- The Regression tool in the Analysis ToolPak performs a complete regression analysis for one criterion and one or more predictors.
- To access this tool, select **Data** > **Analysis** > **Data Analysis** > **Regression**.
- The Regression tool conducts an analysis of variance of the overall regression and calculates various summary statistics.
- This tool calculates the slope and intercept terms, and tests the significance of these terms.
- The Regression tool optionally produces residuals and residual plots.

A Brief Introduction to Time Series and Forecasting

Now that you know how to use the Regression tool, let us revisit forecasting and briefly discuss time series data. In many cases, we are interested in the changes in a dependent or criterion variable over time. Measures of a variable taken at regular intervals over time are a ***time series*** (Moore, McCabe, Duckworth, & Sclove, 2003). In such cases the predictor or X variable is successive periods of time, or more often an index variable based on these periods. An example of a time series is the annual fall enrollment for a college or university. Another example is a bank's monthly deposits for a period of several years. An analysis of time series data can aid in understanding the current situation as well as help us make informed predictions (or forecasts) about the future state of affairs.

A time series can have four different components (Lind, Marchal, & Wathen, 2007). These are the *trend*, the *cyclical variation*, the *seasonal variation*, and *irregular* variation. This book only considers the trend and irregular variation. In the simple examples below, we will allocate irregular variation to error, and the trend will be found either to be linear or curvilinear. When the relationship between time and changes in the dependent variable plots a line or something resembling a straight line, then we can use linear regression and forecasting to model the relationship and to predict future values of the dependent variable. In other cases, the relationship may not be linear, but it might still be monotonic decreasing or increasing in a curvilinear fashion.

There are only two simple cases in this book, but interested readers can consult an econometrics text for other extensions to the regression model for dealing with violations of the classical assumptions of regression as well as for coverage of more sophisticated regression-based models. The common problems to be dealt with in regression generally and time series analysis in particular are autocorrelation (or serial correlation), multicollinearity, and heteroscedasticity. A good basic econometrics text such as Studenmund (2006) discusses these problems and methods for dealing with them. Two examples are discussed below, one for which a linear model appears to be appropriate, one in which an exponential model appears more effective. Advanced techniques provide "smoothing" and "deseasonalizing" methods for dealing with time series data with regular seasonal or cyclical patterns. If a straight line fits the observed or transformed data well, one may use linear forecasting, a direct extension of regression to time series data. If a curved line fits the data well, it is often possible to use models that take the curvature of the line into account via data transformations.

Linear Trend

The trend (sometimes called the *secular trend*) is the smooth long-term direction of a time series. Consider for example the following data (See Table 10.5), which show the per capita personal income of South Carolina residents from the years 1990 to 2006 (source: Bureau of Economic Analysis).

Table 10.5 South Carolina per capita income, 1990 – 2006

Year	Index	Income
1990	1	15894
1991	2	16241
1992	3	16953
1993	4	17531
1994	5	18365
1995	6	19124
1996	7	20058
1997	8	20987
1998	9	22161
1999	10	23075
2000	11	24423
2001	12	24974
2002	13	25348
2003	14	25852
2004	15	27039
2005	16	28460
2006	17	29767

A time series plot of these data (see Figure 10.7) shows a relatively smooth and steady increase in personal income over the years, and a linear model would appear to be appropriate for describing the trend. We can fit a line to the observed data points using linear regression. By formatting the data with a trend line using the Scatterplot tool discussed in Chapter 3, we can also display the equation for the line of best fit and the value of r^2 on the scatterplot (see Figure 10.7).

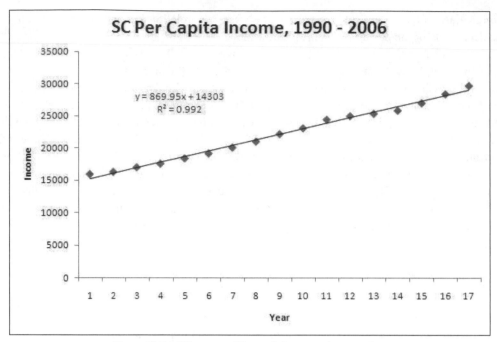

Figure 10.7 Adding a trend line and the regression equation

To test the significance of the regression, we will use the Regression tool. The output is in Table 10.6.

Table 10.6 Regression analysis of income data (after cell formatting)

SUMMARY OUTPUT

Regression Statistics	
Multiple R	0.996
R Square	0.992
Adjusted R Square	0.991
Standard Error	407.754
Observations	17

ANOVA

	df	SS	MS	F	Significance F
Regression	1	308776921.19	308776921.19	1857.16	0.000
Residual	15	2493945.05	166263.00		
Total	16	311270866.24			

	Coefficients	Standard Error	t Stat	P-value	Lower 95%	Upper 95%
Intercept	14302.96	206.85	69.15	0.00	13862.06	14743.85
Index	869.95	20.19	43.09	0.00	826.92	912.97

After verifying that the regression is significant, you can now use the slope and intercept terms to predict the per capita incomes for subsequent years. This is simplified by Excel's built-in FORECAST function discussed earlier (See Table 10.7).

Table 10.7 Forecasts for 2007–2010

Year	Index	Forecast
2007	18	29961.99
2008	19	30831.93
2009	20	31701.88
2010	21	32571.82

Nonlinear Trend

Consider the following hypothetical annual sales data (in thousands of dollars) for a growing business over the years 1995–2009 (Table 10.8).

Table 10.8 Hypothetical sales figures for a growing business

Index	Year	Sales	LogSales
1	1995	124.2	2.09412
2	1996	175.6	2.24452
3	1997	306.9	2.48700
4	1998	524.2	2.71950
5	1999	714.0	2.85370
6	2000	1052.0	3.02202
7	2001	1638.3	3.21439
8	2002	2463.2	3.39150
9	2003	3358.2	3.52611
10	2004	4181.3	3.62131
11	2005	5388.5	3.73147
12	2006	8027.4	3.90457
13	2007	10587.2	4.02478
14	2008	13537.4	4.13154
15	2009	17515.6	4.24343

Examination of the time series (Figure 10.8) indicates that a straight line would be a poor fit to these data. However, a smooth curved line would appear to fit the data well. Such data can easily be accommodated in a trend analysis by the use of a logarithmic transformation. We simply find the base 10 logarithm of each year's data and then use the logarithms as the dependent variable and the year (or the coded index number) as the independent variable. To transform a variable to a base 10 logarithm, use the following Excel function:

$$= LOG10(Y)$$

substituting the raw sales values for Y. Now, we can use a linear regression equation to determine the model fit.

Figure 10.8 The data appear to be curvilinear

To simplify our calculations, we will use the index variable 1 to 15 rather than the year for the X variable in the regression analysis, though the results would be equivalent if we used the actual year. Figure 10.9 shows the linear relationship between the transformed sales data and the index year. Clearly, the transformation produced a very nearly perfect linear relationship.

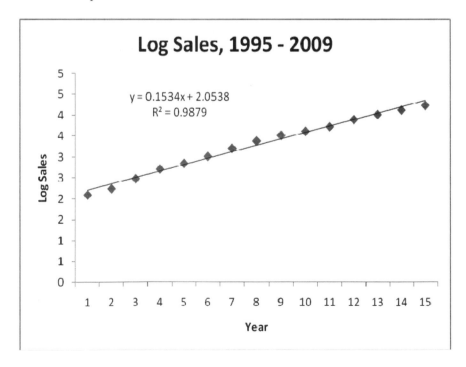

Figure 10.9 The log transformation produces a linear relationship

The regression analysis of the log-transformed sales data appears as follows (see Table 10.9).

Table 10.9 Regression analysis for log-transformed data

SUMMARY OUTPUT

Regression Statistics	
Multiple R	0.994
R Square	0.988
Adjusted R Square	0.987
Standard Error	0.079
Observations	15

ANOVA

	df	SS	MS	F	Significance F
Regression	1	6.585	6.585	1065.228	0.000
Residual	13	0.080	0.006		
Total	14	6.666			

	Coefficients	Standard Error	t Stat	P-value	Lower 95%	Upper 95%
Intercept	2.054	0.043	48.074	0.000	1.962	2.146
Index	0.153	0.005	32.638	0.000	0.143	0.164

Because the regression is significant, we can forecast the estimated log sales for future years by use of the regression equation, and then find the "antilog" of the estimated log sales for each year (see Figure 10.10) to convert the logarithm back to dollars. Remember we used base 10 logarithms, so we find the forecasted sales simply by taking 10 to the power of the estimated log sales for a given year. As you will recall from an earlier chapter, we perform exponentiation in Excel by using the caret symbol (^) as shown in the Formula Bar in Figure 10.11).

C19			f_x	=10^D19	
	A	B	C	D	
16	15	2009	17515.6	4.24343	
17					
18	Index	Year	Sales	LogSales	
19	16	2010	32175.2	4.50752	
20	17	2011	45801.4	4.66088	
21	18	2012	65198.2	4.81424	
22	19	2013	92809.7	4.96759	
23	20	2014	132114.5	5.12095	

Figure 10.10 Forecast future sales by finding the antilog of the predicted log sales

As mentioned earlier, advanced time series analyses include additional kinds of nonlinear relationships and methods for "smoothing" data and for dealing with cyclical and seasonal variations. Such methods are beyond the scope of this basic text, though most time series analyses are possible in Excel.

THE BOTTOM LINE
- Time series data are repeated observations over regular time periods.
- Time series data showing a linear trend can be analyzed directly by using the time period or an index number as the predictor.
- Time series data showing a curvilinear trend can often be transformed by logarithmic transformations to allow the use of regression models.
- Advanced time-series analyses are beyond the scope of this text, though the Regression tool in Excel can handle such analyses.

An Introduction to the General Linear Model

In Chapters 7 – 9, you learned how to conduct t tests and analyses of variance. Regression provides a general model of linear relationships that allows us to repurpose t tests and ANOVAs as regression problems. Let us take one example, the independent-samples t test, and see how the same problem is a special case of ANOVA and of correlation. Similar demonstrations can show ANOVA is a special case of multiple regression.

Recall the example from Chapter 7 used to illustrate the independent-samples t test. Student leaders had a significantly higher need for competence than did members of a randomly selected classroom at the same university. The results from the Analysis ToolPak's t-test tool are repeated below (Table 10.10).

Table 10.10 t-test results from Chapter 7

t-Test: Two-Sample Assuming Equal Variances

	Leaders	Control
Mean	79.705	70.917
Variance	133.946	186.054
Observations	19	23
Pooled Variance	162.606	
Hypothesized Mean Difference	0	
df	40	
t Stat	2.223	
P(T<=t) one-tail	0.016	
t Critical one-tail	1.684	
P(T<=t) two-tail	0.032	
t Critical two-tail	2.021	

Let us now use the same data (the original data are in Table 7.3) and conduct an analysis of variance using the Analysis ToolPak. With only two groups, the ANOVA results are identical to those of the t test. Because you have already seen them illustrated, the steps of the analysis are omitted. The ANOVA summary table appears in Table 10.11. The F ratio, 4.942, has 1 and 40 degrees of freedom, and the value of t reported previously, 2.223, with 40 degrees of freedom, is the square root of the F ratio. The two-tailed p value for both F and t is precisely .032. This equivalence is not at all accidental, as the F distribution for 1 and n degrees of freedom is equal to the square of the t distribution for n degrees of freedom, as we discussed earlier.

Table 10.11 ANOVA summary table

Anova: Single Factor

SUMMARY

Groups	Count	Sum	Average	Variance
Leaders	19	1514.4	79.71	133.95
Control	23	1631.1	70.92	186.05

ANOVA

Source of Variation	SS	df	MS	F	P-value	F crit
Between Groups	803.525	1	803.525	4.942	0.032	4.085
Within Groups	6504.223	40	162.606			
Total	7307.748	41				

Recall we can calculate eta squared as the ratio of the between-groups sum of squares to the total sum of squares: η^2 = 803.525 / 7307.748 = .11. This value, of course, agrees with the one we calculated in Chapter 7 using a slightly different but algebraically equivalent formula.

Now, let us recast this as a regression problem . Remember that the t test used to test the significance of a correlation coefficient has the following form, with $n - 2$ degrees of freedom, where n is the number of pairs of observations:

$$t_{(n-2)} = r_{XY}\left(\sqrt{\frac{n-2}{1-r_{XY}^2}}\right)$$

Recall from our previous discussion in this chapter the square of this value of t is the value of F found in the test of the significance of the overall regression. Let us return to the t test example and use a vector of dummy-coded (1, 0) indicator variables to indicate group membership. We will use the "stacked" data format discussed earlier (see Figure 10.11). Now, instead of doing a t test or an ANOVA, let us "regress" the dependent variable onto the dummy-coded group membership vector using Excel's Regression tool (see Figure 10.12). The result will be informative.

	A	B
1	Value	Group
2	78.6	1
3	76.2	1
4	85.7	1
5	81.0	1
6	97.6	1
7	61.9	1
8	88.1	1
9	59.5	1
10	73.8	1
35	85.7	0
36	50.0	0
37	69.1	0
38	92.9	0
39	61.9	0
40	61.9	0
41	66.7	0
42	73.8	0
43	85.7	0

Figure 10.11 Dummy-coded group membership vector (partial data)

The use of named ranges makes the purpose of the analysis clearer. The dialog box appears in Figure 10.12.

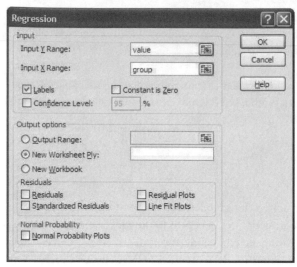

Figure 10.12 Regressing the dependent variable onto the group membership vector

The results of the regression analysis appear in Table 10.11. "Multiple R" is the correlation between the dependent variable and the dummy-coded group membership vector, and by our earlier formula, t is

$$t_{(n-2)} = r_{XY}\left(\sqrt{\frac{n-2}{1-r_{XY}^2}}\right) = .332\left(\sqrt{\frac{42-2}{1-.332^2}}\right) = 2.22$$

This, of course, agrees with the value we calculated for the independent-samples t test. Locate this value in Table 10.12 as the test of the significance of the slope term. Apart from labeling, the Regression output in Table 10.12 agrees completely with the ANOVA output in Table 10.11. The value of "R Square" is equal to the value of eta squared we calculated earlier. Finally, note the intercept term, 70.917, is the mean for the control group and the slope term, 8.788, when added to the intercept term, is the mean for the experimental group, 79.705. None of these equivalences occurred by chance, because the general linear model underlying the analysis of variance and t tests is the same model as that of regression.

Table 10.12 Regression analysis produces the same result as ANOVA and t test.

SUMMARY OUTPUT

Regression Statistics	
Multiple R	0.332
R Square	0.110
Adjusted R Square	0.088
Standard Error	12.752
Observations	42

R Square equals eta squared

ANOVA

	df	SS	MS	F	Significance F
Regression	1	803.525	803.525	4.942	0.032
Residual	40	6504.223	162.606		
Total	41	7307.748			

	Coefficients	Standard Error	t Stat	P-value	Lower 95%	Upper 95%
Intercept	70.917	2.659	26.672	0.000	65.544	76.291
Group	8.788	3.953	2.223	0.032	0.798	16.778

Intercept equals mean for control group. Intercept plus regression coefficient equal mean for experimental group

THE BOTTOM LINE
- Regression provides a general linear model that allows t tests and ANOVAs to be repurposed as regression problems.
- In the example of an independent-samples t test, the same results are achieved by use of ANOVA and by regressing the dependent variable onto the dummy-coded group membership vector.

Chapter 10 Exercises

1. Using the data from Exercise 3.5, calculate the correlation between 2007 unemployment rate and 2007 weekly wage for the eight educational attainment groups. Determine the regression coefficient (slope) and intercept term for the line of best fit. Test the significance of the correlation. Note: use unemployment rate as the Y variable and weekly wage as the X variable. What can you conclude?

2. Explain the following terms: covariance, correlation, regression, slope, intercept.

3. Using the data from Table 2.1, calculate the correlation between 2001 wages and 2002 wages. Determine the regression coefficient (slope) and intercept term for the line of best fit. Test the significance of the correlation. Note: use 2002 wages as the Y variable and 2001 wages as the X variable. What can you conclude?

4. Calculate and test the significance of the correlation between the Time1 and Time2 scores for the data in Table 7.5 (repeated below). Determine the regression coefficient (slope) and intercept term for the line of best fit. Note: use Time2 as the Y variable and Time1 as the X variable.

Student	Time1	Time2
1	84	88
2	45	54
3	32	43
4	48	42
5	53	51
6	64	73
7	45	58
8	74	79
9	68	72
10	54	52
11	90	92
12	84	89
13	72	82
14	69	82
15	72	73

5. A common use of correlation is to estimate the reliability of tests. One form of reliability is test-retest reliability. The following table shows scores for 30 test takers on the same test taken at two different times. Calculate and interpret the correlation between the two scores. Is the correlation significant?

Person	Score1	Score2	Person	Score1	Score2	Person	Score1	Score2
1	100	95	11	49	51	21	39	29
2	23	46	12	92	89	22	61	60
3	90	87	13	48	54	23	78	79
4	60	55	14	61	54	24	56	62
5	45	54	15	98	94	25	60	63
6	52	48	16	64	73	26	52	54
7	54	52	17	63	82	27	81	83
8	35	33	18	42	53	28	66	61
9	98	94	19	61	43	29	60	57
10	63	73	20	40	40	30	23	22

6. The following data represent final grades in a statistics class and self-reported weekly study hours. Construct a scatterplot of the relationship between study hours and grades. Calculate the correlation coefficient and test its significance. Does studying lead to better grades?

Student	StudyHrs	Grade	Student	StudyHrs	Grade
1	15	90	11	13	68
2	13	80	12	10	68
3	12	76	13	13	86
4	18	95	14	10	74
5	14	83	15	15	82
6	12	80	16	13	79
7	11	74	17	13	92
8	15	90	18	17	94
9	11	70	19	14	88
10	10	75	20	9	65

Using the regression equation from Exercise #6, above, predict the final course grade for a student who studies 9 hours per week. What is the predicted course grade for a student who studies 11.5 hours per week?

7. In your spring term statistics class, you notice more students tend to be missing on days when the temperature is warm. Because you get to the lab earlier than most of the class, you decide to use the computer to check the outside temperature, and then you count the number of students in class. For a period of 10 class sessions, you record the following data. Conduct a regression analysis and test the significance of the correlation. Using the regression equation, predict the class attendance on a day when the temperature is 85 degrees.

Temperature	Students
76	14
82	13
71	16
80	14
69	20
75	13
77	12
68	19
73	20
70	19

8. The following data show the annual sales of JC Penney for the years 2003 to 2007 (source: www.jcpenney.net):

Year	Sales($Millions)
2003	17513
2004	18096
2005	18781
2006	19903
2007	19860

Develop a time series plot of these data and fit a trend line. Conduct a regression analysis of these sales. Test the significance of the correlation. If the overall correlation is significant, use your regression equation to forecast sales for 2008 – 2010.

11 Chi-Square Tests

Like the product-moment correlation coefficient, the chi-square distribution was a contribution of statistician Karl Pearson. This chapter covers both one-way (chi-square goodness-of-fit) tests and two-way chi-square tests of independence. The chi-square distribution has many other uses besides the ones discussed here.

Excel does not directly calculate the value of chi square for either the test of goodness of fit or the test of independence, but it has several built-in chi-square functions. These functions include:

- CHIINV—this is the "inverse" of the chi-square distribution, and will return a value of chi square for a given degrees of freedom and probability level.[7]
- CHIDIST—this function returns the p value for a given value of chi square at the stated degrees of freedom.
- CHITEST—this feature is actually a tool that compares a range (array or matrix) of observed values with its associated range of expected frequencies. It reports the probability (p value) of the chi-square test result, but not the computed sample value of chi square. The CHITEST tool can be used for goodness-of-fit tests or tests of independence.

To use the CHITEST tool, you must provide to Excel the observed frequencies and the frequencies expected under the null hypothesis. After you find the p level from the CHITEST tool, you could use that value and the degrees of freedom to determine the computed value of chi-square by use of the CHIINV function with the proviso noted in the footnote.

Chi-Square Goodness-of-Fit Tests

The chi-square goodness-of-fit test compares an array of observed frequencies for levels of a single categorical variable with the associated array of expected frequencies under some null hypothesis. The data may be nominal, or they may be grouped frequencies for a test of the fit of observed cases to a theoretical model such as the normal or some other continuous distribution. The null hypothesis may state the expected frequencies are uniformly distributed across the levels of the variable, or that they follow some theoretical distribution of values. For example, we can use intervals of a continuous distribution like the normal distribution for expected values and compare the observed with the expected frequencies. We can also use chi-square tests with discrete distributions like the binomial or the Poisson distributions, making chi-square tests a very flexible tool.

Chi-Square Test of Goodness of Fit for Equal Expected Frequencies

Table 11.1 shows hypothetical data concerning the reasons consumers switch brands even when they report an initial high level of satisfaction with their brand of choice. Two hundred customers were asked to identify their most

---

[7] The CHIINV function algorithms in Excel do not calculate values for the extremes ($p < .0000003$ or $p > .0000097$) of the chi-square distribution or for very large degrees of freedom. In these cases, the CHIINV function returns a #NUM error. Thus the only currently reliable application of CHIINV is to find critical values for hypothesis tests. The CHITEST and CHIDIST functions continue to work correctly in the extreme tails of the distribution.

important reason for switching brands. To make the categories mutually exclusive and collectively exhaustive, a category called "other" was added to the survey. Assume the reasons were distributed as follows:

Table 11.1 Reasons for switching brands (hypothetical data)

Reason for Switching	Observed
Preferred Brand not Available	32
Less Expensive Alternative	17
New Brand Available	16
Dissatisfaction with Preferred Brand	37
Just Looking for a Change	33
Negative Publicity about Preferred Brand	35
Positive Promotion of Alternative Brand	14
Other	16
	200

There are eight reasons (categories). If the reasons were uniformly distributed, the expected frequency for each reason would be 200 / 8 = 25. Calculate the value of chi square from this formula:

$$\chi^2 = \sum_{i=1}^{k} X_i \frac{(f_{o_i} - f_{e_i})^2}{f_{e_i}}$$

where k is the number of categories, f_{o_i} is the observed frequency for a given category, and f_{e_i} is the expected frequency for the same category. The degrees of freedom for the goodness of fit test are $k - 1$. The CHITEST tool reports the probability of the obtained value of chi square if the null hypothesis is true. However, this tool does not calculate the value of chi square.

The following screenshot (Figure 11.1) shows how to use formulas to calculate the expected frequencies, the value of chi square (cell D10), and the p level of the obtained chi square using the CHIDIST function (cell D11). Figure 11.2 shows the results of the test.

	A	B	C	D	E
1	Reason for Switching	Observed	Expected	(O - E)^2/E	
2	Preferred Brand not Available	32	=200/8	=(B2-C2)^2/C2	
3	Less Expensive Alternative	17	=200/8	=(B3-C3)^2/C3	
4	New Brand Available	16	=200/8	=(B4-C4)^2/C4	
5	Dissatisfaction with Preferred Brand	37	=200/8	=(B5-C5)^2/C5	
6	Just Looking for a Change	33	=200/8	=(B6-C6)^2/C6	
7	Negative Publicity about Preferred Brand	35	=200/8	=(B7-C7)^2/C7	
8	Positive Promotion of Alternative Brand	14	=200/8	=(B8-C8)^2/C8	
9	Other	16	=200/8	=(B9-C9)^2/C9	
10		Total =SUM(B2:B9)	=SUM(C2:C9)	=SUM(D2:D9)	χ^2
11				=CHIDIST(D10,7)	$p(\chi^2)$

Figure 11.1 Formulas used for chi-square test

	A	B	C	D	E
1	Reason for Switching	Observed	Expected	(O - E)^2/E	
2	Preferred Brand not Available	32	25	1.96	
3	Less Expensive Alternative	17	25	2.56	
4	New Brand Available	16	25	3.24	
5	Dissatisfaction with Preferred Brand	37	25	5.76	
6	Just Looking for a Change	33	25	2.56	
7	Negative Publicity about Preferred Brand	35	25	4.00	
8	Positive Promotion of Alternative Brand	14	25	4.84	
9	Other	16	25	3.24	
10	Total	200	200	28.16 χ^2	
11				0.000 $p(\chi^2)$	

Figure 11.2 Chi-square test results

The chi-square test revealed the reasons for brand switching are not equally distributed, $\chi^2(7, N = 200) = 28.16$, $p < .001$.

Chi-Square Goodness-of-Fit Test Template for Equal Expected Frequencies

Although the calculations shown above are routine, they are laborious. A worksheet template for the chi-square goodness of fit test makes the calculations less time consuming. The user inserts the observed data values, and the template automates the calculations. The current problem is shown in the template (See Figure 11.3).

	A	B	C	D	E	F	G	H	I	J	K
1	Level	Observed	Expected		Results						
2	1	32	25		Count (k)	8					
3	2	17	25		Sum	200					
4	3	16	25		χ^2	28.16					
5	4	37	25		df (k - 1)	7					
6	5	33	25		$p(\chi^2)$	0.0002					
7	6	35	25								
8	7	14	25		This worksheet template performs a chi-square test of goodness of fit.						
9	8	16	25		The expected values are based on the null hypothesis of no difference in						
10					distribution of observations in the different levels of the categorical variable.						
11											
12					Enter up to 100 observed frequencies in the green-shaded data entry area,						
13					beginning in cell B2. Each row should represent a level of the categorical						
14					variable. The template counts the number of categories, calculates expected						
15					frequencies according to the null hypothesis, calculates chi-square, and						
16					calculates the probability of the observed value of chi-square if the null						
17					hypothesis is true.						
18					The worksheet is protected to keep you from accidentally changing the formulas.						
19											
20											

Figure 11.3 Chi-square goodness-of-fit template

Chi-Square Goodness-of-Fit Test with Unequal Expected Frequencies

The chi-square goodness-of-fit test also applies to unequal expected frequencies. For example, a college dean collected the following data, which represent the numbers of D, F, and W (withdrawn) grades for different freshman courses in his college (Table 11.2). There are 80 biology students, 200 English students, 100 history students, 175 math students, and 150 psychology students. Let us conduct a chi-square test of goodness of fit to determine if the "DFWs" are distributed in equal proportions among the courses.

Table 11.2 Observed frequencies of D, F, and W grades

Course	DFWs
Biology	44
English	95
History	48
Math	108
Psychology	76

The null hypothesis would dictate equal proportions of DFW grades if there is no association between the department and the grade distribution. However, because there are different numbers of students in the various classes, the expected frequencies are not equal. There are 371 DFW grades altogether for the 705 students enrolled in the courses. Thus, to determine expected frequencies under the null hypothesis, we must multiply the number of students in each course by the expected proportion, 371 / 705 or .53 (see Table 11.3).

Table 11.3 Expected frequencies under the null hypothesis

Course	Observed	Students	Expected
Biology	44	80	42.10
English	95	200	105.25
History	48	100	52.62
Math	108	175	92.09
Psychology	76	150	78.94
Total	371	705	371.00

The chi-square template for unequal expected frequencies is shown in Figure 11.4. The user must calculate the expected frequencies separately, and must enter both observed and expected frequencies. The expected values calculated by Excel formulas appear with higher precision than in Table 11.3.

	A	B	C	D	E	F	G
1	Level	Observed	Expected		Results		
2	1	44	42.09929078		Count (k)	5	
3	2	95	105.248227		Sum	371	
4	3	48	52.62411348		χ^2	4.35	
5	4	108	92.09219858		df (k - 1)	4	
6	5	76	78.93617021		$p(\chi^2)$	0.361	
7							

Figure 11.4. Chi-square template for unequal expected frequencies

The subject was not related to the frequency of DFW grades, $\chi^2(4, N = 371) = 4.35, p = .36$. Failure to reject the null hypothesis indicates the data are adequately described by or "fit" the expected distribution. Statistical significance, on the other hand, would mean the data depart from the expected distribution under the null hypothesis. The observed counts clearly must be whole numbers because they are discrete, but expected counts can be fractional (see Figure 11.4).

Chi-Square Test of Independence

The chi-square test of independence is used with two or more levels for each of two categorical variables. We want to determine the degree of association or independence among the categories.

Use the following formula to calculate the value of chi-square for a test of independence:

$$\chi^2 = \sum_{i=1}^{R} \sum_{j=1}^{C} \frac{(f_{o_{ij}} - f_{e_{ij}})^2}{f_{e_{ij}}}$$

where R is the number of rows (representing one categorical variable) and C is the number of columns (representing the other categorical variable). The double summation simply means to add up $(f_o - f_e)^2 / f_e$ for every cell in the table.

The expected frequencies under the null hypothesis are based on a presumed lack of association between the row and column variables. To calculate expected frequencies for the chi-square test of independence, the row and column marginal subtotals are multiplied for a given cell, and the product is divided by the total number of observations. The degrees of freedom for the test of independence are $(R - 1) \times (C - 1)$. Once the expected frequencies are calculated, the CHITEST tool can return the p level for the chi-square the test of independence, though not the value of chi-square.

The following hypothetical data represent the frequency of use of various computational tools by statistics professors in departments of psychology, business, and mathematics (see Table 11.4).

Table 11.4 Computational tools used in statistics classes

Department	SPSS	Excel	Minitab	Total
Psychology	21	6	4	31
Business	6	19	8	33
Mathematics	5	7	12	24
Total	32	32	24	88

Calculating Expected Frequencies for Chi-Square Tests of Independence

To calculate the expected frequencies, multiply the row marginal total for the given cell by the column marginal total for the same cell, and divide the product by the total number of observations. To illustrate, the expected frequency for the first cell of the table is $(31 \times 32) / 88 = 11.27$, the number of users of SPSS in psychological statistics classes we would expect if there is no association between the department and the computational tool used. Similarly, the expected frequency of SPSS in business departments under the null hypothesis would be $(33 \times 32) / 88 = 12.00$. We will use this procedure to calculate the expected frequencies. Excel provides matrix multiplication operations that allow the user to calculate all the expected frequencies at once. See Figure 11.5 for an example of an array formula using the MMULT function. To employ this formula, enter the data for the row totals in column E and the column totals in row 5, leaving the cell entries in the range B2:D5 empty. Then select the range B2:B5, click in the Formula Bar and enter

$$= \text{MMULT(E2:E4,B5:D5)/E5}$$

Then press <**Shift**> + <**Ctrl**> + <**Enter**> to enter the array formula and calculate the expected frequencies all at the same time. As a reminder, Excel supplies the curly braces surrounding the array formula, and you cannot enter them directly.

B2   {=MMULT(E2:E4,B5:D5)/E5}

	A	B	C	D	E
1	Department	SPSS	Excel	Minitab	Total
2	Psychology	11.27	11.27	8.45	31
3	Business	12.00	12.00	9.00	33
4	Mathematics	8.73	8.73	6.55	24
5	Total	32	32	24	88

Figure 11.5 Use of MMULT function and array formula to calculate expected frequencies (after cell formatting)

Using a Pivot Table for Cross Tabulations

Assume the data for Table 11.4 were in raw form (see Figure 11.6) with 1 used to indicate use of the tool and 0 to indicate the professor did not use the tool.

	A	B	C	D	E
1	ID	Department	SPSS	Excel	Minitab
2	1	Psychology	1	0	0
3	2	Psychology	1	0	0
4	3	Psychology	1	0	0
5	4	Psychology	1	0	0
6	5	Psychology	1	0	0
7	6	Psychology	1	0	0
8	7	Psychology	1	0	0
9	8	Psychology	1	0	0
10	9	Psychology	1	0	0
11	10	Psychology	1	0	0
12	11	Psychology	1	0	0
13	12	Psychology	1	0	0
14	13	Psychology	1	0	0
15	14	Psychology	1	0	0
76	75	Mathematics	0	1	0
77	76	Mathematics	0	1	0
78	77	Mathematics	0	0	1
79	78	Mathematics	0	0	1
80	79	Mathematics	0	0	1
81	80	Mathematics	0	0	1
82	81	Mathematics	0	0	1
83	82	Mathematics	0	0	1
84	83	Mathematics	0	0	1
85	84	Mathematics	0	0	1
86	85	Mathematics	0	0	1
87	86	Mathematics	0	0	1
88	87	Mathematics	0	0	1
89	88	Mathematics	0	0	1

Figure 11.6 Preference for computational tools by department (partial data)

We can use the PivotTable tool discussed in detail in Chapter 3 to cross tabulate the raw data (see Figure 11.7). Remember the PivotTable tool organizes the text entries for departments alphabetically for lack of any other organizing principle.

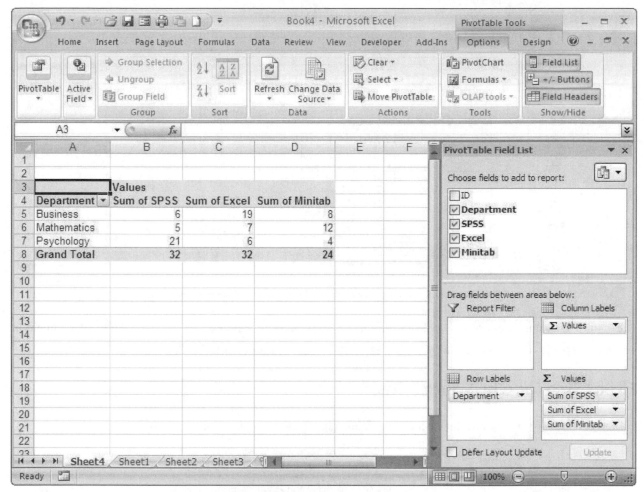

Figure 11.7 Using the PivotTable tool to summarize raw data

Because the calculations for the chi-square test of independence are repetitive, it is beneficial to create and save a generic worksheet template and then replace the observed values with different values for new tests. The worksheet template shown in Figure 11.8 was used to calculate the value of chi-square and test its significance. The results of the test appear in Figure 11.8. The template also Cramér's V (or the ϕ coefficient for 1 df) as a measure of effect size for the chi-square test of independence (Gravetter & Wallnau, 2008).

The worksheet template applies Yates' correction for continuity when the data are a 2×2 contingency table (1 degree of freedom). This correction is required because the binomial distribution is discrete while the normal distribution is continuous, as discussed earlier in Chapter 4 (see also Hays, 1973). The chi-square test for a two-way contingency table, even with the Yates correction, is an approximate test. When expected frequencies are low, the Fisher exact test is an alternative to chi-square for examining a 2×2 table of independent observations. The Fisher test gives the one-tailed probability that the particular level of association or one even stronger would be observed if the null hypothesis of no relationship was true (Rosenthal & Rosnow, 2008).

▲	A	B	C	D	L
1		Observed Frequencies			
2		Column1	Column2	Column3	Total
3	Row1	6	19	8	33
4	Row2	5	7	12	24
5	Row3	21	6	4	31
27	Total	32	32	24	88
28					
29		Test Results			
30		0	Correction		
31		26.88	χ^2		
32		3	Rows		
33		3	Columns		
34		4	df		
35		0.000	$p\,(\chi^2)$		
36		0.39	V (or ϕ)		

Figure 11.8 Worksheet template for chi-square test of independence

The significant value of chi square indicates the choice of a computational tool is associated with the department in which the statistics course is taught: $\chi^2\,(4, N = 88) = 26.88, p < .001$, Cramér's $V = .39$.

Effect Size for Chi-Square Tests

For the goodness-of-fit test, we can calculate the following effect-size index (Cohen, 1988):

$$r = \sqrt{\frac{\chi^2}{N(C-1)}}$$

where N is the total number of observations and C is the number of categories. For this effect-size index, a value lower than .30 is considered a small effect, a value between .30 and .50 is considered a medium effect, and a value greater than .50 is considered a large effect.

The phi coefficient provides an appropriate effect-size index for a 2 × 2 contingency table:

$$\varphi = \sqrt{\frac{\chi^2}{N}}$$

When working with summary data, you can use the following shortcut formula to calculate phi:

$$\varphi = \frac{ad - bc}{\sqrt{efgh}}$$

Where $a, b, c, d, e, f,$ and g are the observed frequencies and totals as shown in Table 11.5 below.

Table 11.5 letters represent observed frequencies and totals

	Col1	Col2	Total
Row1	a	b	e
Row2	c	d	f
Total	g	h	N

Cramér's V is the extension of the phi coefficient for 3 or more columns or rows:

$$V = \sqrt{\frac{\chi^2}{N(df^*)}}$$

where df^* is the smaller of $(R-1)$ or $(C-1)$. Cohen (as cited in Gravetter & Wallnau, 2008) provides the following interpretation for Cramér's V (Table 11.6):

Table 11.6 Guidelines for interpreting Cramér's V

df^*	V	Effect Size
1	.10	Small
	.30	Medium
	.50	Large
2	.07	Small
	.21	Medium
	.35	Large
3	.06	Small
	.17	Medium
	.29	Large

Rea & Parker (1992) provide an additional guide to interpreting the magnitude of the effect size for chi-square tests of independence (Table 11.7).

Table 11.7 Guide to interpreting effect size for φ or Cramér's V

Value of φ or Cramér's V	Strength of Association
.00 and under .10	Negligible association
.10 and under .20	Weak association
.20 and under .40	Moderate association
.40 and under .60	Relatively strong association
.60 and under .80	Strong association
.80 to 1.00	Very strong association

THE BOTTOM LINE
- Chi-square tests compare expected frequencies under a null hypothesis with observed frequencies. Chi-square tests are suitable for categorical or qualitative data.
- One-way chi-square tests (multiple categories of a single qualitative variable) are called goodness-of-fit tests.
- Two-way chi-square tests (two or more categories of two qualitative variables) are called tests of independence.

- Excel provides the CHIDIST, CHIINV, and CHITEST functions. There is no chi-square test in the Analysis ToolPak.
- The CHIINV function does not work in the extremes of the chi-square distribution.
- Chi-square test templates assist in goodness-of-fit tests for both equal and unequal frequencies and for tests of independence.

Chapter 11 Exercises

1. Recall the data from Table 3.3, in which 40 college students who like Peanut M&Ms expressed their color preferences. If the six colors are preferred equally, we would expect 40/6 = 6.67 students to choose each color. Perform and interpret a chi-square test of goodness of fit. Use an alpha level of .05.

Row Labels	Count of Color
Blue	14
Brown	3
Green	10
Orange	2
Red	8
Yellow	3
Grand Total	40

2. Fifty-nine college students expressed their number one reason for choosing a fast-food restaurant. Use a chi-square test of goodness of fit to determine whether the reasons are equally distributed. Use an alpha level of .05.

Reason	Observed
Food taste	23
Habit	10
Food quality	9
Convenience	7
Price	4
Food variety	4
Atmosphere	2

3. A researcher used a computer program to assign 88 participants to three different experimental conditions. The program produced the following results, and the researcher wonders whether the program is working properly. Use a chi-square test of goodness of fit to determine if the data depart significantly from what you would expect if the assignments were completely random. Use an alpha level of .05.

	Condition1	Condition2	Condition3
Number	30	38	20

4. According to DuPont Corporation's 2008 Automotive Color Popularity survey, automobile purchasers in North America prefer white over any other color. The color preferences are distributed as follows (by percentage).

Color	Popularity(%)
White	20
Black	17
Silver	17
Blue	13
Gray	12
Red	11
Other	10

You wonder whether the same preferences exist in your region, so you record the colors of the first 50 cars passing in front of your house. Using DuPont's reported percentages to calculate expected frequencies, conduct a chi-square test of goodness of fit to determine whether color preferences in your region are the same as or different from the national preferences. Use an alpha level of .05.

Color	Observed	Expected
White	7	10.0
Black	15	8.5
Silver	10	8.5
Blue	3	6.5
Gray	4	6.0
Red	9	5.5
Other	2	5.0

5. The following data show the distribution by sex and college of 383 professors at a large state university. Conduct and interpret a chi-square test of independence. Use an alpha level of .05. Calculate and interpret Cramér's V as a measure of effect size.

College	Female	Male	Total
Business	14	36	50
Liberal Arts	47	82	129
Eduation	17	22	39
Engineering	13	81	94
Sciences	37	34	71
Total	128	255	383

6. Anderson AutoPlex keeps track of monthly new automobile sales and whether the car was domestic or foreign. Sales at or above the median price are considered "high cost" while sales below the median are considered "low cost." The following are sales for July 2010. Conduct and interpret a chi-square test of independence to determine if there is an association between the source of the vehicle and the price. Use an alpha level of .05. What is the phi coefficient?

	Domestic	Foreign
High Cost	24	16
Low Cost	6	34

7. Ninety college students participated in a study in which they assumed the role of a juror and read a description of a crime. Students were randomly assigned to one of three conditions: 1 (*no eyewitness present*), 2 (*eyewitness present whose testimony was discredited at trial*), and 3 (*eyewitness present whose testimony was corroborated at trial*). After reading the scenario, the student decided whether the alleged

suspect was guilty or not guilty. The results of the study were as follows. Conduct and interpret a chi-square test of independence. Calculate and interpret Cramér's V as a measure of effect size.

	No Eyewitness	Discredited Eyewitness	Unrefuted Eyewitness	Total
Guilty	15	22	28	65
Not Guilty	14	7	4	25
Total	29	29	32	90

8. Assume the data in Table 11.3 were expanded to include the following additional information:

Department	SPSS	Excel	Minitab	SAS	Matlab	Fathom	Total
Psychology	21	6	4	4	4	8	47
Business	6	19	8	10	5	4	52
Mathematics	5	7	12	4	11	3	42
Education	3	4	5	4	5	12	33
	35	36	29	22	25	27	174

Conduct and interpret a chi-square test of independence using an alpha level of .05. Calculate and interpret Cramér's V as a measure of effect size.

9. The American Sociological Association reported the following results from a 2001 survey of more than 4,000 full-time sociology department faculty members. Conduct and interpret a chi-square test of independence using an alpha level of .05. Is faculty rank associated with sex? Calculate and interpret Cramér's V as a measure of effect size.

Rank	Sex Male	Female
Professor	1313	461
Associate	648	489
Assistant	530	575

12   Additional Nonparametric Tests

When scale (interval and ratio) data fail to meet the distributional assumptions required for parametric tests, or when your data are ordinal (ranks) to begin with, you can use nonparametric alternatives to the t test, ANOVA, and correlation coefficient. These tests are nonparametric because they make few if any assumptions about population parameters or because they make no estimates of population parameters. Some authors call these tests distribution-free (e.g., Downie & Heath, 1983; Howell, 2008). In the sense we have just described, chi-square tests of goodness of fit and independence are nonparametric tests, as is the sign test you learned in Chapter 4.

Because they use ranks, these tests are not particularly difficult to calculate. Excel functions and formulas are still helpful in the computations, as you will see, and once you build or acquire an Excel template for these analyses, you can reuse it. For convenience and for comparison with their parametric alternatives, we present the tests in the same order as in Chapters 7 and 8, covering the between-groups tests before their within-groups counterparts. We will discuss the Mann-Whitney U test for two independent groups, the Wilcoxon matched-pairs signed ranks test for paired samples, the Kruskal-Wallis test for three or more independent groups, and the Friedman test for three or more repeated observations of the same cases or participants.

The Mann-Whitney *U* Test

The Mann-Whitney U test is a nonparametric alternative to the independent-samples t test. This test is appropriate when your data do not meet the assumptions of normality or homogeneity of variance. The test is also appropriate when your data are ordinal when you collect them. Wilcoxon originally devised this test, and it is sometimes called the Wilcoxon rank sum test, simply the rank sum test, or even the Wilcoxon-Mann-Whitney sum of ranks test, which is the most accurate though most cumbersome of the several names. Wilcoxon's original test was for equal sample sizes, and Mann and Whitney extended the test to unequal sample sizes. Most modern authors use the term Mann-Whitney U test to distinguish this from the Wilcoxon matched-pairs signed-ranks test. The Mann-Whitney test is not available in Excel, but Excel add-ins, such as MegaStat, and dedicated statistics packages routinely include this test.

Although the Mann-Whitney U test is sensitive to differences in central tendency between the two independent samples, it is not strictly a test of means or medians. Though some authors insist it is a test of the "locations" of the two distributions, this is not strictly true either. Instead, the Mann-Whitney U test considers a more general hypothesis that the two samples of observations have equal distributions. If the two distributions are equal, the ranks from the two groups should overlap. As the distributions move apart, the ranks overlap less and less.

Rationale and Procedure

We have two independent groups of observations and want to compare the groups, but are unwilling to assume our data meet the traditional assumptions of the independent-samples t test. By converting our data to ranks, we can test the null hypothesis that the observed differences in ranks between the groups are attributable to chance against the alternative that the observed differences are larger than what we could expect based on chance alone. For illustrative purposes, we will call the groups 1 and 2. Group 1 has n_1 observations, and Group 2 has n_2 observations. Because the groups are independent, there is no requirement that $n_1 = n_2$. We will rank all $n_1 + n_2 = N$ observations from 1 to N, using the customary correction for ties, which is to assign the average rank to tied values. For example, if two equal values tie for first place, instead of both receiving the rank of 1, each will be assigned the rank 1.5. The test statistic, U, has the following expected value when the null hypothesis that the two groups have equal distributions is true:

$$E(U) = \frac{n_1 n_2}{2}$$

To calculate the sample value of the U statistic, we sum the ranks for Groups 1 and 2 separately. Let us call these sums R_1 and R_2, respectively. For the statistic, U, find the *smaller* of the following values:

$$U_1 = n_1 n_2 + \frac{n_1(n_1+1)}{2} - R_1$$

$$U_2 = n_1 n_2 + \frac{n_2(n_2+1)}{2} - R_2$$

You can also find the value of U_2 from the following formula, which provides a convenient check on the calculations:

$$U_2 = n_1 n_2 - U_1$$

Tables of critical values of U are available for small sample sizes (see Table 12.1). If the obtained value of U is *smaller than* the critical value for n_1 and n_2, the test is significant at $p < .05$ (two-tailed).

Table 12.1 Critical values of U for $n_1 \leq 20$ and $n_2 \leq 20$ and alpha = .05 (two-tailed)

n_2																			

n_2	2	3	4	5	6	7	8	9	10	11	12	13	14	15	16	17	18	19	20
2	-	-	-	-	-	-	0	0	0	0	1	1	1	1	1	2	2	2	2
3	-	-	-	0	1	1	2	2	3	3	4	4	5	5	6	6	7	7	8
4	-	-	0	1	2	3	4	4	5	6	7	8	9	10	11	11	12	13	13
5	-	0	1	2	3	5	6	7	8	9	11	12	13	14	15	17	18	19	20
6	-	1	2	3	5	6	7	10	11	13	14	16	17	19	21	22	24	25	27
7	-	1	3	5	6	8	10	12	14	16	18	20	22	24	26	28	30	32	34
8	0	2	4	6	7	10	13	15	17	19	22	24	26	29	31	34	36	38	41
9	0	2	4	7	10	12	15	17	20	23	26	28	31	34	37	39	42	45	48
10	0	3	5	8	11	14	17	20	23	26	29	33	36	39	42	45	48	52	55
11	0	3	6	9	13	16	19	23	26	30	33	37	40	44	47	51	55	58	62
12	1	4	7	11	14	18	22	26	29	33	37	41	45	49	53	57	61	65	69
13	1	4	8	12	16	20	24	28	33	37	41	45	50	54	59	63	67	72	76
14	1	5	9	13	17	22	26	31	36	40	45	50	55	59	64	67	74	78	83
15	1	5	10	14	19	24	29	34	39	44	49	54	59	64	70	75	80	85	90
16	1	6	11	15	21	26	31	37	42	47	53	59	64	70	75	81	86	92	98
17	2	6	11	17	22	28	34	39	45	51	57	63	67	75	81	87	93	99	105
18	2	7	12	18	24	30	36	42	48	55	61	67	74	80	86	93	99	106	112
19	2	7	13	19	25	32	38	45	52	58	65	72	78	85	92	99	106	113	119
20	2	8	13	20	27	34	41	48	55	62	69	76	83	90	98	105	112	119	127

(n_1 heads the set of columns 2–20.)

The distribution of U is approximately normal when n_1 and n_2 are both larger than 10 (Ott, Mendenhall, & Larson, 1978), and programs like SPSS use the normal approximation regardless of sample size. The normal approximation is:

$$z = \frac{U - \dfrac{n_1 n_2}{2}}{\sqrt{\dfrac{n_1 n_2 (n_1 + n_2 + 1)}{12}}}$$

When there are many tied ranks, the accuracy of the z score can be improved by a correction factor (Roscoe, 1975). For tied ranks, an improved estimate of the z score can be obtained by calculating the quantity $T = (f^3 - f)/12$ for each score value where ties exist, and where f is the number of tied scores at that level. The quantity ΣT is the sum of all the values of T, and the statistic adjusted for tied ranks is

$$z = \frac{U - \dfrac{n_1 n_2}{2}}{\sqrt{\left(\dfrac{n_1 n_2}{N^2 - N}\right)\left(\dfrac{N^3 - N}{12} - \Sigma T\right)}}$$

We will not use the tie correction here. Interested readers should consult a book on nonparametric statistics for more information.

Example

Students in business statistics and psychological statistics took an Excel mastery test with scores ranging from 0 to 100. Table 12.2 shows the hypothetical data. These data do not meet the assumptions of normality or of homogeneity of variance.

Table 12.2 Hypothetical Excel mastery scores

Business	Psychology	Rank1	Rank2
100	100	15.5	15.5
100	77	15.5	9
100	50	15.5	7
98	48	13	6
90	30	12	5
83	25	11	4
82	10	10	3
75	0	8	1.5
	0		1.5
		100.5	52.5 Sum

To perform the test, rank the values from 1 to N without regard to group membership, using the correction for tied ranks. Next, sum the ranks separately for each group to calculate R_1 and R_2. These values are $R_1 = 100.5$ and $R_2 = 52.5$, respectively. Then calculate the test statistic U, as follows:

$$U_1 = n_1 n_2 + \frac{n_1(n_1+1)}{2} - R_1 = 8(9) + \frac{8(9)}{2} - 100.5 = 7.5$$

$$U_2 = n_1 n_2 + \frac{n_2(n_2+1)}{2} - R_2 = 8(9) + \frac{9(10)}{2} - 52.5 = 64.5$$

The test statistic U is the smaller of these two values, 7.5. In the current case, we can use the table of critical values of U. With $n_1 = 8$ and $n_2 = 9$ observations, the critical value is 15 (see Table 12.1), and we reject the null hypothesis. As we might expect, business students exhibit higher Excel mastery than psychology students, $U = 7.5, p < .05$.

It is also instructive to employ the normal approximation:

$$z = \frac{U - \frac{n_1 n_2}{2}}{\sqrt{\frac{n_1 n_2 (n_1 + n_2 + 1)}{12}}} = \frac{7.5 - \frac{8(9)}{2}}{\sqrt{\frac{8(9)(8+9+1)}{12}}} = \frac{7.5 - 36}{\sqrt{\frac{1296}{12}}} = \frac{-28.5}{10.392} = -2.74$$

We can use the NORMSDIST function to find the two-tailed probability of the obtained value of z as follows. The ABS function ensures the correct p value for positive or negative z scores.

$$= 2 * (1 - \text{NORMSDIST}(\text{ABS}(-2.74))) \approx .006$$

When the data violate the assumption of homogeneity of variance, but not the normality assumption, the independent-samples t test assuming unequal variances may be a more powerful alternative than the Mann-Whitney U test. Figure 12.1 shows the current problem solved by use of a generic worksheet template.

	A	B	C	D	E	F	G	H	I	J	K
1	Group1	Group2		Rank1	Rank2		Value	Group1	Group2		
2	100	100		15.5	15.5		ΣR	100.5	52.5		
3	100	77		15.5	9		Count	8	9		
4	100	50		15.5	7						
5	98	48		13	6		U_1	7.5		For small samples, use tabled values	
6	90	30		12	5		U_2	64.5		Critical U for $\alpha = .05$, two-tailed	15
7	83	25		11	4		U	7.5		$U \le U_{crit}$?	Yes, Reject
8	82	10		10	3		z	-2.742			
9	75	0		8	1.5		$p(z)$ One-tailed	0.003			
10		0			1.5		$p(z)$ Two-tailed	0.006			
11											

Figure 12.1 Generic Mann-Whitney U test template

THE BOTTOM LINE

- The Mann-Whitney U test is a nonparametric alternative to the independent-samples t test.
- The test is not available in Excel, but it is not difficult to build a reusable template for it.
- Excel add-ins such as MegaStat and dedicated statistics packages provide the Mann-Whitney U test.

The Wilcoxon Matched-Pairs Signed-Ranks Test

The Wilcoxon matched-pairs signed-ranks test is a nonparametric alternative to the paired-samples t test. The Wilcoxon test requires data at least on an ordinal scale. This test does not require the data to be normally distributed. Just as with the paired-samples t test, we are interested in the differences between the paired observations. However, for the Wilcoxon matched-pairs signed-ranks we convert the differences to ranks (Roscoe, 1975). This test is more powerful than the sign test you learned in Chapter 4 because it uses more information.

Rationale and Procedure

The rationale for the Wilcoxon matched-pairs signed-ranks test is straightforward. Imagine a random sample of N pairs of observations from a population of interest. Calculate the difference between each pair of observations and then rank these differences in absolute value, ignoring the sign of the difference. If the sample is random and there are no differences between the observations except those attributable to chance, the positive and negative differences would be roughly the same in number. If a difference is zero, omit that pair and reduce N by 1. If any nonzero differences are tied, assign the average rank to these differences, as discussed above.

After ranking the differences, revisit the signs, and sum the ranks separately for positive and negative signs. The test statistic T is the smaller of these two sums. If the positive and negative differences are random, we would expect the value of T to be

$$E(T) = \frac{N(N+1)}{4}$$

The test statistic is the smaller of the positive or negative sums of ranks, so the value of T becomes lower as the observed value of T departs from expectation. Tables of critical values for T are available for sample sizes up to $N = 25$ (see Table 12.3).

Table 12.3 Critical values of T for alpha levels of .05, .02, and .01 (two-tailed probabilities)

N	.05	.02	.01
6	0	-	-
7	2	0	-
8	4	2	0
9	6	3	2
10	8	5	3
11	11	7	5
12	14	10	7
13	17	13	10
14	21	16	13
15	25	20	16
16	30	24	20
17	35	28	23
18	40	33	28
19	46	38	32
20	52	43	38
21	59	49	43
22	66	56	49
23	73	62	55
24	81	69	61
25	89	77	68

When the sample size is larger than 25, the distribution of T is approximately normal, and you can use the following formula to find a z score (Hays, 1973):

$$z = \frac{T - \dfrac{N(N+1)}{4}}{\sqrt{\dfrac{N(N+1)(2N+1)}{24}}}$$

Example

A professor developed an individualized instruction program in critical thinking. She believes this program will improve her students' quiz scores. She chooses a random sample of eight students and measures their grades on two equivalent forms of the chapter quiz before and after the instructional program. To control for order effects, the professor gives half the students Form A first, and the other half Form B first. The scores are as follows (Table 12.4):

Table 12.4 Hypothetical quiz scores

Student	Before	After
1	57	65
2	60	64
3	66	70
4	69	72
5	84	94
6	87	87
7	90	97
8	100	97

To perform the Wilcoxon matched-pairs signed-ranks test, calculate the difference between the two scores for each student and rank these differences from 1 to N in absolute value without regard to sign. Discard any pairs with no difference. We assign the average of 1 and 2 (1.5) to the lowest tied values, both of which are 3, and the average of 3 and 4 (3.5) to the next tied values, both of which are 4. Correcting ranks for ties is possible but somewhat cumbersome in Excel, so the template automates the ranking and correction. The interested reader should consult the Excel help files. We sum the ranks for positive and negative differences separately. The smaller of these sums, 1.5, is the test statistic, T (see Figure 12.2). Because there was no difference for Pair 6, we reduce N by 1 and refer to $N = 7$ in Table 12.1. The value of $T = 1.5$ is lower than the critical value, 2. The p value for our significance test is $p < .05$, and we conclude the instruction in critical thinking was effective.

	A	B	C	D	E	F	G	H	I	J		K
1	Pair	Observation1	Observation2	Diff	AbsDiff	Rank	Signed Rank1	Signed Rank2		T		1.5
2	1	57	65	8	8	6		6		N		7
3	2	60	64	4	4	3.5		3.5		z		-2.11
4	3	66	70	4	4	3.5		3.5		$p(z)$		0.035
5	4	69	72	3	3	1.5		1.5				
6	5	84	94	10	10	7		7				
7	6	87	87	0								
8	7	90	97	7	7	5		5				
9	8	100	97	-3	3	1.5	1.5					

Figure 12.2 Wilcoxon matched-pairs signed-ranks test template

Programs such as SPSS use the normal approximation regardless of sample size. Let us use the formula shown earlier and calculate z:

$$z = \frac{T - \frac{N(N+1)}{4}}{\sqrt{\frac{N(N+1)(2N+1)}{24}}} = \frac{1.5 - \frac{7(8)}{4}}{\sqrt{\frac{7(8)(14+1)}{24}}} = \frac{1.5 - 14}{\sqrt{\frac{(56)(15)}{24}}} = \frac{-12.5}{\sqrt{35}} = -2.11$$

Because we are doing a two-tailed test, we find the total probability associated with $z \leq -2.11$ and $z \geq 2.11$. As you learned in Chapter 5, you can find this area by adding the probabilities in the tails:

$$= \text{NORMSDIST}(-2.11) + (1 - \text{NORMSDIST}(2.11)) = .035.$$

It is also possible because of the symmetry of the normal distribution to double the probability in the upper tail of the standard normal distribution:

$$= 2 * (1–NORMSDIST(2.11)) = .035$$

The conclusion is the same in either case. The normal approximation is quite effective, and the result agrees closely with the critical value method using the tabled values of T.

THE BOTTOM LINE

- The Wilcoxon matched-pairs signed ranks test is a nonparametric alternative to the paired-samples t test.
- This test is based on the sums of the ranks of positive and negative differences. The test is not available in Excel.
- For larger sample sizes, the normal distribution provides an effective test statistic.
- Excel add-ins such as MegaStat provide the Wilcoxon matched-pairs signed-ranks test.

The Kruskal-Wallis Test

The Kruskal-Wallis "analysis of variance" for ranks is a nonparametric alternative to the one-way ANOVA when the data do not meet the assumptions of homogeneity of variance or normality of distribution. As with the other tests in this chapter, the Kruskal-Wallis test makes use of ranks, either converted from the raw data or collected as ordinal data originally. This test is a direct extension of the Mann-Whitney U test to three or more groups..

Rationale and Procedure

Imagine three or more independent groups of observations, in which each observation is represented by a numerical value. We can pool all the observations, and rank them from 1 to N, where $n_1 + n_2 + n_3 + \ldots + n_k = N$, applying the customary correction for tied ranks. We can then sum the ranks separately for each group and compare these sums. If the null hypothesis that the ranks are equal is true, and each n_j is at least 5 (Aczel & Sounderpandian, 2009), the test statistic, H, is distributed approximately as χ^2 with $k - 1$ degrees of freedom (Roscoe, 1975):

$$H = \frac{12}{N(N+1)} \left(\sum_{j=1}^{k} \frac{R_j^2}{n_j} \right) - 3(N+1)$$

As with the one-way ANOVA, there is no requirement that the groups contain equal numbers of observations. Evaluate H as chi-square with $k - 1$ degrees of freedom. You can do this with the CHIDIST function, as you have learned previously.

An adjustment for ties can improve the approximation of the chi-square distribution. For each score value where ties are encountered, calculate the quantity $T = f^3 - f$, where f is the frequency of the score interval (f is the number of tied ranks at that level). The correction is the following quantity:

$$CFT = 1 - \frac{\sum T}{N^3 - N}$$

Then, calculate H' as

$$H' = \frac{H}{CFT}$$

Use H' as the test statistic with $k-1$ degrees of freedom. The correction factor will never exceed one, and the effect of the correction when there are ties present is to increase the value of the test statistic (Roscoe, 1975). We will not illustrate the tie correction further. The interested reader should consult a book on nonparametric statistics for additional information.

Example

The following data show extraversion scores for engineering, marketing, and psychology majors.[8] The data do not meet the assumption of equality of variance. As with the other nonparametric tests, we rank all observations from 1 to N, correcting for tied ranks (Table 12.5).

Table 12.5 Extraversion scores for engineering, marketing, and psychology majors

Engineering	Marketing	Psychology	Rank1	Rank2	Rank3	
16	36	19	5	27	9	
11	18	23	1	7	18.5	
26	37	34	20.5	28.5	25.5	
26	18	14	20.5	7	4	
20	27	12	11	22.5	2	
22	37	34	17	28.5	25.5	
18	23	30	7	18.5	24	
20	40	20	11	30	11	
21	27	21	14.5	22.5	14.5	
21	21	13	14.5	14.5	3	
			122	206	137	Sum

The test statistic H is

$$H = \frac{12}{N(N+1)}\left(\sum_{j=1}^{k}\frac{R_j^2}{n_j}\right) - 3(N+1) = \frac{12}{30(31)}\left(\frac{122^2}{10}+\frac{206^2}{10}+\frac{137^2}{10}\right)-3(31)$$
$$= 0.0129032(1488.4+4243.6+1876.9)-93 = 5.18$$

We can use the CHIDIST function to evaluate the probability of this value under the null hypothesis of no group differences in distribution. There are $k-1=2$ degrees of freedom.

$$= \text{CHIDIST}(5.18, 2)$$

The obtained p value of .075 is greater than our alpha level of .05, and we retain the null hypothesis. We conclude there are no differences in extraversion among the different majors. Figure 12.4 shows a generic Kruskal-Wallis template that automates all our calculations.

---

[8] These are a sample of data collected by the author.

Group	Score	Rank		Groups	3	
1	16	5		N	30	
1	11	1				
1	26	20.5		Group	R	n
1	26	20.5		1	122	10
1	20	11		2	206	10
1	22	17		3	137	10
1	18	7				
1	20	11				
1	21	14.5				
1	21	14.5				
2	36	27				
2	18	7				
2	37	28.5				
2	18	7				
2	27	22.5		H	p	
2	37	28.5		5.18	0.075	
2	23	18.5				
2	40	30				
2	27	22.5				
2	21	14.5				
3	19	9				
3	23	18.5				
3	34	25.5				
3	14	4				
3	12	2				
3	34	25.5				
3	30	24				
3	20	11				
3	21	14.5				
3	13	3				

This template performs a Kruskal-Wallis "analysis of variance by ranks." Enter a group identifier in the green-shaded data entry area in column A, beginning with 1, and the data value in column B. The data do not have to be in order. The template calculates ranks for all N observations, correcting for tied ranks.

The template is protected to keep the user from accidentally deleting the formulas. To unprotect the template, select **Review > Changes > Unprotect Sheet**. There is no password.

This template is freely available for personal and educational use.

Copyright © 2009, Larry A. Pace, Ph.D.

Figure 12.3 Generic Kruskal-Wallis test template

Pairwise Comparisons for the Kruskal-Wallis Test

Aczel and Sounderpandian (2009) offer a critical-value method similar to the Tukey HSD criterion for pairwise comparisons after a significant Kruskal-Wallis test. Calculate the average rank for each of the k groups,

$$\bar{R}_k = \frac{R_k}{n_k}$$

Then calculate the absolute value of the differences between the pairs of average ranks.

$$D = \left| \bar{R}_i - \bar{R}_j \right|$$

Compare this value D to the critical point based on the chi-square distribution using the same alpha level as the one used for the overall test.

$$C_{KW} = \sqrt{\chi^2_{\alpha,k-1}\left(\frac{N(N+1)}{12}\right)\left(\frac{1}{n_i} + \frac{1}{n_j}\right)}$$

In our case, the critical value of χ^2 for $\alpha = .05$ and 2 degrees of freedom is

$$= \text{CHIINV}(0.05, 2) = 5.99$$

As the overall test we just discussed was not significant, we would not perform pairwise comparisons in this case. Let us illustrate pairwise comparisons with another example. Each of three randomly selected groups learns a different problem solving strategy. The dependent variable is task performance, with higher scores indicating better performance. The hypothetical data are as follows (Table 12.6)

Table 12.6 Hypothetical task performance scores

Group1	Group2	Group3
26	17	30
23	15	25
19	14	20
17	12	18
15	10	16

The calculations are left for the reader. The value of H is 7.44, and $p = .024$. Table 12.7 shows the average ranks for the three groups.

Table 12.7 Average ranks for three groups

Group	R	n	$\bar{R}$
1	48	5	9.6
2	18	5	3.6
3	54	5	10.8

Calculate the absolute difference scores as described above (Table 12.8).

Table 12.8 Absolute difference scores

	Group1	Group2	Group3
Group1	-	6	1.2
Group2	-	-	7.2*
Group3	-	-	-

$*p < .05$

With 2 degrees of freedom, the critical difference is

$$C_{\text{KW}} = \sqrt{\chi^2_{\alpha,k-1}\left(\frac{N(N+1)}{12}\right)\left(\frac{1}{n_i}+\frac{1}{n_j}\right)} = \sqrt{5.99\left(\frac{15(16)}{12}\right)\left(\frac{1}{5}+\frac{1}{5}\right)}$$

$$= \sqrt{5.99(20)(.40)} = 6.92$$

Because the samples are of the same size, we need to calculate only one critical difference. By this measure, only the difference between groups 2 and 3 is significant at the .05 level.

Thorne & Giesen (2003) recommend a slightly different approach for follow-up comparisons after a significant H test. Their approach is to use the Mann-Whitney U test for pairwise comparisons. The reader should be aware of the probability of compounding Type I error if this approach is chosen. A good strategy would be to use a lowered alpha level for these tests, perhaps the Bonferroni correction. In the current case, each of the three tests could be performed at $\alpha = .05 / 3 = .0167$.

THE BOTTOM LINE

- The Kruskal-Wallis test is a nonparametric alternative to the one-way between groups ANOVA.

- The test is not available in Excel.

- A critical difference method can be used for pairwise comparisons after a significant Kruskal-Wallis test.

- Excel add-ins such as MegaStat provide the Kruskal-Wallis test.

The Friedman Test

The Friedman test is a nonparametric alternative to the repeated-measures ANOVA. The repeated measures for each participant or case are ranked, and these ranks are then compared. This test is an extension of the Wilcoxon matched-pairs signed-ranks test discussed earlier to three or more repeated measurements.

Rationale and Procedure

As mentioned in Chapter 9, the repeated-measures ANOVA is a special case of two-way ANOVA with one observation per cell. The Friedman test applies the same logic as the repeated-measures ANOVA to data ranked across three or more measures for the same participants. The data are collected as ranks initially or are converted to ranks within each row. We sum the ranks for each of the k treatments, and compute the following chi-square statistic:

$$\chi^2 = \frac{12}{nk(k+1)} \sum_{j=1}^{k} R_j^2 - 3n(k+1)$$

When the null hypothesis that the ranks do not differ among the treatment conditions is true, the resulting value approaches the chi-square distribution with degrees of freedom equal to $k - 1$.

The calculations for the Friedman test are not complicated, as the ranks occur within each row. When there are tied ranks within a row, Hays (1973) suggests the conservative approach of breaking the ties in a way that assures the column sums are as close together as possible. A more common approach would be simply to apply the customary tie correction we have used thus far. As with the Mann-Whitney U test, a correction for ties can improve the approximation of the chi-square distribution. For the sake of simplicity, we will not employ the tie correction here.

Example

Twelve frequent travelers ranked four major hotel chains from 1 (*best*) to 4 (*worst*). The hypothetical data appear in Table 12.9. As with other nonparametric tests, we assign the average rank to ties.

Table 12.9 Hypothetical hotel rankings

ChainA	ChainB	ChainC	ChainD	
1	2	4	3	
2	1	3	4	
1	2	3	4	
2	3	4	1	
2	3	1	4	
1	2	4	3	
1	2	3	4	
1.5	1.5	3.5	3.5	
1	2	4	3	
2	3	4	1	
1	2	3.5	3.5	
1	2	3	4	
16.5	25.5	40	38	Sum

Calculating the test statistic, we find

$$\chi^2 = \frac{12}{nk(k+1)}\sum_{j=1}^{k} R_j^2 - 3n(k+1) = \frac{12}{12(4)(5)}\left(16.5^2 + 25.5^2 + 40^2 + 38^2\right) - 3(12)(5)$$

$$= \frac{12}{240}\left(272.25 + 650.25 + 1600 + 1444\right) - 180 = 18.33$$

The Friedman test indicates the hotel chains do not have equal ranks, χ^2 (3, $N = 12$) = 18.33, $p < .001$. A generic Friedman test template shown in Figure 12.4 automates these calculations.

	A	B	C	D	E	F	G	H	I	J	K	L	M	N	O
1	Subject	Meas1	Meas2	Meas3	Meas4	Meas5	Meas6	Meas7	Meas8	Meas9	Meas10				
2	1	1	2	4	3								n	12	
3	2	2	1	3	4								k	4	
4	3	1	2	3	4										
5	4	2	3	4	1								Measure	Sum	Avg. Rank
6	5	2	3	1	4								Meas1	16.5	1.38
7	6	1	2	4	3								Meas2	25.5	2.13
8	7	1	2	3	4								Meas3	40	3.33
9	8	1.5	1.5	3.5	3.5								Meas4	38	3.17
10	9	1	2	4	3								Meas5		
11	10	2	3	4	1								Meas6		
12	11	1	2	3.5	3.5								Meas7		
13	12	1	2	3	4								Meas8		
14													Meas9		
15													Meas10		
16															
17													χ^2	18.33	
18													$p(\chi^2)$	0.000	

Figure 12.4 Generic Friedman test template

THE BOTTOM LINE

- The Friedman test is a nonparametric alternative to the repeated-measures ANOVA.
- The test is not available in Excel, but it is not difficult to build a reusable template for it.
- Excel add-ins such as MegaStat provide the Friedman test.

Chapter 12 Exercises

1. The following hypothetical data compare male and female drivers on an index of safe driving practices, such as wearing a seatbelt, using turn signals, and driving within the speed limit. The higher the number, the more safe driving practices the participant uses. Perform and interpret a Mann-Whitney U test.

Male	Female
10	12
10	13
12	15
13	16
13	17
14	18
14	19
15	19
16	19
20	20

2. The following hypothetical ordinal data represent two independent groups of observations. Perform and interpret a Mann-Whitney U test.

Group1	Group2
1	2
3	5
4	8
6	9
7	11
10	12
13	16
14	17
15	18

3. Perform and interpret a Wilcoxon matched-pairs signed-ranks test for the data used in Chapter 4 (Table 4.2) to illustrate the sign test. As a reminder, the data represent students' attitudes toward the use of the computer by the student compared to the use of the computer by the teacher. Comment on any differences between the two tests. The data are as follows.

Pair	Student	Teacher
1	4	3
2	3	3
3	5	2
4	3	2
5	4	5
6	4	1
7	4	1
8	4	1
9	5	1
10	4	3
11	5	3
12	4	2
13	3	4
14	2	1
15	5	4

4. Perform and interpret a Wilcoxon matched-pairs signed-ranks test for the following data, which represent measures on an Attitude Toward Statistics scale before and after a statistics course. Higher numbers indicate more positive attitudes.

Before	After
50	48
40	50
55	60
48	53
42	51
45	49
51	78
55	62
62	57

5. Conduct and interpret a Kruskall-Wallis test with the data from Chapter 8 (Table 8.1) used to illustrate the one-way ANOVA. As a reminder, the data represent the statistics test scores from three different groups, each of which received a different form of instruction. The data are repeated below. If the overall test is significant, use the critical difference method to perform pairwise comparisons.

Online	Classroom	Hybrid
65	72	87
75	82	94
83	87	75
80	82	95
64	69	70
81	85	80
85	90	86
62	70	91
84	92	87
80	86	93

6. A dean ranked professors in her college from 1 (*highest*) to 15 (*lowest*) according to student ratings of teaching effectiveness. The dean then separated the professors into three groups (*low, medium,* and *high*) based on research productivity and service. Use a Kruskal-Wallis test to determine whether the teaching effectiveness rankings of the three groups of professors are equal. If the overall test is significant, use the critical difference method to perform pairwise comparisons.

Low	Medium	High
7	2	1
11	5	3
13	9	4
14	10	6
15	12	8

7. Consumer ratings of their satisfaction with their cell phone provider for seven major metropolitan areas revealed the following rankings from 1 (*best*) to 4 (*worst*). Perform and interpret a Friedman test to determine if the providers' ranks are equal.

BrandA	BrandB	BrandC	BrandD
1	2	4	3
2	1	3	4
1	2	3	4
2	1	4	3
1	2	3	4
2	3	1	4
1	3	1	4

8. A random sample of nine sufferers of acid reflux disease received each of three medications. To control for order effects, researchers counterbalanced the order of the medications. Patients ranked the medications in terms of their effectiveness from 1 (*best*) to 3 (*worst*). The hypothetical data are as follows. Perform and interpret a Friedman test to determine if the medications are equally effective.

Patient	Drug1	Drug2	Drug3
1	2	1	3
2	3	2	1
3	2	3	1
4	3	2	1
5	3	2	1
6	2	3	1
7	1.5	3	1.5
8	2.5	2.5	1
9	2	2	1

Appendix A—Statistical Functions in Excel

Statistical Term	Definitional Formula	Excel Function/Formula
Summation	$\displaystyle\sum_{i=1}^{n} X_i$	= SUM(X)
Mean	$\displaystyle\bar{X} = \frac{\sum_{i=1}^{n} X_i}{n}$	= AVERAGE(X)
Sum of Squares	$SS = \sum\left(X - \bar{X}\right)^2$	= DEVSQ(X)
Population Variance	$\sigma^2 = \dfrac{\sum\left(X - \mu\right)^2}{N}$	= VARP(X)
Sample Variance	$s_X^2 = \dfrac{\sum\left(X - \bar{X}\right)^2}{n-1}$	= VAR(X)
Population Standard Deviation	$\sigma = \sqrt{\sigma^2}$	= STDEVP(X)
Sample Standard Deviation	$s_X = \sqrt{s_X^2}$	= STDEV(X)
Population Covariance	$\sigma_{XY} = \dfrac{\sum\left(X - \mu_X\right)\left(Y - \mu_Y\right)}{N}$	= COVAR(X, Y)
Sample Covariance	$\mathrm{Cov}(X,Y) = \dfrac{\sum\left(X - \bar{X}\right)\left(Y - \bar{Y}\right)}{n-1}$	= COVAR(X, Y) * (n / (n–1))
Correlation	$r_{XY} = \dfrac{\mathrm{Cov}(X,Y)}{s_X s_Y}$	= CORREL(X, Y)
Slope (Regression Coefficient)	$b_1 = r_{XY}\left(\dfrac{s_Y}{s_X}\right)$	= SLOPE(Y, X)
Intercept	$b_0 = \bar{Y} - b_1\bar{X}$	= INTERCEPT(Y, X)

Replace X or Y in the Excel function with the reference to the applicable value, data range, e.g., A1:A25, or the name of the range. Replace n or N with the number of observations (or pairs of observations for covariance and correlation).

Appendix B—Writing Statistical Results in APA Format

Many disciplines in the social and behavioral sciences and many academic institutions require APA formatting for articles, reports, and student papers, theses, and dissertations. The recently released sixth edition of the *Publication Manual of the American Psychological Association* (APA, 2010) provides direction for reporting statistical results. These instructions cover what to report and how to report it. In this appendix you will find a brief overview and some examples of APA format.

What to Report

A minimally adequate set of statistics includes per-cell sample size, observed cell means or frequencies, cell standard deviations, and an estimate of the pooled within-cell variance (APA, 2010). When reporting the results of inferential tests such as t tests, F tests, and chi-square tests, you should report the obtained value or magnitude of the test statistic, the degrees of freedom, and the exact p value. You should also report a measure of effect size or relationship so the reader can understand the importance of your results. State the actual p value for both significant and nonsignificant results. You should also indicate when you use one-tailed statistical tests.

"Assume your reader has a professional knowledge of statistics" (APA, 2010, p. 33). You do not need to give references for commonly used statistical tests or indicate which computer program or computational aid you used to conduct your analyses, unless there is some reason for justifying the test you chose or the particular tool you used. It is not necessary to review common assumptions or interpret effect-size indexes.

How to Report Statistical Results

The APA manual provides specific direction for the number of decimals to report and for the use of leading zeros. Some statistical symbols should be in italics, while others should not, as explained below. The APA manual also has strict rules concerning the use and misuse of hyphens.

The Number of Decimals

As a rule, two decimal places are sufficient for properly scaled measures (APA, 2010). You should always report statistics such as t, F, χ^2, z, correlations, and proportions to two decimal places. You should report exact p values and carry these to two or three decimal places, but should report p values less than .001 as $p < .001$ (2010, p. 114).

Leading Zeros

Values that cannot exceed 1 should have no zero before the decimal (APA, 2010, p. 113). You should therefore report the values of correlations, proportions, and probabilities without leading zeros. For values less than 1, but which could exceed 1, you should use a leading zero. You should therefore write $r = .84$ and $p < .001$, but write $z = 0.49$, $F = 0.93$, $SD = 0.38$, and Cohen's $d = 0.61$.

Italics and Hyphens

Common practice in many statistics texts is to use constructions such as t-test, F-ratio, z-score, and p-value as noun forms. APA format requires t test, F ratio, z score, and p value. The hyphen should be restricted to the use of the compound form as an adjective before the word it modifies. Thus, you should write "*t*-test results," but write "the results of *t* tests" (APA, 2010, p. 100).

Latin letters used to represent sample statistics and inferential tests should appear in italics. Greek letters used to represent population parameters or identifiers should not be in italics. The APA manual provides an extensive list of statistical symbols and abbreviations (APA, 2010, pp. 119-122). The following table presents some common statistical symbols and their definitions summarized from the APA manual and personal experience.

Table A.1 Common statistical symbols and definitions

Symbol	Definition
b	Unstandardized regression coefficient
d	Cohen's measure of effect size
f	Frequency
F	Fisher's F ratio
M	Mean (arithmetic average)
MS	Mean square
n	Number in a subsample
N	Number in a sample (or population)
ns	Nonsignificant
p	Probability
P	Percentage, percentile
r	Pearson product-moment correlation
R	Multiple correlation
r^2	Pearson product-moment correlation squared; coefficient of determination
R^2	Multiple correlation squared; measure of strength of relationship
SD	Standard deviation
SS	Sum of squares
t	Computed value of t test
T	Computed value of Wilcoxon's or McCall's test
U	Computed value of Mann-Whitney test
V	Cramér's statistic for contingency tables
z	Standard score
α	Probability of Type I error; Cronbach's index of internal consistency
β	Probability of Type II error; standardized regression coefficient
η^2	Eta squared (measure of effect size)
μ	Mu (population mean)
σ	Sigma (population standard deviation)
σ^2	Sigma squared (population variance)
χ^2	Computed value of chi square

Examples

The following examples show how to report statistical results in APA format. For more examples, consult the APA manual.

Reporting a Significant *t*-Test Result

Moore and Johnson (2008) studied the phenomenon of mental rotation in human infants. Previous research had found males perform mental rotation on average more effectively than females, but these differences had not been studied in children younger than 4 years of age. Moore and Johnson found that male 5-month-old infants looked significantly longer at a mirror-image test object than at a familiar object rotated through a novel angle, indicating male infants were able to distinguish the rotated original object from its mirror image. The following summary statement (adapted from Moore & Johnson, 2008) reports this difference:

> Male 5-month-old infants looked longer at the mirror-image test object than at the familiar object rotating through the novel angle, $t(19) = 4.07, p < .001, d = 0.61$.

Reporting a Nonsignificant *t*-Test Result

In the same study, Moore and Johnson (2008) found no sex differences in accumulated habituation times. A summary statement adapted from their article follows:

> Male and female infants did not differ in accumulated habituation times, $t(38) = 0.86, p = .395, d = 0.27$.

Reporting *t*-Test Results—Commentary

Moore and Johnson's (2008) article reported the value of *t* with the degrees of freedom in parentheses. Although they did not state it, it is clear from the context the *t* test of the differences between the times spent looking at the mirror image and the familiar object for male infants was a paired-samples *t* test. The test of sex differences in habituation times is an independent-samples *t* test. The reader can infer these facts by noting there were 20 male infants and 20 female infants. The degrees of freedom for a paired-samples *t* test for one group are 19, and the degrees of freedom for an independent-samples *t* test are 38.

The value of *t* is reported to two decimals. The *p* value has no leading zero. The reported value of Cohen's *d* has a leading zero because this index can exceed 1. The value of Cohen's *d* is shown for both the significant *t* test and the nonsignificant test, but is not interpreted in either case.

Reporting a Significant *F*-Test Result

In a study of reciprocity, Keysar, Converse, Wang, and Epley (2008) examined the effects of selfish and generous behaviors by a "dictator" (a person who decides how to split a sum of money with another player) on the resulting choices of participants when the roles were reversed. The dictator assumed the role of either giver or taker in splitting a pot of $100. In the objectively generous condition, the dictator gave $70 or took $30. In the objectively fair condition, the dictator gave or took $50. In the objectively selfish role, the dictator gave $30 or took $70. After the split, the research participant "reciprocators" in the first game became the dictators in the second game and decided how to split a new $100 pot. Pairs of participants were randomly assigned to one of the six cells of the 2 (*frame*: Giving vs. taking) by 3 (*outcome*: Selfish, fair, or generous) between-participants design (Keysar, Converse, Wang, & Epley, 2008). A summary statement adapted from their article follows:

People reciprocated more selfishly after the dictator took from them ($M = \$37$ left for the other player) than after the dictator gave to them ($M = \$51$). A 2 (*frame*) × 3 (*outcome*) ANOVA revealed a significant main effect of frame, $F(1,52) = 5.79$, $p = .020$, $\eta^2 = .10$.

Reporting a Nonsignificant F-Test Result

Smith, Sansone, and White (2007) studied the effect of interest and achievement motivation on women's motivation to select and persist in domains for which negative competence stereotypes about women exist. They studied a computer science task and examined whether women higher and lower in achievement motivation were differentially likely to adopt performance-avoidance goals when a math-gender stereotype was salient. As part of their study, they compared the achievement motivation of the three conditions created through the experimental design (stereotype threat versus nullified stereotype versus control, i.e., nothing said about stereotypes). Before conducting their hypothesis tests, they used an ANOVA to compare the achievement motivation scores of the three groups. Their summary statement follows (Smith, Sansone, & White, 2007):

> First, we wanted to ensure that achievement motivation did not differ between conditions, and it did not, $F(2, 55) = 1.58$, $p = .215$, $R^2 = .05$ (p. 105).

Reporting F-Test Results—Commentary

The researchers reported p values and effect-size indexes for both significant and nonsignificant F tests. As the discussion in this book indicates, eta-squared and R^2 are equivalent measures of effect size. The degrees of freedom for the F ratio appear in parentheses. The value of F is reported to two decimal places, and no leading zeros appear before the p values or effect-size measures. The exact p value is reported to two or three decimal places. In the case of the Keysar et al. (2008) study, the p value rounds to .020 and thus could be reported effectively to two decimals as $p = .02$. There is no interpretation of the effect-size measures.

Reporting the Results of a Chi-square Test

Rinn and Nelson (2009) studied the effects of biased and unbiased information forms on the diagnosis by participants of Attention Deficit Hyperactivity Disorder of a hypothetical student described in a vignette. The biased form included the diagnosis and a statement that the child was gifted and talented. The unbiased form used a free recall method and asked for the underlying cause of the behavior. The researchers use a chi-square test of independence to determine the relationship between the type of form and the diagnosis. The summary statement adapted from their article (Rinn & Nelson, 2009) appears below:

> Results of the chi-square analysis indicate a significant relationship between the type of form (Form A or form B) and the diagnosis made by the participant, $\chi^2(3, N = 32) = 12.61$, $p = .006$.

Reporting Chi-Square Tests—Commentary

The value of chi-square is reported to two decimals, while the exact p value is reported to two or three decimal places. Because the degrees of freedom for chi-square tests are based on the number of levels of the variables rather than the sample size, information for both degrees of freedom and sample size appears in parentheses). For a chi-square analysis to be complete, the authors should also include a measure of effect size.

A "Different" Way to Report Probabilities

The Association for Psychological Science (APS) generally follows APA style, but now encourages authors of articles for APS journals such as *Psychological Science* to report the probability of replication, p_{rep}, instead of, or in addition to, the standard p value. This value has a direct correspondence to the p value and can be approximated by the following equation (Killeen, 2005):

$$p_{rep} \approx \left[1 + \left(\frac{p}{1-p} \right)^{2/3} \right]^{-1}$$

The above uses the logistic approximation to the normal distribution. Users of Excel can evaluate p_{rep} using the normal distribution and the obtained p value as

$$= \text{NORMSDIST(NORMSINV}(1 - p) / \text{SQRT}(2))$$

The probability an effect will be replicated is a different way to examine the importance of the findings from a particular study, and is a step away from null hypothesis statistical tests (NHST). The Moore and Johnson (2008) article discussed earlier was published in the APS journal *Psychological Science*, and reported p_{rep}. The summary statement appearing in their article and reporting the probability of replication follows:

> Male 5-month-old infants looked longer at the mirror-image test object than at the familiar object rotating through the novel angle, $t(19) = 4.07$, $p < .001$, $p_{rep} = .99$, $d = 0.61$.

Appendix C—Answers to Odd-Numbered Exercises

Chapter 1 Exercises

1. The answers are as follows:
    a. 570.40
    b. 16528
    c. 1185921
    d. 4.5
3. The answers are as follows:
    a. 100
    b. 3.75
    c. 129
    d. 3628800
5. The answers are as follows:
    a. 72.545
    b-d . See the following:

X	5b	5c	5d
73	0.455	0.207	0.455
80	7.455	55.570	7.455
60	-12.545	157.388	12.545
91	18.455	340.570	18.455
59	-13.545	183.479	13.545
64	-8.545	73.025	8.545
77	4.455	19.843	4.455
77	4.455	19.843	4.455
53	-19.545	382.025	19.545
84	11.455	131.207	11.455
80	7.455	55.570	7.455

7. The answers are as follows:
    a. Minimum = 53
    b. Maximum = 91
    c. Squares and square roots (see the following)

X	SQRT(X)	X^2
73	8.544	5329
80	8.944	6400
60	7.746	3600
91	9.539	8281
59	7.681	3481
64	8.000	4096
77	8.775	5929
77	8.775	5929
53	7.280	2809
84	9.165	7056
80	8.944	6400

9. You can assign a name to a cell or a range of cells. Named ranges offer the advantages of simplicity and of clarity. You cannot name a range something that will conflict with Excel's use of letters and numbers referring to worksheet cells.
10. *Descriptive statistics* summarize, organize, and present numerical information in a meaningful way. A *sample* is a subset of a population. As *statistic* is a measurable

characteristic of a sample. A *variable* is a quantity that can take on two or more different values. *Measurement* is the assignment of numbers to objects to represent quantities of attributes.

Chapter 2 Exercises

1. The answers are as follows:
    a. Mean = 4.125
    b. Mode = 5
    c. Median = 4
    d. Count = 24
    e. Minimum = 2
    f. Maximum = 8
    g. Range = 6
    h. Variance = 2.90
    i. Standard deviation = 1.70
3. The answers are as follows:
    a. Mean = 73.69
    b. Mode = 67
    c. Median = 73
    d. Count = 36
    e. Minimum = 52
    f. Maximum = 90
    g. Range = 38
    h. Variance = 63.76
    i. Standard deviation = 7.99
5. The answers are as follows:
    a. Mean = 2.32
    b. Mode = 2.9
    c. Median = 2.6
    d. Count = 51
    e. Minimum = –0.9
    f. Maximum = 4.5
    g. Range = 5.4
    h. Variance = 1.23
    i. Standard deviation = 1.11
    The average percent change is 2.32, indicating modest growth in wages.
7. The answers are as follows:
    a. The 2001 wage 25th percentile is $28,837
    b. The 2001 wage 75th percentile is $36,733
    c. The 2001 wage percentile rank for D.C. is 100%

9.   See the following:

UpperLimit	Frequency
30000	13
35000	19
40000	13
45000	2
50000	3
55000	0
60000	1

Chapter 3 Exercises

1.   The pivot table appears below:

Row Labels ▾	Average of Wage2002
Midwest	$ 32,544.25
Northeast	$ 38,987.44
South	$ 34,001.18
West	$ 33,256.85
Grand Total	**$ 34,348.57**

3.   The clustered bar chart follows:

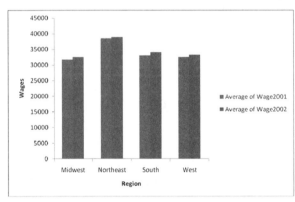

5.   The bar chart follows:

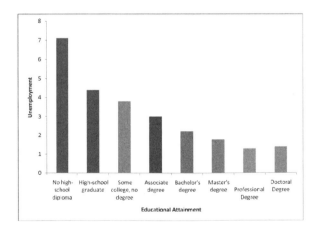

7.   The scatterplot appears below.

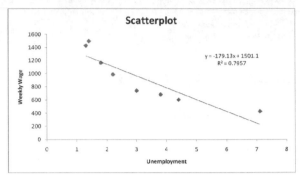

9.   The histogram appears below.

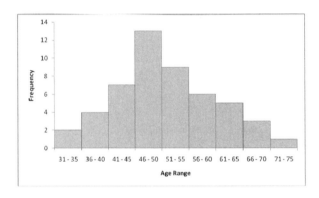

Chapter 4 Exercises

1.   The answers are as follows:
   a.   .09537
   b.   .00742
   c.   .72479

3.   The answers are as follows:
   a.   .37581
   b.   .28941
   c.   .03279

5.   .00259

7.   The answers are as follows:
   a.   .1008
   b.   .4232
   c.   .0839
   d.   .0801

9.   The answers are as follows:
   a.   .9513
   b.   .1251
   c.   .3036

Chapter 5 Exercises

1. The answers are as follows:
   a. $z = -1.30$
   b. About 2.28%
   c. About 15.87%
   d. About 86.64%
3. The answers are as follows:
   a. $z = -2.40$
   b. About 15.87%
   c. About 15.87%
   d. About 68.27%
5. $z = 1.04$
7. The 91st percentile
9. Top 15% cutoff is 116, top 10% cutoff is 119, top 5% cutoff is 125

Chapter 6 Exercises

1. $M = 1.159$, 95% CI = [1.073, 1.246]
3. $M = 1.159$, 99% CI = [1.043, 1.276]. The 99% confidence interval is wider because it encompasses a wider range of possible values for the population mean in order to increase the confidence in the estimate from 95% to 99%.
5. $M = 51.38$, 99% CI = [47.81, 54.95]
7. $\tilde{p} = ..4795$, 99% CI = [.43, .53]
9. $z = -0.24$, $p = .810$ (two-tailed). There is no significant difference.

Chapter 7 Exercises

1. The results from the one-sample t test template appear below. Cohen's d suggests a large effect size.

Sample Size	51
Population Mean	0
Sample Mean	2.317647059
Mean Difference	2.317647059
Standard Deviation	1.11026229
Standard Error	0.155467817
t	14.91
df	50
Two-tailed Probability	0.000
One-tailed Probability	0.000
Cohen's d	2.09

95% Confidence Interval	
Max. Error of Estimate	0.312
Lower Limit	2.005
Upper Limit	2.630

3. The results from the paired-samples t test worksheet template appear as follows. Cohen's d suggests a large effect size.

Statistic	Measure1	Measure2
Count	51	51
Mean	33605.07843	34348.56863
Standard Deviation	6263.733844	6215.071582
Mean Difference	-743.4901961	
Std. Error	54.580	
t	-13.62	
df	50	
$p(t)$ one-tailed	0.000	
$p(t)$ two-tailed	0.000	
95% Confidence Interval		
Lower Limit	-853.118	
Upper Limit	-633.863	
Effect Size		
Cohen's d	-1.91	
Eta squared	0.79	

5. The result from the worksheet template appears as follows. Cohen's d suggests a medium effect size.

Statistic	Measure1	Measure2
Count	38	38
Mean	0.841842105	1.159473684
Standard Deviation	0.164150	0.263725
Mean Difference	-0.317631579	
Std. Error	0.046	
t	-6.97	
df	37	
$p(t)$ one-tailed	0.000	
$p(t)$ two-tailed	0.000	
95% Confidence Interval		
Lower Limit	-0.410	
Upper Limit	-0.225	
Effect Size		
Cohen's d	-1.13	
Eta squared	0.57	

7. The results from the worksheet template appear below. The t test is not significant, and Cohen's d suggests no effect.

Statistic	Group1	Group2
Sum	1796	773
Count	35	15
Mean	51.31428571	51.53333333
Variance	83.51596639	107.8380952
Standard Deviation	9.138707041	10.38451228
Pooled Variance	90.60992063	
Pooled Standard Deviation	9.518924342	
Mean Difference	-0.21904762	
Standard Error of Mean Difference	2.937603828	
df	48	
t obtained	-0.07	
one-tailed probability	0.470	
two-tailed probability	0.941	
Cohen's d	0.02	
Eta squared	0.00	

	Lower Limit	Upper Limit
95% Confidence Interval for Mean Diff.	-6.125	5.687

9. The result from the worksheet template appears below.
    The two-tailed *t* test is not significant. Cohen's *d*
    suggests a medium effect size.

Statistic	Group1	Group2
Sum	135.1	98
Count	15	15
Mean	9.006666667	6.533333333
Variance	11.87209524	17.55380952
Standard Deviation	3.445590695	4.189726665
Pooled Variance	14.71295238	
Pooled Standard Deviation	3.835746652	
Mean Difference	2.473333333	
Standard Error of Mean Difference	1.400616644	
df	28	
t obtained	1.77	
one-tailed probability	0.044	
two-tailed probability	0.088	
Cohen's *d*	0.64	
Eta squared	0.10	

	Lower Limit	Upper Limit
95% Confidence Interval for Mean Diff.	-0.396	5.342

Chapter 8 Exercises

1. The ANOVA summary table from the worksheet
    template appears below. The *F* ratio is not significant.
    Post hoc comparisons are unwarranted.

Source	Sum of Squares	df	MS	F	p
Between	271363844.840	3	90454614.947	2.52	0.070
Within	1690354238.846	47	35964983.805		
Total	1961718083.686	50			

η^2	0.14

3. The ANOVA summary table from the worksheet
    template appears below, along with mean comparisons.
    The LSD test indicates all pairs of means are
    significantly different at *p* < .05.

Source	SS	df	MS	F	p
Between	1524.006	2	762.003	27.49	0.000
Within	554.429	20	27.721		
Total	2078.435	22			

η^2	0.73

	Mean Differences		
	Group1	Group2	Group3
Group1	-	19.500*	8.964*
Group2		-	10.536*
Group3			-

5. The ANOVA summary table from the worksheet
    template appears as follows, along with mean
    comparisons. The LSD test indicates the mean for
    Group1 is significantly higher than the means for all
    other groups at *p* < .05, and all other groups do not
    differ significantly.

ANOVA Summary Table

Source	SS	df	MS	F	p
Between	62.250	3	20.750	6.57	.001
Within	139.000	44	3.159		
Total	201.250	47			

η^2	.31

	Group1	Group2	Group3	Group4
Group1	-	2*	3*	2.5*
Group2		-	1	0.5
Group3			-	0.5
Group4				-

7. The ANOVA summary table from the worksheet
    template appears below, along with mean comparisons.
    The LSD test indicates the mean for poultry hot dogs is
    significantly lower than the means for the other two
    types at *p* < .05, and the other types do not differ
    significantly.

Source	SS	df	MS	F	p
Between	17692.195	2	8846.098	16.07	.000
Within	28067.138	51	550.336		
Total	45759.333	53			

η^2	.39

	Beef	Meat	Poultry
Beef	-	1.86	38.09*
Meat		-	39.94*
Poultry			-

9. The ANOVA summary table from the worksheet
    template appears below, along with mean comparisons.
    The LSD test indicates the mean for Brands A and C do
    not differ at *p* < .05, and the other two pairs of means
    differ significantly.

ANOVA Summary Table

Source	SS	df	MS	F	p
Between	17.049	2	8.525	12.74	.001
Within	8.028	12	0.669		
Total	25.077	14			

η^2	.68

	BrandA	BrandB	BrandC
BrandA	-	1.64*	0.94
BrandB		-	2.58*
BrandC			-

11. The ANOVA summary table from the Analysis
    ToolPak follows. There are significant main effects for
    the type of violence and the length of exposure. The
    interaction is also significant. A plot of cell means
    reveals the interaction is "ordinal."

ANOVA						
Source of Variation	SS	df	MS	F	P-value	F crit
Time of Exposure	5202.00	1	5202.00	165.10	0.000	4.20
Type of Violence	1128.13	1	1128.13	35.80	0.000	4.20
Time x Type Interaction	561.13	1	561.13	17.81	0.000	4.20
Within	882.25	28	31.51			
Total	7773.50	31				

Chapter 9 Exercises

1. The summary output from the worksheet template follows, along with a table of mean comparisons using the LSD criterion. Mean differences marked by an asterisk (*) are significant at $p < .05$.

ANOVA Summary Table

Source	SS	df	MS	F	p(F)
Between groups	147.0750	3	49.0250	33.79	0.000
Subjects	173.7250	9	19.3028		
Error	39.1750	27	1.4509		
Total	359.9750	39	9.2301		
Partial η^2	0.7897				

	Meas1	Meas2	Meas3	Meas4
Meas1	0.00	-1.50*	-3.60*	-5.00*
Meas2	1.50*	0.00	-2.10*	-3.50*
Meas3	3.60*	2.10*	0.00	-1.40*
Meas4	5.00*	3.50*	1.40*	0.00

3. The summary output from the worksheet template follows, along with a table of mean comparisons using the LSD criterion. Mean differences marked by an asterisk (*) are significant at $p < .05$.

ANOVA Summary Table

Source	SS	df	MS	F	p(F)
Between groups	336.8148	5	67.3630	26.11	0.000
Subjects	311.4815	8	38.9352		
Error	103.1852	40	2.5796		
Total	751.4815	53	14.1789		
Partial η^2	0.7655				

	Meas1	Meas2	Meas3	Meas4	Meas5	Meas6
Meas1	0.00	1.67*	3.00*	5.11*	5.89*	7.22*
Meas2	-1.67*	0.00	1.33	3.44*	4.22*	5.56*
Meas3	-3.00*	-1.33	0.00	2.11*	2.89*	4.22*
Meas4	-5.11*	-3.44*	-2.11*	0.00	0.78	2.11*
Meas5	-5.89*	-4.22*	-2.89*	-0.78	0.00	1.33
Meas6	-7.22*	-5.56*	-4.22*	-2.11*	-1.33	0.00

5. The summary output from the worksheet template follows criterion. Mean differences marked by an asterisk (*) are significant at $p < .05$., along with a table of mean comparisons using the LSD criterion.

ANOVA Summary Table

Source	SS	df	MS	F	p(F)
Between groups	67.8519	2	33.9259	15.30	0.000
Subjects	399.8519	8	49.9815		
Error	35.4815	16	2.2176		
Total	503.1852	26	19.3533		
Partial η^2	0.6566				

	Meas1	Meas2	Meas3
Meas1	0.00	-2.67*	-3.78*
Meas2	2.67*	0.00	-1.11
Meas3	3.78*	1.11	0.00

7. The summary output from the worksheet template follows, along with a table of mean comparisons using the LSD criterion. Mean differences marked by an asterisk (*) are significant at $p < .05$.

ANOVA Summary Table

Source	SS	df	MS	F	p(F)
Between groups	1908.0833	2	954.0417	8.83	0.003
Subjects	33718.2917	7	4816.8988		
Error	1512.5833	14	108.0417		
Total	37138.9583	23	1614.7373		
Partial η^2	0.5578				

	Meas1	Meas2	Meas3
Meas1	0.00	-3.38	-20.38*
Meas2	3.38	0.00	-17.00*
Meas3	20.38*	17.00*	0.00

9. The summary output from the worksheet template follows, along with a table of mean comparisons using the LSD criterion. Mean differences marked by an asterisk (*) are significant at $p < .05$.

ANOVA Summary Table

Source	SS	df	MS	F	p(F)
Between groups	387.2667	2	193.6333	11.72	0.001
Subjects	6326.8000	9	702.9778		
Error	297.4000	18	16.5222		
Total	7011.4667	29	241.7747		
Partial η^2	0.5656				

	Meas1	Meas2	Meas3
Meas1	0.00	-4.50*	-8.80*
Meas2	4.50*	0.00	-4.30*
Meas3	8.80*	4.30*	0.00

Chapter 10 Exercises

1. The results from the Regression tool appear below, with the relevant values highlighted. Note the negative sign for the slope term, indicating the correlation is also negative, $r(7) = -.89$, $p = .003$.

SUMMARY OUTPUT

Regression Statistics	
Multiple R	0.892
R Square	0.796
Adjusted R Square	0.762
Standard Error	0.956
Observations	8

ANOVA

	df	SS	MS	F	Significance F
Regression	1	21.336	21.336	23.366	0.003
Residual	6	5.479	0.913		
Total	7	26.815			

	Coefficients	Standard Error	t Stat	P-value	Lower 95%	Upper 95%
Intercept	7.307	0.929	7.868	0.000	5.034	9.579
WeeklyWage	-0.004	0.001	-4.834	0.003	-0.007	-0.002

3. The results from the Regression tool appear below, with the relevant values highlighted. The correlation is positive and nearly perfect, $r(50) = .998$, $p < .001$.

SUMMARY OUTPUT

Regression Statistics	
Multiple R	0.998
R Square	0.996
Adjusted R Square	0.996
Standard Error	388.949
Observations	51

ANOVA

	df	SS	MS	F	Significance F
Regression	1	1923942940.978	1923942940.978	12717.628	0.000
Residual	49	7412797.532	151281.582		
Total	50	1931355738.510			

	Coefficients	Standard Error	t Stat	P-value	Lower 95%	Upper 95%
Intercept	1068.615	300.091	3.561	0.001	465.560	1671.670
Wage2001	0.990	0.009	112.772	0.000	0.973	1.008

5. The correlation indicates high test-retest reliability, $r(29) = .92, p < .001$.

7. The predicted attendance is approximately 10.1 students.

Chapter 11 Exercises

1. The results from the chi-square template follow. There is a significant departure from expectation, $\chi^2(5, N = 40) = 17.30, p = .004$.

Results	
Count (k)	6
Sum	40
χ^2	17.30
df (k - 1)	5
p (χ^2)	0.004

3. The results from the chi-square template follow. There is no significant departure from expectation, $\chi^2(3, N = 88) = 5.55, p = .062$.

Results	
Count (k)	3
Sum	88
χ^2	5.55
df (k - 1)	2
p (χ^2)	0.062

5. The results from the chi-square template follow. There is a significant departure from expectation, $\chi^2(4, N = 383) = 30.36, p < .001$. Cramér's V indicates a moderate effect.

Test Results

0	Correction
30.361	χ^2
5	Rows
2	Columns
4	df
0.000	p (χ^2)
0.282	V (or φ)

7. The results from the chi-square template follow. There is a significant association, $\chi^2(2, N = 90) = 9.99, p = .007$. Cramér's $V = .33$, which suggests a medium effect size. Note the application of the Yates continuity correction.

Test Results

0	Correction
9.99	χ^2
2	Rows
3	Columns
2	df
0.007	p (χ^2)
0.33	V (or φ)

9. The results from the chi-square template follow. There is a significant association, $\chi^2(2, N = 2016) = 213.24, p < .001$. Cramér's $V = .23$, which suggests a small or weak effect .

Test Results

0	Correction
213.24	χ^2
3	Rows
2	Columns
2	df
0.000	p (χ^2)
0.23	V (or φ)

Chapter 12 Exercises

1. The results of the Mann-Whitney U test from the worksheet template appear below. Women's ranks on the safe driving practices index are significantly higher than the ranks of men, $z = -2.04, p = .002$,

Value	Group1	Group2
ΣR	58.5	132
Count	10	10

U_1	96.5
U_2	23
U	23
z	-2.041
$p(z)$ One-tailed	0.021
$p(z)$ Two-tailed	0.041

For small samples, use tabled values	
Critical U for α = .05, two-tailed	23
$U \le U_{crit}$?	Yes, Reject

3. The results of the Wilcoxon matched-pairs signed-ranks test from the worksheet template appear below. The critical value of T for $N = 14$ at $\alpha = .01$ is 13 (Table 12.1). The normal approximation indicates a p value of .005, two-tailed. The one-tailed probability is .003, making the Wilcoxon test more powerful than the sign test, the p value of which was .0065 (one-tailed).

T	8
N	14
z	-2.79
$p(z)$	0.005

5. The Kruskall-Wallis test indicated the three methods produced significantly different test scores, $\chi^2(2, N = 30) = 6.95$, $p = .031$. The Kruskall-Wallis test results are in agreement with those from the ANOVA. A table of the absolute differences in average ranks follows. The critical difference is 9.64, and only the difference between groups 1 and 3 is significant.

Groups	3
N	30

Group	R	n
1	101	10
2	159.5	10
3	204.5	10

H	p
6.95	0.031

	Group1	Group2	Group3
Group1	-	5.85	10.35*
Group2		-	4.50
Group3			-

7. The Friedman test indicated the cell phone providers' ranks were not equal, $\chi^2(3, N = 7) = 9.26$, $p = .026$.

χ^2	9.26
df	3
$p(\chi^2)$	0.026

Appendix D—Critical Values of q (the Studentized Range Statistic)

df_w	α	Number of Means								
		2	3	4	5	6	7	8	9	10
5	0.05	3.64	4.60	5.22	5.67	6.03	6.33	6.58	6.80	6.99
	0.01	5.70	6.98	7.80	8.42	8.91	9.32	9.67	9.97	10.24
6	0.05	3.46	4.34	4.90	5.30	5.63	5.90	6.12	6.32	6.49
	0.01	5.24	6.33	7.03	7.56	7.97	8.32	8.61	8.87	9.10
7	0.05	3.34	4.16	4.68	5.06	5.36	5.61	5.82	6.00	6.16
	0.01	4.95	5.92	6.54	7.01	7.37	7.68	7.94	8.17	8.37
8	0.05	3.26	4.04	4.53	4.89	5.17	5.40	5.60	5.77	5.92
	0.01	4.75	5.64	6.20	6.62	6.96	7.24	7.47	7.37	7.86
9	0.05	3.20	3.95	4.41	4.76	5.02	5.24	5.43	5.59	5.74
	0.01	4.60	5.43	5.96	6.35	6.66	6.91	7.13	7.33	7.49
10	0.05	3.15	3.88	4.33	4.65	4.91	5.12	5.30	5.46	5.60
	0.01	4.48	5.27	5.77	6.14	6.43	6.67	6.87	7.05	7.21
11	0.05	3.11	3.82	4.26	4.57	4.82	5.03	5.20	5.35	5.49
	0.01	4.39	5.15	5.62	5.97	6.25	6.48	6.67	6.84	6.99
12	0.05	3.08	3.77	4.20	4.51	4.75	4.95	5.12	5.27	5.39
	0.01	4.32	5.05	5.50	5.84	6.10	6.32	6.51	6.67	6.81
13	0.05	3.06	3.73	4.15	4.45	4.69	4.88	5.05	5.19	5.32
	0.01	4.25	4.96	5.40	5.73	5.98	6.19	6.37	6.53	6.67
14	0.05	3.03	3.70	4.11	4.41	4.64	4.83	4.99	5.13	5.25
	0.01	4.21	4.89	5.32	5.63	5.88	6.08	6.26	6.41	6.54
15	0.05	3.01	3.67	4.08	4.37	4.59	4.78	4.94	5.08	5.20
	0.01	4.17	4.84	5.25	5.56	5.80	5.99	6.16	6.31	6.44
16	0.05	3.00	3.65	4.05	4.33	4.56	4.74	4.90	5.03	5.15
	0.01	4.13	4.79	5.19	5.49	5.72	5.92	6.08	6.22	6.35
17	0.05	2.98	3.63	4.02	4.30	4.52	4.70	4.86	4.99	5.11
	0.01	4.10	4.74	5.14	5.43	5.66	5.85	6.01	6.15	6.27
18	0.05	2.97	3.61	4.00	4.28	4.49	4.67	4.82	4.96	5.07
	0.01	4.07	4.70	5.09	5.38	5.60	5.79	5.94	6.08	6.20
19	0.05	2.96	3.59	3.98	4.25	4.47	4.65	4.79	4.92	5.04
	0.01	4.05	4.67	5.05	5.33	5.55	5.73	5.89	6.02	6.14
20	0.05	2.95	3.58	3.96	4.23	4.45	4.62	4.77	4.90	5.01
	0.01	4.02	4.64	5.02	5.29	5.51	5.69	5.84	5.97	6.09
24	0.05	2.92	3.53	3.90	4.17	4.37	4.54	4.68	4.81	4.92
	0.01	3.96	4.55	4.91	5.17	5.37	5.54	5.69	5.81	5.92
30	0.05	2.89	3.49	3.85	4.10	4.30	4.46	4.60	4.72	4.82
	0.01	3.89	4.45	4.80	5.05	5.24	5.40	5.54	5.65	5.76
40	0.05	2.86	3.44	3.79	4.04	4.23	4.39	4.52	4.63	4.73
	0.01	3.82	4.37	4.70	4.93	5.11	5.26	5.39	5.50	5.60
60	0.05	2.83	3.40	3.74	3.98	4.16	4.31	4.44	4.55	4.65
	0.01	3.76	4.28	4.59	4.82	4.99	5.13	5.25	5.36	5.45
120	0.05	2.80	3.36	3.68	3.92	4.10	4.24	4.36	4.47	4.56
	0.01	3.70	4.20	4.50	4.71	4.87	5.01	5.12	5.21	5.30
∞	0.05	2.77	3.31	3.63	3.86	4.03	4.17	4.29	4.39	4.47
	0.01	3.64	4.12	4.40	4.60	4.76	4.88	4.99	5.08	5.16

Source: Generated by the author using the *qtukey* function in R.

References

Aczel, A., & Sounderpandian, J. (2009). *Complete business statistics* (7th ed.). New York: McGraw-Hill.

American Psychological Association. (2010). *Publication manual of the American Psychological Association* (6th ed.). Washington, DC: Author.

Bakeman, R., & Robinson, B. F. (2005). *Understanding statistics in the behavioral sciences*. Mahwah, NJ: Lawrence Erlbaum Associates.

Bennett, J., Briggs, W., & Triola, M. (2009). *Statistical reasoning for everyday life* (3rd ed.). New York: Pearson Addison-Wesley.

Cohen, J. (1988). *Statistical power analysis for the behavioral sciences* (2nd ed.). Hillsdale, NJ: Lawrence Erlbaum Associates.

Downie, N. M., & Heath, R. W. (1983). *Basic statistical methods* (5th ed.). New York: Harper & Row.

Dretzke, B. (2009). *Statistics with Microsoft Excel* (4th ed.). Upper Saddle River, NJ: Pearson Prentice Hall.

Gravetter, F., & Wallnau, L. (2008). *Essentials of statistics for the behavioral sciences* (6th ed.). Belmont, CA: Thomson Wadsworth.

Grover, C., MacDonald, M., & Vander Veer, E. A. (2007). *Office 2007: The missing manual*. Sebastopol, CA: O'Reilly.

Hays, W., & Winkler, R. (1970). *Statistics: Probability, inference, and decision* (vol. I). New York: Holt, Rinehart and Winston.

Hays, W. (1973). *Statistics for the social sciences* (2nd ed.). New York: Holt, Rinehart and Winston.

Howell, D. (2008). *Fundamental statistics for the behavioral sciences* (6th ed.). Belmont, CA: Thomson Wadsworth.

Keysar, B., Converse, B. A., Wang, J., & Epley, N. (2008). Reciprocity is not give and take: Asymmetric reciprocity to positive and negative acts. *Psychological Science, 19*(12). 1280-1286.

Killeen, P. (2005). An alternative to null-hypothesis significance tests. *Psychological Science, 16*(5), 345-353.

Lind, D., Marchal, W. & Wathen, S. (2008). *Basic statistics for business & economics* (6th ed.). New York: McGraw-Hill.

Moore, D. (2004). *The basic practice of statistics* (3rd ed.). New York: W. H. Freeman and Company.

Moore, D., McCabe, G., Duckworth, W., & Sclove, S. (2003). *The practice of business statistics: Using data for decisions*. New York: W. H. Freeman and Company.

Moore, D. S., & Johnson, S. P. (2008). Mental rotation in human infants: A sex difference. *Psychological Science*, *19*(11), 1063-1066.

Ott, L., Mendenhall, W., and Larson, R. F. (1978). *Statistics: A tool for the social sciences* (2nd ed.). North Scituate, MA: Duxbury Press.

Pace, L. A. (2006). *Introductory statistics: A cognitive learning approach*. Anderson, SC: TwoPaces, LLC.

Patterson, D. A., & Basham, R. E. (2006). *Data analysis with spreadsheets*. Boston: Pearson Allyn and Bacon.

Rea, L. & Parker, R. (1992). *Designing and conducting survey research*. San Francisco: Jossey-Bass.

Rinn, A. N., & Nelson, J. M. (2009). Preservice teachers' perceptions of behaviors characteristic of ADHD and giftedness. *Roeper Review*, *31*(1), 18-26.

Roscoe, J. (1975). *Fundamental research statistics for the behavioral sciences* (2nd ed.). New York: Holt, Rinehart and Winston.

Rosenthal, R., & Rosnow, R. (2008). *Essentials of behavioral research: methods and data analysis* (3rd ed.). New York: McGraw-Hill.

Smith, J. L, Sansone, C., & White, P. H. (2007). The stereotyped task engagement process: the role of interest and achievement motivation. *Journal of Educational Psychology*, *99*(1), 99-114.

Studenmund, A. (2006). *Using econometrics: A practical guide* (5th ed.). New York: Pearson Addison-Wesley.

Thorne, M., & Giesen, J. M. (2003). *Statistics for the behavioral sciences* (4th ed.). New York: McGraw-Hill.

Tukey, J. (1949). Comparing individual means in the analysis of variance. *Biometrics*, *5*, 99-114.

Tukey, J. (1977). *Exploratory data analysis*. Reading, MA: Addison-Wesley.

Walpole, R. E., & Myers, R. H. (1972). *Probability and statistics for engineers and scientists*. New York: MacMillan.

Welkowitz, J., Cohen, B., & Ewen, R. (2006). *Introductory statistics for the behavioral sciences* (6th ed.). Hoboken, NJ: John Wiley & Sons.

Index

Z